Thinking Otherwise

Philosophy/Communication
Ramsey Eric Ramsey, series editor

Thinking Otherwise

Philosophy, Communication, Technology

David J. Gunkel

Purdue University Press / West Lafayette, Indiana

ISBN 978-1-55753-436-1

Library of Congress Cataloging-in-Publication Data

Gunkel, David J.
  Thinking otherwise : philosophy, communication, technology / David J. Gunkel.
     p. cm. -- (Philosophy/communication)
  Includes bibliographical references and index.
  ISBN 978-1-55753-436-1 (alk. paper)
  1. Other minds (Theory of knowledge) 2. Other (Philosophy) 3. Technology-
- Moral and ethical aspects. 4. Communication and technology. 5. Information
technology--Social aspects. 6. Communication--Social aspects. I. Title.
  BD213.G86 2007
  302.2--dc22

                                                              2006038903

For my son,
Stanisław Józef Gunkel

Contents

Acknowledgments

Once a book is complete, it is often difficult to recall just where and when it all began. Fortunately, this is not the case with *Thinking Otherwise*. I can recall, quite distinctly, the three events that, in one way or another, can rightfully be identified as the beginning. The first was a sabbatical leave granted me during the fall semester of 2002. Having just completed my first book, *Hacking Cyberspace*, the year before, I desperately need time to reorient my research program and to decide upon what would become "the next big thing." Sabbatical was just what I needed. I am grateful to my colleagues at Northern Illinois University for their enthusiastic support of my proposal and their ongoing assistance throughout the sabbatical period. The second event was the Applied Ethics Colloquium and International Conference on Virtual Reality and Communication Ethics convened at the University of Illinois in November of 2002. If sabbatical provided the initial time and space for *Thinking Otherwise*, then it was the colloquium that supplied what would become its content. This unique opportunity, which was hosted by Clifford Christians, brought together scholars of all varieties and backgrounds. Participants worked in pairs to compose original papers that served as the focal point of colloquium discussion. I had the good fortune to work with Debra Hawhee. Although the paper we composed and eventually published is not reprinted in this book, everything that is contained herein is a direct result of the ideas and problems that she and I initially examined together. I am, therefore, grateful to Cliff Christians for organizing and coordinating this pivotal event, to Debbie Hawhee for her remarkable insights and friendship, and to the other participants of the colloquium for their enthusiastic support, critical questions, and valuable comments. The third event, which also took place during the fall semester of 2002, was a chance meeting between myself and Ramsey Eric Ramsey, the editor of the series to which this book belongs. This encounter was facilitated by my former colleague Mary Keehner, who made the introduction during the 2002 National Communication Association (NCA) convention in New Orleans. As a result of this and subsequent conversations, Dr. Ramsey not only encouraged me to expand my research into a book-length investigation but, more importantly, challenged me to push the analysis beyond the rather safe boundaries that I had initially provided for it. Consequently, I am thankful for having the opportunity to have worked with a truly skilled series editor, someone who not only shepherds the manuscript through the process of publication but also possesses that unique ability to draw out of an author work that he himself did not think possible.

Although the chapters that comprise *Thinking Otherwise* were all written for inclusion in the book, the research they contain has been tested at academic conferences, presented during invited lectures, and rehearsed in scholarly journals. The first chapter was initially written for and presented at the 2005 NCA convention. It has benefited from my interactions with the other panelists (Lenore Langsdorf, Ramsey Eric Ramsey, and Larry Williamson) and from the response composed and delivered by Cliff Christians. The second chapter, "What's the Matter with Books?" was originally written for and presented to the Center for Writing Studies at the University of Illinois in October of 2002. I am grateful to Debra Hawhee and Gail Hawisher for coordinating this event and to the faculty, staff, and students of the Center for their warm reception, challenging questions, and insightful comments. A draft of the current chapter was published under the same title in *Configurations* vol. 11, no. 3 (Fall 2003). I graciously acknowledge the editorial support and advice of James Bono and the critical feedback provided by the journal's two anonymous reviewers. Preliminary versions of the third chapter, "Second Thoughts: Toward a Critique of the Digital Divide," were presented at the NCA convention in 2001 and 2002. And a draft of this chapter was published in *New Media and Society*, vol. 5, no. 4 (December 2003). This early version benefited from comments provided by thoughtful readers and editors, including Jan A. G. M. van Dijk, Lawrence Grossberg, William Keith, Andrew Glikman, Steve Jones, and two anonymous reviewers at the journal. Chapter 4, "VRx: Media Technology, Drugs, and Codependency," was presented at the 2006 NCA convention in the context of a panel on the rhetoric of new media technology. I am grateful for the participation and assistance of the other two panelists, Heidi Campbell and Ian Weber, and thoughtful comments and questions from Brett Lunceford and David Heineman. The fifth chapter, "The Virtual Dialectic: Rethinking *The Matrix* and Its Significance," was originally composed at the invitation of Cliff Christians, who graciously offered me the opportunity to address his graduate seminar in the philosophy of technology at the University of Illinois in November of 2003 and again in 2005. I am grateful to Dr. Christians for his kind invitation and ongoing support of this project and to the seminar members of both semesters, who provided the thoughtful questions and comments that have proved to be essential for the development of this material. The research that is contained in this chapter was also presented at the 2004 NCA convention and the 2005 meeting of the Midwest Popular Culture Association (MPCA). I graciously acknowledge the participation and comments of the other panelists at the MPCA conference, Matt Duncan and Paul Booth, and the insightful questions supplied by Philip Fagen and the other members of the audience. The sixth chapter, "The Machine Question: Ethics, Alterity, and Technology," was initially written for and presented at the 2004 NCA convention. This early version evolved into its current form as a result of comments and questions from Heidi Campbell, Leslie Dart, Peter Krapp, Cliff Christians, and Joanna Bryson. And an abridged version of the text was published in a special edition of *Explorations in Media Ecology*, vol. 5, no. 4 (Winter 2006). My thanks to the journal's editor, Lance Strate, for his interest in and support of this project and to Cheryl Casey for her attentive copyediting.

In addition to the people named above, there are a number of other individuals who contributed, in one way or another, to the composition and writing of this book. First and foremost is Margaret Hunt of Purdue University Press, who edited the manuscript and patiently tolerated all my typos, errors, and malformed sentences. Robert Brookey provided weekly reality checks, helping in the refinement of ideas and providing much needed advice concerning a multitude of practical matters. Paul Taylor offered timely guidance and graciously agreed to read the entire manuscript. Mark Amerika not only donated an image for chapter 2 but entertained and commented on the ideas that it presents. Michael Anderson provided much needed advice concerning my reading and interpretation of his "machine ethics" and, in doing so, contributed to the composition of chapter 6. Kevin Breutzmann of Northern Illinois University prepared the index. And the students in both my undergraduate (COMS 465) and graduate (COMS 547) seminars asked all the right questions and taught me how to look at my own research from new and fresh perspectives. Most importantly, however, none of this would be possible without the unqualified support of my family: my wife, Ann Hetzel Gunkel, who completes my life and work in every way imaginable; my son, Stanisław, who opens my eyes and teaches me the joy of wonder; my parents, Peter and Judith Gunkel, who read everything I write with enthusiasm and interest; my mother-in-law, Florence Hetzel, who keeps an eye on the kid while I'm working; and my dogs, Pączek and Paluszka, who force me to get out of the chair and go for a run.

Thinking Otherwise

Introduction

> Everyone will readily agree that it is of the highest impor-
> tance to know whether we are not duped by morality.[1]
> —Emmanuel Levinas

Ethical evaluations of computer-generated virtual environments, of which computer games remain one of the more accessible and popular examples, inevitably
take one of two forms, which Philip Brey terms the pro-censorship and anti-censorship positions. The former argues that the virtual worlds that are created and
sustained by this technology not only permit but often induce users to behave
unethically toward other human beings in the real world. "In the standard pro-
censorship position," Brey writes, "it is claimed that such games are immoral,
that they hinder moral development, that they cause immoral or antisocial behavior in the real world, and that under these circumstances the state has the
right to impose censorship."[2] This argument operates on the assumption that
there is some kind of causal relationship between user activity in the virtual
environment and his/her actual behavior in the "real world." As explicated by
Blay Whitby, one of the first theorists to address the ethical aspects of virtual
reality (VR) technology, such an argument "suggests that people who regularly
perform morally reprehensible acts such as rape and murder within VR are as a
consequence more likely to perform such acts in reality."[3] This position is often
justified by and follows in the wake of decades of media effects research, which
has argued, through numerous empirical investigations done on television in
particular, that exposure to media violence contributes to a general desensitiza-
tion to real-life violence, as well as to an increased likelihood of actual aggression.[4] In fact, the United States military is counting on this. The U.S. Marines,
for example, have employed commercially available first-person shooter games,
like specially modified versions of *Doom II*, to condition their personnel to conduct actual combat operations more effectively.[5]

The anti-censorship position advances, as is indicated by its name, an opposing claim. "In the standard anti-censorship position," Brey writes, "the libertarian viewpoint is defended that since immoral acts in a virtual environment do not cause harm to others, the decision to engage in such behavior is private, and the morality of these games or the right of individuals to use them should be decided by private citizens individually and not by the state or other acting body. It is often added that there is no evidence that such games would cause individuals to act immorally in the real world, and it is sometimes claimed that such games may even be beneficial by allowing individuals to release pent-up frustrations and act out fantasies or desires that they might otherwise act out in the real world."[6] According to this line of argument, violent or aggressive behavior in a computer-generated virtual world causes no actual harm to any other person and is therefore either a benign form of entertainment or a mechanism that could effectively defuse and redirect potentially violent tendencies. The latter claim derives from what Seymour Feshbach called the catharsis hypothesis, which, according to Barrie Gunter, "posits that violent media content can be used as a safe outlet for aggressive thoughts and feelings."[7] In other words, simulated experiences might provide an artificial environment in which to both exercise and exorcise violent behavior and, as such, could have a positive effect on its users and the real social world they inhabit. Or as Whitby explains it, "performing morally reprehensible acts within VR would tend to reduce the need for the user to perform such acts in reality."[8] And evidence for this position does not just rest on Aristotelian aesthetics. It too has been tested and demonstrated in empirical studies with computer games and gamers.[9]

Binary Logic

As long as inquiry remains defined by the terms and conditions of this debate, very little will change. Investigators will continue to deploy and entertain what are by now easily recognizable arguments, somewhat predictable evidence, and, in the final analysis, unresolved controversies. For this reason, the debate between the pro- and anti-censorship positions appears to be not only persistent but ultimately irreducible. According to Whitby, for example, "the question as to which of these two arguments is correct is a purely empirical one. Unfortunately, it is not clear what sort of experiment could ever resolve the issue. A high correlation, for example, between those who perform rape and murder in VR and those who do it in reality does not establish a causal link. It may be that there is a level of motivation to perform morally reprehensible acts in some individuals which even the most effective catharsis cannot assuage. . . . There is little prospect in resolving this debate in a scientific fashion."[10] Whitby's conclusion, which identifies something of an impasse in scholarship, is supported by recent empirical investigations. In his meta-analysis of studies addressing game violence, John Sherry found little evidence to support either side of the current debate. "Unlike the television controversy, the existing social science research on the impact of video games is not nearly as compelling. Despite over 30 studies, researchers cannot agree if violent-content video games have an effect on aggression."[11] According to Sherry's investigation, both the pro- and anti-censorship positions lack sufficient evidence to demonstrate the presence or absence of a causal connection between game violence and actual aggressive behavior. In the face of this demonstration, there are at least two options available. On the one hand, investigations of virtual violence can continue to operate according to the pro- and anti-censorship debate in an attempt to better define the issue and eventually construct studies that will hopefully generate definitive data. This is, not surprisingly, the suggestion provided by both Whitby and Sherry. Whitby, for instance, cautions against dismissing the debate simply because we have not yet devised an appropriate method to test the claims. In his mind, the stakes are simply too high. "With many Western societies showing both a rise in civil violence and crime and an increase in the portrayal of such actions by entertainment media, there is at least the possibility of causal link. There is also the possibility that VR might pose more of a problem than previous more 'passive media. This is because it involves physically 'practicing,' in an important sense, the morally reprehensible acts which we would not wish performed in reality."[12] For Whitby, then, there is something of a moral imperative that motivates and justifies this line of research. "Morally speaking, it behooves scientists to commit a vast research effort to devising some way of answering these empirical questions."[13] What Whitby suggests, therefore, is a kind of brute force approach that will, if nothing else, keep social scientists gainfully employed and do so under the umbrella of a moral imperative. Sherry concludes his analysis in a similar vein, suggesting that "further research is needed to explore the relationships among a variety of variables implicated in the potential violent video game and aggression connection."[14] Like Whitby, Sherry calls for increased attention to this problem and a serious attempt to define appropriate empirical solutions.

On the other hand, we can admit that this particular debate, like so many of the binary oppositions that have structured Western thought, convey thinking into a kind of intellectual cul-de-sac. And because of this, we can attempt to define the issue in a way that proceeds otherwise. This alternative does not, it is important to note, simply dismiss the issue of game violence and aggression, but recontextualizes and reconsiders it from an altogether different perspective. Instead of adhering to the terms and conditions of the current debate and trying to devise an appropriate study to prove one side or the other, we can also focus on and question what it is they already hold in common. Such an investigation would target not the differences between the pro- and anti-censorship positions but the shared values and assumptions that both sides must endorse, whether conscious of it or not, in order to engage each other and enter into debate in the first place. Although the pro- and anti-censorship arguments appear to be situated in direct opposition to each other, they essentially value the same thing and are involved in protecting the same investments and interests. Both sides of the debate invest value in the real and endeavor to protect appropriate moral behavior toward other human beings in the so-called "actual world." The point of contention only concerns the *effect* that the virtual world of the computer is perceived to have on this real behavior in social reality. One side argues the effect is negative; the other argues that it is positive. Despite this difference, both sides ostensibly agree that it is the real world and the other human beings who inhabit it that really matter. For both sides of the debate, then, the crucial issue is not what transpires within the virtual world per se but the subsequent effect of these activities on one's behavior toward other, real human beings who exist outside of and beyond the computer-generated virtual environment. At bottom, then, both positions affirm and agree upon the same fundamental values—an unquestioned anthropocentric ethics and metaphysics that has already made specific decisions about who qualifies as an appropriate moral subject, what is really valuable and important, and where responsible activity may or may not be properly situated. When considered from this perspective, what is needed is not more research data to prove one side or the other but a qualitatively different way of considering the philosophical dimensions of information and communication technology (ICT), our responsibilities in the face of what can only amount to other forms of otherness, and a mode of critical thinking that is able to operate and proceed otherwise.

Thinking Otherwise

Thinking Otherwise pursues this alternative. It is, therefore, not interested in simply joining, contributing to, or participating in the available debates involving ICT. Instead it is concerned with challenging, criticizing, and even changing the terms and conditions by which these apparent controversies have been organized, articulated, and configured. For this reason, *Thinking Otherwise* does not take sides, argue for one position against another, or seek to resolve extant disputes by negotiating a reasonable solution. It does so not to avoid controversy but to demonstrate that the range of available controversies surrounding ICT have not been controversial enough and to introduce alternatives that open the field to other possibilities. The first chapter, "Critique of Digital Reason: Toward a Method of Thinking Otherwise," investigates the binary logic that organizes, for better or worse, both the technical operations and critical reception of ICT. As is already apparent in what Brey calls the "pro- and anti-censorship" positions, assessments of computer technology are more often than not organized according to a binary structure where the two terms of the debate are defined and understood as the opposite of each other. In colloquial discourse this is often indicated in schematic form as *x* or *not-x*, in formal logic *x* or $\neg x$, and in the binary alphabet of the digital computer 0 or 1. The first chapter considers the intellectual expense and structural limitations of this particular form of thinking, assesses the various methods that have been proposed for dealing and dispensing with these logical dichotomies, and considers the consequences and stakes of these attempts to think binary opposition otherwise. In this way then, the first chapter describes something like a method of thinking otherwise, although the word "method" is not quite right in this particular context. "Methods," as Rodolphe Gasché explains, "are generally understood as roads (from *hodos:* 'way,' 'road') to knowledge. In the sciences, as well as in the philosophies that scientific thinking patronizes, method is an instrument for representing a given field, and it is applied to the field from the outside."[15] In scientific discourse or any kind of investigation that aspires to be called science, it is commonly assumed that a method of inquiry can and should be able to be articulated and justified in advance of its subsequent and particular applications. This understanding employs and trades on a number of old and well-established metaphysical oppositions: universal/particular, abstract/concrete, method/application, means/end, inside/outside, etc. *Thinking Otherwise*, if it is to be consistent and rigorous in its engagement with the logic of binary opposition, does not and cannot in practice adhere to these traditional dichotomies but must also submit them to critical questioning and analysis. Consequently, the first chapter does not propose a method in the usual sense of the word but describes and models the kind of engagements (always in the plural) that are necessary to intervene in and to think binary oppositions otherwise.

Following from this beginning, subsequent chapters take up and consider some of the more influential and persistent logical dichotomies that have organized thinking about and the evaluation of ICT. The second chapter, "What's the Matter with Books?" addresses the tension that is already situated between the book's subject matter and material, and it does so by engaging what Nicholas Negroponte has called "the paradox of a book."[16] One of the great ironies of contemporary culture's obsession with computer technology, digital media, and cyberspace is the remarkable proliferation of print publications that announce, in one way or another, the end of the book, the obsolescence of print, or the death of literature. In book after book, one can read about how the computer, the Internet, and virtual reality will eventually replace the "civilization of the book" with the wired and now wireless civilization of digital information and computer-mediated communication. Such publications are obviously involved in a curious and potentially contradictory form of self-effacement. That is, what these publications state about their subject matter appears to question and even invalidate the material in which these statements have been made. Consequently, what's the matter with books is that the subject matter of so many print publications in this, the so-called "late age of print," effectively negates the material in which it necessarily appears. This is of course not a new problem or recent dilemma. It is already present in and characterizes the first recorded debate about the oldest form of information technology, which takes place in Plato's *Phaedrus*. Toward the end of this dialogue, Plato reflects on and writes about the relatively new technology of writing. Writing, Plato has Socrates say, constitutes a threat to real knowledge and effective communication and, for this reason, should not be taken seriously. In fact, whoever is worthy of the title *philosopher*, Socrates argues, "has the power to show by his own speech that the written words are of little worth."[17] Interestingly this argument against writing is presented in and by writing. Like recent publications addressing ICT, the *Phaedrus* is involved in what appears to be a potentially contradictory form of self-effacement, where the subject matter of its argument seems to be at odds with the actual material in which it comes to be presented. The second chapter examines this problem, which inevitably affects any and all writing on technology. It traces the history and mechanisms of "the paradox of a book," investigates how it has been explained or negotiated, and suggests some alternatives for understanding this strange occurrence and situation. In pursuing this matter, the book's second chapter cannot help but address and become increasingly involved with its own material. In other words, what is presented in the second chapter about texts that address information technology will need to be applied to the texture and technology of its own presentation. This self-reflectivity, which is both unavoidable and deliberate, not only interrupts the assumed instrumental transparency that is so often assigned to media technology but opens up, in both theory and practice, alternative ways to understand the role and function of both technology and text.

The third chapter, "Second Thoughts: Toward a Critique of the Digital Divide," employs this alternative understanding of text in an investigation of what many individuals, including technologists, academics, politicians, journalists, and social activists, consider to be the leading moral crisis involving ICT—the unequal distribution of access to information technology, or what is now routinely called the "digital divide." Recent attention to this problem is significant, because it challenges and attenuates the often unrestrained optimism that has characterized much of the popular and scholarly assessments of ICT. In particular, the digital divide provides something of a "reality check," reminding those of us who enjoy the unique opportunities afforded by ICT that the material conditions of access, which we often take for granted, have not been distributed across the globe in a way that approaches anything close to equitable. In defining the characteristics of this particular issue, the numerous scholarly publications, empirical studies, government reports, and popular discussions addressing the digital divide have more often than not organized things by distinguishing and documenting the separation that exists between what the U.S. National Telecommunications and Information Administration (NTIA) calls "the information haves" and "the information have-nots."[18] In formulating its problematic in these terms, the debates and discussions about the digital divide arrange and proceed according to what is clearly a binary structure. The third chapter engages and investigates the terms and conditions of this particular arrangement. Its analysis, however, is distinguished from other attempts to address this subject matter insofar as it does not seek to document or analyze the empirical problems of unequal access but considers the logical structure and form that have defined and directed work on this important socio-ethical issue. For this reason, the investigation does not collect empirical data on the actual distribution and use of ICT, nor does it reevaluate the numbers that these kinds of studies generate. Instead it targets and investigates the extant texts, reports, and studies on the digital divide in order to track how this particular problem has been organized and to question whether and to what extent there might not be philosophical complications already encoded in the way the issue has been defined and characterized. To have second thoughts about the digital divide is not to question the validity or importance of the various socio-technological inequalities that have been documented in recent empirical studies of computer usage and ICT distribution. Instead "second thoughts" means reconsidering the entire problematic that is organized by the digital divide, examining its underlying binary structure and form, and explicating how such preconditions authorize, regulate, and ultimately restrict its investigation and proposed reparation.

The fourth and fifth chapters take up and investigate the logical distinction situated between material reality and its various opposites (immateriality, artifice, illusion, fiction, simulation, falsity, appearance, etc.) that already is, in one way or another, deployed by and operative in the previous chapters. The fourth chapter, "VRx: Media Technology, Drugs, and Codependency," examines the way the logical distinction situated between the real or true world and the fiction of computer-generated artifice is dependent on both a rhetoric and logic of drugs. A perfect example of this affiliation is evident in the first *Matrix* film. At a crucial point early in the narrative, Morpheus presents the protagonist Neo with a pivotal choice between two pills. The blue pill, Morpheus claims, leads to a life of illusion and fantasy in a fully immersive virtual reality. The red pill deposits one, body and soul, outside the computer matrix in what is determined to be the real and true world.[19] This curious confluence of computer technology and drugs is not something that is limited to or first introduced in Andy and Larry Wachowski's cyberpunk narrative. It is part and parcel of an old and often unacknowledged codependency. Already in Plato's *Phaedrus*, the technology of writing had been connected to and described in terms of drugs. In fact, the *Phaedrus* is a dialogue on drugs. It begins with Socrates falling under the influence of a book and ends with a consideration of writing that is, quite literally, all about pharmaceuticals. Consequently, media technology and drugs, from the time of the Platonic dialogues to the *Matrix*, share a common intellectual heritage, endeavor to achieve virtually the same objectives, and, as Avital Ronell suggests, often suffer similar crackdowns in the face of moral evaluation and the law.[20] The fourth chapter tracks the codependency of ICT and drugs, traces this interaction to its Platonic origins in the *Phaedrus*, and examines the way this ancient pharmacology already controls and parses understanding and evaluation of media technology. The goal of this investigation, it is important to note, is neither to endorse experimentation nor to institute something like an intellectual 12-step program. Instead it endeavors to understand the mechanisms of and to intervene in the dialectic of drugs that is already operative in and has already determined critical investigations of technology in general and ICT in particular. In other words, the fourth chapter is neither for nor against drugs and technology but proceeds in such a way as to open this rather restricted binary pairing to other opportunities, alternative kinds of questions, and new arrangements that are and remain otherwise.

If the fourth chapter provides the opening to an alternative, the fifth pursues its exigencies and consequences. This chapter, titled "The Virtual Dialectic: Rethinking *The Matrix* and Its Significance," not only continues examination of the logical oppositions that have organized critical thinking about ICT but also defines another arrangement that remains, in ways that will need to be characterized in some detail, outside the scope of the recognized options, decisions, and values. Like the previous chapter, this investigation also leverages the imagery that has been presented in the *Matrix* films. This is done, it is important to note, not out of some mistaken perception concerning the role and status of this or any other science fiction narrative. Slavoj Žižek is right about this one: "There is something inherently stupid and naïve in taking the *philosophical* underpinnings of the *Matrix* trilogy seriously and discussing its implications. The Wachowski brothers are obviously *not* philosophers. They are just two guys who superficially flirt with and exploit in a confused way some postmodern and New Age notions."[21] Heeding such advice, this chapter, quite deliberately and unlike so many books recently published on this subject,[22] does not endeavor to expose, explain, or evaluate the "philosophical themes" that are supposedly contained in and exemplified by *The Matrix* and its numerous spin-offs. Instead, it proceeds otherwise, not only submitting these philosophical interpretations of the *Matrix* franchise to philosophical scrutiny but also addressing this pop-culture material from an entirely different perspective. "What is interesting," Žižek argues, "is to read The *Matrix* movies not as containing a consistent philosophical discourse, but as rendering, in their very inconsistencies, the antagonisms of our ideological and social predicament."[23] This is precisely how the *Matrix* franchise in particular and science fiction literature and cinema in general are employed in this chapter and throughout the text of *Thinking Otherwise*. Understood in this fashion, science fiction constitutes something like contemporary parables or myths that articulate, often in very melodramatic terms, the various antagonisms and binary oppositions that comprise the contemporary situation. Consequently, chapter 5 takes up and employs the conceptual opposition situated between the red and blue pill as a mechanism for investigating the philosophical dilemmas and the choices that are commonly associated with ICT. This investigation is divided into two parts. The first reconsiders the logical structure of this decision, arguing that the choice between these two alternatives originates in the history of Western thought and that this dialectic informs both the theories and practices of ICT. The second questions the choice of the red pill. It critiques the assumed value of "true reality" that is expressed in the cinematic narrative and validated within much of ICT research, and it suggests alternative ways to think technology beyond the limited either/or logic that supports such a decision. The objective of such an undertaking is not simply to question the philosophical assumptions of what has been typically defined as the "right choice" but to learn, through such questioning, to suspend the very system that already delimits the understanding of and the range of possible decisions that are made within this field. This chapter, therefore, suggests alternative methods to question and to respond to ICT that are no longer limited by the two terms of this particular logical opposition.

Although each chapter of the book is clearly concerned with some aspect of ICT and ethics, it is the sixth chapter that takes up and explicitly investigates ethics in particular. It does so, however, in a way that is significantly different from what would typically be described under the terms "computer ethics," "cyberethics," "Internet ethics," and "media ethics." To put it in rather blunt philosophical terms, this chapter, which goes by the name "The Machine Question: Ethics, Alterity, and Technology," is interested in advancing within the field of ICT an approach to ethics that is oriented otherwise. In doing so, the investigation leverages recent innovations in moral philosophy, especially what has been called, in the wake of Emmanuel Levinas's influential work, "an ethics of otherness."[24] This does not mean, however, that the chapter simply applies Levinasian ethics to computer technology. Instead, "The Machine Question" asks about the moral status of those other forms of otherness, most notably the animal and the machine, which have been, even in Levinas's own work, systematically excluded from the rank and file of ethics. An example might help to illustrate this rather abstract characterization. In a now well-known and often reproduced *New Yorker* cartoon by Peter Steiner, two dogs sit in front of an Internet-connected PC (personal computer). The one operating the machine says to his companion, "On the Internet, nobody knows you're a dog."[25] The cartoon has often been employed to address issues of identity and anonymity in computer-mediated communication.[26] As Richard Holeton interprets it, "the cartoon makes fun of the anonymity of network communications by showing a dog online, presumably fooling some credulous humans about its true identity."[27] On this reading, what the cartoon portrays is that who or what one *is* in computer-mediated communication (CMC) is, as Allucquère Rosanna Stone, Sherry Turkle, and others have demonstrated, something that can be easily and endlessly reconfigured.[28] This reading of the cartoon, although not necessarily incorrect, misses the more interesting and suggestive insight that is provided by the wired canines. What the cartoon demonstrates is not the anonymity and indeterminacy of others in ICT but the unquestioned assumption that despite this anonymity, users assume that the other with whom they interact online is another human. The other who confronts us in cyberspace is always, it is assumed, another human being, like ourselves. These others may be "other" in a "celebrate diversity" sense of the word—another race, another gender, another ethnicity, another social class, etc.

But they are never a dog. Consequently, what the cartoon shows, through a kind of clever inversion, is the standard operating presumption (SOP) of mainstream moral philosophy and ICT ethics. Online identity is, in fact, reconfigurable. You can be a dog, or you can say you are. But everyone knows, or so it is assumed, that what is on the other end of the line is another human user, someone who is, despite what are often interpreted as minor variations in physical appearance and background, essentially like what we assume ourselves to be. The cartoon works, because in ICT everyone always already assumes that the other is human. "Inside the little box," Stone concludes, "are other people."[29] This chapter of *Thinking Otherwise* responds to and seeks to intervene in this deep-seated and often unquestioned anthropocentric assumption. In doing so, it does not simply rage for the animal and machine, but shows through an engagement with these other forms of otherness the structural limits of ethics as it has been previously thought and practiced.

Chapter One

Critique of Digital Reason

Toward a Method of Thinking Otherwise

> Dualism lies at the heart of life. It should not then be surprising that given the chance to build the ultimate machine, we based it on zeros and ones.[1]—Peter Lurie

Digital information is composed of two discrete variables, off or on, which are commonly represented by the binary digits, or bits, 0 and 1. All information in digital form, whether alpha-numeric characters, images, audio, video, or computer-generated 3d models, consists of nothing more than a complex sequence of 0's and 1's. Interestingly this dualistic structure not only defines the technical aspects of digital information but also characterizes much of its critical reception. The debates, discussions, and controversies involving digital media and technology have typically been defined by two different and opposed positions. Michael Heim, for example, finds contemporary debate about the social impact of the computer, the Internet, and cyberspace to be organized around and motivated by two different alternatives, which he terms "network idealism" and "naïve realism."[2] For the "network idealist," the computer constitutes a virtual techno-utopia—a new world of uninhibited freedom, boundless opportunity, and unrestricted growth. The "naïve realist" opposes this overly optimistic assessment and warns of increased surveillance, compromised security, loss of a sense of reality, and the erosion of human connection and face-to-face interaction. Where the network idealist sees utopian possibilities and virtual redemption, the naïve realist perceives a threat to real human relations, real communities, and reality in general. Characterized in this way, network idealism and naïve realism are positioned and function as opposites. They are, as Heim describes it, "binary brothers." "One launches forth with unreserved optimism; the other lashes back with a cry to ground ourselves outside technology."[3] A similar characterization has been provided by Derek Stanovsky in his philosophical evaluation of virtual reality (VR) technology. Although Stanovsky does not use Heim's rather specific terminology, he charts the same oppositional structure. "Virtual reality is equally prone to portrayals as either the bearer of bright utopian possibilities or dark dystopian nightmares, and both of these views have some basis to recommend them."[4] Although Heim and Stanovsky both identify a general binary structure in the current debates about information and communication technology (ICT), it is perhaps Andrew Calcutt who has provided the most comprehensive survey of the logical dichotomies that have come to organize contemporary understandings of this technology. Calcutt's *White Noise: An A–Z of the Contradictions in Cyberculture* is composed of an alphabetical listing of 26 oppositional pairs that are evident in the debates and discussions about technology and culture. Some of the pairings are immediately recognizable as classic philosophical oppositions: Anarchy/Authority, Community/Alienation, Play/Work, Subject/Object, Universal/Particular. Others appear to be less intuitive: Free/Fee, Gates/Anti-Gates, Journalism/Personalism, Knockers/Boosters. According to Calcutt's demonstration, digital technology is best characterized and described according to a set of logically irreducible and contradictory terms. Consequently it appears that digital information systems are binary not only at the level of their technical operations but also in the way they have been discussed, understood, and evaluated.

This conclusion is both theorized in and justified by structuralism, a twentieth-century intellectual movement that found application in fields as diverse as linguistics, anthropology, literary theory, and philosophy. Although structuralism does not constitute a formal discipline or singular method of investigation, its particular innovations are widely recognized as the result of developments in semiology in general and the "structural linguistics" of Ferdinand de Saussure in particular. In the posthumously published *Course in General Linguistics*, Saussure argued for a fundamental shift in the way that language is understood and analyzed. "The common view," as Jonathan Culler describes it, "is doubtless that a language consists of words, positive entities, which are put together to form a system and thus acquire relations with one another. . . ."[5] Saussure turns this common-sense view on its head. For him, the fundamental element of language is the sign, and "the constitutive structure of signs is," as Mark Taylor points out, "binary opposition."[6] "In language," Saussure argues in one of the most often quoted passages of the *Course*, "there are only differences. Even more important: a difference generally implies positive terms between which the difference is set up; but in language there are only differences *without positive terms*."[7] For Saussure, then, language is not composed of linguistic units that have some intrinsic value or positive meaning and that subsequently comprise a system of language through their interrelationships. Instead, a sign, any sign in any language, is defined by the differences that distinguish it from other signs within the linguistic system to which it belongs. According to this way of thinking, the sign is not a positive term but an effect of difference, and language itself consists in a system of differences. This characterization of language, although never explicitly described in this fashion by Saussure, mirrors the logic of the digital computer, where the binary digits 0 and 1 have no intrinsic or positive meaning but are simply indicators and an effect of difference—a switch that is either on or off. If structuralism is right, then binary opposition does not just describe the technical operations of the computer or define the terms of its critical evaluation but characterizes fundamental structures of human cognition and communication. And this conclusion, although not always identified with the name "structuralism," has received increasing support in recent years. Daniel Chandler, for instance, argues that "people have believed in the fundamental character of binary oppositions since at least classical times" and that it would be difficult, if not impossible, to operate otherwise.[8] Likewise Peter Elbow argues that "there's no hope of getting away from binary oppositions given the nature of the human mind and situation. Binary thinking seems to be the path of least resistance for the perceptual system, for thinking, and for linguistic structures. . . . It may be that the very structure of our bodies and our placement in phenomenal reality invite us to see things in terms of binary oppositions."[9] And Peter Lurie has even suggested that "dualism may be hardwired into our genes" and presents as evidence the structure of the DNA molecule.[10] Whatever its origin and justification, the fact is that binary opposition has played and continues to play a constitutive role in shaping how we understand and describe innovations in ICT. For this reason, the issue is not whether to proceed in binary terms or not, which ironically would be just one more binary opposition, but concerns how one dispenses with and manages the effect of these various dichotomies. As Elbow explains it, "the question, then, is not whether to deal with dichotomies but how to deal with them."[11] And when it comes to contending with the dualisms and dichotomies that characterize ICT, there have been at least four different techniques, which, for the sake of convenience, can be identified with the following names: either/or, balance, dialectic, and poststructuralism.

Either/or

> The universe is not dialectical: it moves toward the extremes, and not towards equilibrium.[12]—Jean Baudrillard

One way to dispense with binary opposition is to privilege one side of the debate over the other. In this situation, one side is claimed to be correct or positive, rendering the opposing side incorrect or negative. The network idealists, for example, argue that digital technology and computer networks will improve our lives by eliminating distance and delay in human communication, providing for better ways to work and play, and expanding the human community to encompass all peoples in all corners of the globe. Arguments like these are evident in J. C. R. Licklider and Robert W. Taylor's prescient paper "The Computer as a Communication Device," Nicholas Negroponte's *Being Digital*, Howard Rheingold's *Virtual Community*, Pierre Lévy's *Cyberculture*, William Mitchell's *City of Bits*, and numerous "cyber-anthologies."[13] For many idealists, however, the computer and the network are not just useful technologies for the purpose of better entertainment, more effective work, or improved connectivity. Instead cyberspace has been situated as "paradise found" or at least reengineered. According to these unreserved utopian pretensions, the computer is imbued, as Michael Benedikt explains it, with the hope for redemption that has traditionally been assigned to the mythical "Heavenly City."[14] In the computer-generated world of cyberspace, users can live in a near-perfect, or at least vastly improved, environment where, as Mark Dery once described it, they can "float free of biological and sociocultural determinants,"[15] inhabiting a world where users "communicate mind to mind," as was promoted in a late-twentieth-century television advertisement for the telecommunications giant MCI. Surveying the various publications by theorists and practitioners of computer technology at the end of the previous century, Margaret Wertheim concludes that cyberspace has been rhetorically positioned as "a technological substitute for the Christian space of Heaven."[16] In her book-length study, appropriately titled *The Pearly Gates of Cyberspace*, she notes that "today's proselytizers of cyberspace proffer their domain as an idealized realm 'above' and 'beyond' the problems of a troubled material world. Just like the early Christians, they too promise a 'transcendent' haven of radiance and light, a utopian arena of equality, friendship, and virtue."[17] In this rhetorical construction, the computer and cyberspace are not just efficient and useful technologies, they promise redemption. And nothing says "my side is right" like allying yourself with the forces of heaven.

Despite and in direct confrontation with this utopian rhetoric, the other side also claims victory. The naïve realists (although they seldom refer to themselves with this particular moniker) not only oppose this unreserved optimistic assessment of technology but also argue that the promises of the techno-utopians are misguided at best and purposefully deceptive at worst. Advocates of this position include not only neo-luddites, like Ted Kaczynski (aka The Unabomber), who has become, for better or worse, the poster-child *du jour* for any anti-technology stance, but also thoughtful cultural critics and computer practitioners who are not opposed to technology *tout court* but find good reasons to be suspicious of the seemingly unrestrained hyperbole that has been issued by the starry-eyed techno-utopians. Neil Postman, for example, initiates his critique of techno-culture, which is aptly titled *Technopoly*, by recalling the judgment offered by Thamus in Plato's *Phaedrus* and siding with the assessment made by the ancient king. In words that echo Thamus's warning against the invention of writing, Postman cautions that "the uncontrolled growth of technology destroys the vital source of our humanity" and "undermines certain mental processes and social relations that make human life worth living."[18] Similarly Mark Slouka's *War of the Worlds: Cyberspace and the High-Tech Assault on Reality* critiques and opposes what he identifies as "our growing separation from reality."[19] According to Slouka's analysis, information technology like print, television, and now the Internet has almost completely replaced the actual experience of reality with "notoriously unreliable" representations and images. And the philosopher Hubert Dreyfus concludes his assessment of the Internet by deploying similar language: "My answer is that, if we managed to live our lives in cyberspace, we would lose a lot more than the face-to-face conversations, verbal promises, and memory power Plato saw were endangered by writing. We would lose our only reliable way of finding relevant information, the capacity for skill acquisition, a sense of reality, and the possibility of leading meaningful lives."[20] Clearly, it is tempting to try to write off these evaluations as polemics written by individuals who are simply opposed to any form of technology whatsoever. Although this may be possible with Postman, who is, by his own account, a neo-luddite[21] of sorts, it is certainly not applicable in the other cases. Slouka, for example, anticipates this charge and addresses it directly: "Let me be as clear as possible. I have no problem with what Andrew S. Grove, President and CEO of Intel Corporation, has called 'the ubiquitous PC.' I own and use one. Nor do I have any argument, for example, with the millions of people who crowd the 'chat groups' available on the Net. My quarrel is with a relatively small but disproportionately influential group of self-described 'Net-religionists' and 'wannabe gods' who believe that the physical world can (and should) be 'downloaded' into a computer, who believe that the future of mankind is not in RL (real life) but in some form of VR (virtual reality)."[22] For Slouka, the computer and the Internet remain useful tools as long as they are employed to augment real human interaction, community, and expression. They only become pernicious when one tries to substitute the virtual for the real. In all these cases, what makes the naïve realist argument persuasive is the fact that they seem to provide a much needed "reality check" to the unrestrained utopianism of the network idealists. Clearly the computer, the Internet, and cyberspace are not some kind of *deus ex machina*. They are products of a particular culture, invented at a particular time, and deployed within particular circumstances. Unlike the fantastic transcendental dreams of the network idealists, the naïve realists appear to have their feet on the ground and reality on their side.

   This method for dealing with binary oppositions, where, as Elbow describes it, you "choose one side as right or better,"[23] is also the preferred mode of operation in many science fiction narratives, which arguably comprise our own era's parables about technology and its consequences. *The Matrix* franchise, for example, is not only organized around a series of oppositions—the survival of the human race versus the domination of the machines, the virtual reality of the matrix versus the real world that exists outside computer-generated experience, the red pill versus the blue pill, etc.—but capitalizes on the either/or option in order to animate its various story lines. At the beginning of *The Matrix*, for example, the machines are in a position of dominance over human beings; they not only control the human population through complex computer simulations but derive power from the bioelectrical energy generated by the human organism. The dramatic action of the narrative concerns the struggle of a band of rebels who oppose this machinic domination and, in the end, turn the tables and initiate what appears to be a new order. Structurally speaking, then, *The Matrix* is organized around the reversal of opposing forces, where the initial arrangement is inverted but the two terms of the polemic remain in conflict. This structure is extended and explained in the film's prequel, which is presented in an anthology of animated shorts called *The Animatrix*. In the two-part episode titled "The Second Renaissance," the origin of *The Matrix*'s principal dramatic conflict between the machines and the human beings is detailed and, not surprisingly, is shown to be derived from a conflict that ultimately takes the form of all-out war, where the machines were victorious. Similar struggles and outcomes have been employed in the *Star Trek* franchise and the recent reimagining of *Battlestar Galactica* (*BSG*). *Star Trek* episodes, whether the original series from the mid-1960s or its numerous sequels and prequel, are often structured around conflicts that are situated between the anthropocentric federation and various opposing alien forces, whether organic, machinic, or a hybrid of the two like the Borg. The Borg, in fact, persist as one of the franchise's enduring villains insofar as they are presented as and represent a complete inversion of everything that is valued by the predominantly human federation. The Borg episodes (especially *Star Trek: The Next Generation*'s "The Best of Both Worlds"), like *The Matrix* films, mobilize and are organized around what philosophers would recognize as traditional metaphysical oppositions—human versus machine, free will versus determination, and individualism versus collectivism—and end, somewhat predictably, with the federation's victory. A similar struggle structures the narrative trajectory of *BSG*, whether the original series from the 1980s or its recent reimagining. Like *The Matrix* and *Star Trek*'s Borg episodes, the organizing principle of *BSG* is a life-and-death struggle between the human race and the robotic cylons. The series begins with a war where the machine are victorious and, from this polemical beginning, documents the struggle of the remaining members of the human race against this opposing force. However, unlike *Star Trek*, where the Borg are visibly differentiated from what is properly human, the cylons of the recent version of *BSG* are virtually indistinguishable from their human counterparts. This inability to distinguish the two factions does not reduce the fundamental conflict but deepens the struggle by allowing for misidentification, confusion, and even reversal.

Although making for good drama, especially in situations involving a serialized narrative, the either/or option does not so much resolve the conflict as it preserves and perpetuates the opposition. Even when the position of "winner" changes hands, as it seems to do so in the first *Matrix* film, the basic conflict that structures the narrative remains in place and is ultimately unaffected—the humans are still situated in opposition to and rage against the machines. Consequently, as Elbow summarizes it, "even when people try to overturn or reverse the traditional dominance in a polar opposition—proclaiming for example that dark is better than light, passion than reason, female than male—it just means that the underdog is defined as overdog, and we are still left with thinking in terms of dominance or hierarchy."[24] This situation is clearly evident in the debates concerning ICT and digital media. The network idealists and proselytizers of cyberspace publish articles and books announcing the next big thing that will supposedly revolutionize the way we work, play, and live. Conversely the naïve realists respond with cautionary tales and warnings that are grounded in what are more often than not reasonable concerns and justifiable reservations. No matter which side gains the upper hand, the terms and conditions of the struggle remain essentially untouched and unaffected. Consequently, the either/or option is less a method for dispensing with binary opposition as it is the condition by which such an arrangement comes to be defined, maintained, and elaborated. When considered in this fashion, the opposition appears to be engaged in an eternal and fundamentally irreducible struggle.

Balance

> Μηδὲν Ἄγαν (Nothing in Excess).
> —Delphic Oracle

Given two opposing and apparently irreconcilable positions, it is *balance* that is so often assumed to be the rational and judicial solution. Between any two extremes, this kind of reasoning presumes, there is an equitable middle point that balances the one against the other. This balancing act, it is important to note, does not seek to reduce the two opposed positions to some intermediate or third term. Instead it endeavors to maintain the opposition as such and juggle their competing perspectives. "This tradition," Elbow writes, "sees value in accepting, putting up with, indeed seeking the nonresolution of the two terms: not feeling that the opposites must be somehow reconciled, not feeling the itch must be scratched. This tradition goes as far back as the philosophy of yin/yang. In the West we see it in Socrates/Plato, in Boethius, and in Peter Abelard's *Sic et Non*, and it continues down through the present. The goal is lack of resolution of opposites."[25] This way of thinking neither chooses sides nor endeavors to mediate and reduce the conflict. It sustains conflict and endeavors to maintain a kind of equilibrium between two contradictory terms without permitting one side to gain the upper hand. It aims, as Elbow describes it, "to have situations of balance, irresolution, nonclosure, nonconsensus, nonwinning."[26]

According to this approach, the best way to deal with binary oppositions is to work with them, allowing the truth of the one to confront and question the truth of the other.

Perhaps the best illustration of this approach in recent work on computer technology is Heim's *Virtual Realism*. Considering the opposing positions represented by the "network idealist" and the "naïve realist," Heim argues that resolution does not consist in siding with one over the other or reducing their conflict through some act of mediation but in the dynamic balancing of the one against the other. "We must," Heim writes, "balance the idealist's enthusiasm for computerized life with the need to ground ourselves more deeply in the felt earth affirmed by the realist as our primary reality. This uneasy balance I call 'virtual realism.'"[27] Heim's virtual realism does not choose sides but maintains the two opposed positions in such a way that one side calls the other into question and vice versa. Such balance charts a middle course between the two extreme positions of network idealism and naïve realism. It respects the insights and contributions that can be made by both sides without resolving or reducing their essential differences. "Virtual realism," Heim writes, using an appropriate metaphor, "walks a tight rope. The delicate balancing act sways between the idealism of unstoppable Progress and the Luddite resistance to virtual life. . . . The challenge is not to end the oscillation between idealism and realism but to find the path that goes through them."[28] A similar approach is proffered by Andrew Shapiro in *The Control Revolution* and demonstrated in Calcutt's *White Noise*. Shapiro's book makes a case for balance not only in its content but also in the structure of its composition. The book is divided into four parts. The first, provocatively titled "Revolution," "explains how new technology is allowing individuals to take power from large institutions such as government, corporations, and the media."[29] It is an admittedly optimistic assessment of ICT and articulates many of the same arguments ascribed to Heim's network idealist—democratization, autonomy, virtual communities, etc. The second and third parts, titled "Resistance" and "Oversteer" respectively, "take a less sanguine view"[30] and present the two forces that threaten and oppose this social revolution—the backlash or "Resistance" of the previous order and the "Oversteer" of excessive and unchecked individualism. Like Heim's naïve realist, Shapiro is concerned that "cherished values like community, free speech, and privacy could be diminished."[31] This tension and opposition is resolved in the fourth and final part, which is called, not surprisingly, "Balance." The final part, therefore, "charts a path between this Scylla and Charibdis" and "attempts to harmonize these competing voices."[32] Like Heim's "virtual realism," Shapiro's "Balance" mediates the conflicts that characterize new technology by charting a middle course between competing values. Similarly Calcutt's *White Noise* exemplifies and practices balance in its formal composition. By arranging an alphabetical listing of the contradictory perspectives that have been assigned to new technology, Calcutt's text deliberately resists decision of one over the other and presents the competing possibilities in a manner that exemplifies balance. In other words, *White Noise*, in a way that is in accord with the American journalistic tradition of "objective reporting," presents the two sides of a debate without itself taking sides or seeking to resolve the conflict. This approach, which is demonstrated in practice but not explicitly theorized as such within the course of the A–Z catalogue, is described on the text's dust cover: "Born out of frustration with recent attempts to pigeon-hole 'the information revolution' as either the i-way utopia or the devil's own dystopia, *White Noise: An A–Z of the Contradictions in Cyberculture* cuts through the vapourware surrounding the Internet and shows how the paradoxical aspects of new media (Is it masculine or feminine? Will it mean peace or war? Does it enhance community or confirm alienation?) are the expression of the inherent contradictions underlying our whole society. Moreover, these contradictions have reached an unprecedented pitch, and their articulation in cyberculture is all the more intense."[33] *White Noise*, therefore, is a deliberate attempt to resist the pull of either side of the conflict. Instead of leaning to one side or the other, Calcutt's text, like any good "objective" account, stakes out a middle path and presents both sides of the conflict without apparent bias for one or the other.

By far, however, the most elaborate attempt to articulate a systemic method of balance is Marshall McLuhan's *Laws of Media*, a book that was published posthumously with the assistance of McLuhan's son Eric. *Laws of Media* was, as Eric McLuhan explains in the preface, initially motivated by a publisher's request to revise *Understanding Media* and McLuhan's desire to answer criticisms of the book by making its insights and procedures "scientific."[34] Toward this end, McLuhan theorized that there are four fundamental properties that apply to and characterize any form of media in particular and every human artifact in general. These "laws of media" are initially presented in the form of four related questions, which McLuhan termed a *tetrad:* "What does it [the artifact] enhance or intensify? What does it render obsolete or displace? What does it retrieve that was previously obsolesced? What does it produce or become when pressed to an extreme?"[35] Despite the sequential mode of presentation, these four elements are not themselves organized in a linear sequence or series. "The tetrads of *Laws of Media*," McLuhan argues, "present not sequential but simultaneous facets of media effects."[36] This simultaneity is visually evident in and exemplified by the numerous examples that are employed by the text. These examples, which include artifacts like booze, refrigerator, drugs, number, computer, Newton's Law of Motion, etc., are presented in a unique format where the four aspects are juxtaposed in two dimensions on the printed page (figure 1).

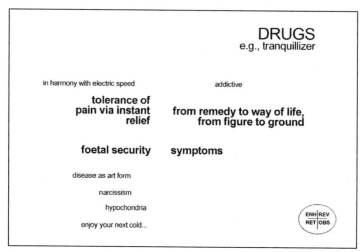

Figure 1
Drug tetrad from *Laws of Media*[37]

As is immediately apparent from this appositional arrangement and as McLuhan explicitly points out, "there is no 'right way' to read a tetrad, as the parts are simultaneous."[38] They can, therefore, be read from left to right, top to bottom, or in reverse. No matter how it is accessed, however, what the tetrad demonstrates is a complex and multidimensional balancing act situated between the four different elements that constitute the artifact in question. In this unique mode of presentation, no one aspect has precedence or privilege over the others, each one is situated in relationship to every other one, and their differences are preserved and remain unresolved. Consequently, what McLuhan describes is, according to his own estimations, a new mode of scientific analysis that is significantly different from the traditional trinary and sequential form of thinking that has been exemplified in both the logical syllogism of the Scholastics and the dialectical process of G. W. F. Hegel. And for this reason, he claims, the *Laws of Media* comprise an entirely *new science* that addresses and explains every aspect of human endeavor.

No matter how it is presented, balance sounds good. The balance that is advocated by Heim and Shapiro and demonstrated in the texts of Calcutt and McLuhan seems so simple, so rational, so commonsense—even if the details of such equilibrium turn out to be somewhat complicated and involved. There is something about this approach that immediately strikes one as reasonable, measured, and equitable. And this is true not only for an English-speaking, American audience where the political struggle for the middle, the social value of moderation and temperance, and a general suspicion of any kind of excessiveness or extremism defines the predominant ethos. In fact, the desire for balance seems to be universal. That is, it appears to be one of those principal "human values" that extend across different cultures—from East to West—and times—from the ancient to the contemporary period. For Heim, the privileged model of balance is found in medieval China. It is rooted in the discipline of Tai Chi Chuang, which he describes as a series of bodily movements initially designed to overcome the imbalance caused by excessive meditation.[39] In the Western tradition, the emphasis on balance and moderation is inscribed, in the form of a general prohibition against any form of overindulgence, above the gate of the Delphic Oracle—"nothing in excess." It also constitutes the cornerstone of Aristotelian ethics, which is organized around the concept of the "golden mean"—the middle course between two extremes.[40] And it is the figure of the balance, a scale held by a blindfolded woman, that constitutes the principal image of Western understandings of justice, both in terms of law and moral conduct. Finally, it is with balance that the *Matrix* trilogy ends. The various elements that make up the *Matrix* universe are organized around and directed by a fundamental conflict that is situated between human beings and the machines. *The Matrix* introduces the terms of the conflict, the animated prequel, *Animatrix*, explicates its origins, and the two sequels, *Reloaded* and *Revolutions*, add complexity by detailing the conflict's gradual intensification into all-out war. Resolution of the struggle, which is presented at the end of *Revolutions*, does not consist in the victory of one side over the other, which would simply reproduce or "reload" the conflict. Instead the narrative achieves closure with a cease-fire and tenuous peace. Like the balance advocated by Elbow, Heim, and Shapiro, the *Matrix* concludes by charting a middle course between the two opposing factions, holding them together without reducing the one to the other.

Despite its intuitive attraction as an equitable means for dealing with differences, balance does have its problems. Ironically the method of balance is often articulated and explicated in counter-distinction to what is defined as its opposite. Elbow, for example, argues for balance by distinguishing it from the other forms by which binary oppositions have customarily been addressed, most notably the either/or option and the synthetic third term that resolves the conflict through compromise in a kind of "happy medium or golden mean."[41] Similarly, Heim advances the cause of "virtual realism" by differentiating it from the synthetic resolution he claims is represented by Hegelianism: "It [virtual realism] is not a synthesis in the Hegelian sense of a result achieved through logic. Rather, virtual realism is an existential process of criticism, practice, and conscious communication."[42] Consequently, in distinguishing balance from other modes of dealing with binary opposition, the advocates of balance not only employ a dichotomy (e.g., balance vs. either/or and balance vs. synthesis) but do so in such a way that is, according to their own descriptions, out of balance. Instead of balancing the opposition that is situated between balance and these other techniques for dealing with binary opposition, the advocates of balance advance their position over and against these others, utilizing an either/or approach in order to advance an argument for something that is said to be an alternative to simple dichotomy. In this way, those who argue for balance, it appears, do not practice what they preach. What they do (describe and advocate balance in opposition to other methods of dealing with binary opposition) remains in conflict with what they espouse (the need to balance competing perspectives without choosing sides). And when one tries to explain or dispense with this difficulty, s/he often does so by introducing an additional logical dichotomy that only makes matters worse. Elbow, for example, provides the following clarification, which is anything but clear: "Of course, I'm not going so far as to say that we should balance every dichotomy we encounter. Certainly, it sometimes makes sense to choose one side as right, the other wrong. Indeed, when we need to make difficult value judgments or sort out slippery distinctions, pairings are an enormous help. . . . And this whole essay could be called an exercise in saying, 'There are two kinds of binary thinking, the good kind and the bad kind.' In short, I acknowledge that now and then we need the invidious kind of binary opposition. I'm just pleading for more effort to notice the many situations where the easy, good/bad distinction gets us in trouble and we need balance and irresolution."[43] With this comment, Elbow organizes binary oppositions into "the good kind of opposition" and "the bad kind of opposition." The "bad kind" needs to be balanced, while the "good kind" can be used to describe and articulate the features of this particular kind of balance. This explanation is not only open to significant equivocation—who or what decides whether an opposition is "good" or "bad"—but leaves one wondering whether the opposition situated between the good and bad opposition is itself a good or bad kind of opposition. Instead of resolving the initial difficulty, this "solution" reinscribes and exacerbates it.

Dialectic

> The history of the term "dialectic" would by itself
> constitute a considerable history of philosophy.[44]
> —Barbara Cassin

In the process of presenting their arguments, Heim, Elbow, and McLuhan all distinguish and oppose the balancing of oppositions to "Hegelian dialectic." Although the concept of "dialectic" goes back as far as Plato, who employed the term in order to distinguish the Socratic practice of philosophy from rhetoric, it is Hegel who, for better or worse, is usually identified as the originator of this method of contending with and resolving conflict between opposites. Hegelian dialectic, as Peter Lunenfeld characterizes it in his introduction to *The Digital Dialectic*, "is commonly understood to be a dynamic process in which one proposition is matched against another (often its opposite) in order to bring a third, combinatory proposition into being. Formulaically, the dialectic is the thinking or acting through of the thesis and the antithesis to reach a synthesis."[45] Understood in this way, dialectic, unlike balance, does not tolerate or maintain binary opposition but mediates the conflict by combining the two opposed perspectives in a new unity or third term. In other words, the conflict that is situated between any two opposing terms, a thesis and its opposite or antithesis, is only a temporary and transitory moment. Eventually the conflict is mediated and resolved in a third term that mixes together or combines the two. Consequently dialectic, as Elbow describes it, "uses binary thinking as a motor always to press on to a third term or higher category that represents a transcendent reconciliation or unity: thesis and antithesis are always harnessed to yield synthesis."[46]

Although the thesis-antithesis-synthesis formula has been routinely attributed to Hegel and can "still be readily found," as Jon Stewart points out, "in encyclopedias and handbooks of Philosophy,"[47] it actually does not appear, in this particular form, in any of Hegel's published texts. As Gustav Mueller points out in his seminal essay addressing this issue, "the Hegel legend of thesis-antithesis-synthesis" is just that, a legend. It has little or no basis in Hegel's writings and is, in fact, the result of a misrepresentation and distortion of Hegelian philosophy.[48] According to Stewart, who includes this essay in the anthology *The Hegel Myths and Legends*, Mueller "irrefutably exposes this legend for what it is, by tracing the regrettable dissemination of this view back to Marx, who inherited it from a certain Heinrich Moritz Chalybäus, a long since forgotten expositor of the philosophy of Kant and Hegel."[49] Consequently, the thesis-antithesis-synthesis formula is not so much a characterization of Hegelian philosophy as it is a caricature. To put it schematically, the method of Hegelian philosophy, as it is described by Hegel, consists not in the three stages of thesis-antithesis-synthesis but in a dynamic process that is animated by two moments of *negation*. It all begins, as Hegel explains in the conclusion to the *Science of Logic*, at the beginning. This beginning is, at the beginning, an abstract universal that is simple, immediate, and thoroughly indeterminate. It is, as Hegel describes, "merely the abstract relation-to-self" or "the *in-itself* that is without a *being-for-itself*."[50] The *Science of Logic*, for example, begins with *being*. Not any particular being but "being, pure being, without any further determination."[51] The means of advancement, which constitutes not only the mediation of this abstract beginning but the process of determination in general, is not a mere subjective operation imposed by consciousness from the outside but an objective occurrence arising out of the first term itself. Hence, "the immediate of the beginning must be *in its own self* deficient and endowed with the *urge* to carry itself further."[52] This self-imposed differentiation, "by which the universal of the beginning of its own accord determines itself as the *other of itself*, is to be named the *dialectical* moment."[53] The dialectical moment, therefore, results in the kind of oppositional pairing where one term is situated as the negative of the other. Being, for example, comes to be determined in opposition to its negative and other, which is, not surprisingly, *nothing*. The opposition of being and nothing, however, does not remain static and fixed as it customarily is in ordinary thinking but is itself negated. This "second negative," which is in fact the negative of a negative, is what Hegel calls the *Aufheben* of the opposition.[54] Although usually translated by the rather archaic

English word "sublation," *Aufheben* names a unique operation, which Hegel argues is fundamental to all of philosophy.[55] According to Hegel's characterization, "'*to sublate*' has a twofold meaning in language: on the one hand it means to preserve, to maintain, and equally it also means to cause to cease, to put an end to.... Thus what is sublated is at the same time preserved; it has only lost its immediacy but is not on that account annihilated."[56] The sublation of the dialectic of being and nothing, for instance, is *becoming*. Becoming constitutes a third term that both puts an end to the mere opposition of being and nothing and at the same time preserves their difference in itself. Or as Hegel describes it in that kind of dense prose for which he is famous, "*Becoming* is the unseparatedness of being and nothing, not the unity which abstracts from being and nothing; but as the unity of *being* and *nothing* it is this *determinate* unity in which there *is* both being and nothing."[57]

This rather technical explanation entails two important consequences. First, Hegelian dialectic, as it is characterized by Hegel, includes within it the other two methods of contending with opposition that were considered previously. This insight is consistent with Hegel's own understanding of the dialectic, which is claimed to be not an alternative method of philosophy that is situated alongside others as a competitor but *the* proper method of philosophy that incorporates all others in its own movement.[58] In particular, the first negative, what Hegel calls "the dialectical moment," generates the binary oppositions that define the two possible options that comprise the either/or approach. For Hegel, however, dialectical thinking does not remain at this point of mere opposition and contradiction. It is submitted to a second negation, the *Aufhebung*, which does not simply annihilate the opposition but preserves it, striking a kind of balance, or what Hegel calls "equilibrium."[59] In this way, then, the dialectic incorporates, as constitutive elements of its own process, the other methods for addressing and dealing with binary opposition. Second, here one can also perceive the points of intersection and differentiation between Hegel's own description and the Marxian formula, which has, for better or worse, come to replace it in the popular understanding. Hegel's description of the method of philosophy focuses attention on process and, in particular, the two moments of negation that animate the process. For Hegel what is, in the beginning, merely *in-itself*, is posited *for-itself* in the ordeal of the dialectical moment, and becomes *in-* and *for-itself* through the unique activity of *Aufheben*. The thesis-antithesis-synthesis formula, on the contrary, identifies, through a kind of abstract and general characterization, the three substantive elements that would be involved in this process. Although Hegelians like Mueller argue that such a general and substantive description does not hold up across all the particular expressions of Hegel's philosophy,[60] there is another point of differentiation that is equally if not more important. When it is characterized substantively as involving three static components, one could get the mistaken impression that the dialectic has a simple end point. That is, it appears that thesis and antithesis are resolved by synthesis, which concludes the conflict and puts an end to opposition. For Hegel, however, the process is on-going and cyclical. The result of sublation, what would ostensibly be the "third term" in the process, is not simply the end but is also a new beginning that, in accordance with the process of philosophy, immediately passes over into dia-lectical differentiation by positing its own negation in its other.[61] Consequently, the entirety of Hegelian philosophy "exhibits itself as a *circle* returning upon itself, the end being wound back to the beginning through the mediation; this circle is moreover a *circle of circles*, for each individual member as ensouled by the method is reflected into itself, so that in returning to the beginning it is at the same time the beginning of a new member."[62] Interestingly, this description, which accounts for both the points of intersection and differentiation between Hegelian philosophy and its formulaic representation, performs the very thing that it seeks to describe. It does not simply differentiate Hegel from the carica-ture of Hegelianism but sublates this difference and, in the process, produces what one might be tempted to call a "synthesis" of the two.

Application of the dialectic, in either the form of its substantive (mis)rep-resentation or a more attentive reading of the Hegelian description of the pro-cess, is readily apparent in recent work addressing computer technology and is exemplified in those situations where theorists and practitioners have attempted to define new, hybrid concepts like the "virtual," the "cyborg," and "remedia-tion." The "virtual" and "virtual reality" are terms that have often been situated in contradistinction to the real. As Pierre Lévy explains it, "the word 'virtual' often signifies unreality, 'reality' here implying some material embodiment, a tangible presence. The expression 'virtual reality' sounds like an oxymoron, some mysterious sleight of hand. We generally assume that something is either real or virtual, and that it cannot possess both qualities at once."[63] Understood in this way, the "virtual" is not only situated in opposition to the real but is also allied with all those other terms that have customarily been differentiated from what is real—representation, fantasy, image, illusion, fiction, fabrication, etc. Despite this rather common characterization, which has been usefully employed by both advocates and critics of VR technology,[64] there has been a concerted ef-fort to define things otherwise. In particular, theorists have opposed this simple characterization, contenting, as Peter Horsfield does, that "it is mistaken to contrast the virtual to 'the real'"[65] and arguing for, as Mark Poster describes it, "a perception of the virtual as a new combination of real and imaginary."[66] Benjamin Woolley, for example, traces the concept of the "virtual" back to the introduction, in the early 1970s, of "virtual memory." Virtual memory, which is now a common design feature of most operating systems for the personal computer, comprises a method for adding RAM (random access memory) to a computer system without actually having to add any memory chips. Accord-ing to Woolley, everything the computer does can be called "virtual" in this particular sense of the word. "Using a computer gives some experience of what 'virtual' really means. Personal computer users generally become comfortable with the idea of the system being at once a word processor, a calculator, a drawing pad, a reference library, a spelling checker. If they pulled their system apart, or the disks that contain the software, they would find no sign of any of these things any more than the dismemberment of an IBM 370 would reveal all that extra memory provided by the virtual memory system. They are purely abstract entities, in being independent of any particular physical embodiment, but real nonetheless."[67] According to this characterization, "virtual" names not the opposite of the real but something that is functionally real and, at the same time, not really real in terms of having some material or physical embodiment.[68] As Michael Heim defines it, the virtual is that which is "not actually, but as if."[69] This particular conceptualization of the virtual has also been applied to explain the features and characteristics of VR. For Stanovsky, who is not alone in this assessment, the images produced by VR technology do not simply conform to the traditional metaphysical divisions that have been used to differentiate the real from its opposites but constitute something entirely different. "It is not," he writes, "simply that the representations of virtual reality are false (not genuine) like the reflections in a mirror. It is not even analogous to Plato's view of theater, which was to be banned from his Republic because of its distortions and misrepresentations of reality. Instead, virtual reality may summon up a whole new reality, existing without reference to an external reality, and requiring its own internal methods of distinguishing true from false, what is genuine or authentic from what is spurious or inauthentic."[70] According to this description, VR creates representations that are not simply false, fictitious, or illusory. Instead they constitute an entirely "new reality" that exists outside external reality and operates according to its own internal laws and mechanisms. Characterized in this way then, the virtual is not the mere opposite of the real but comprises a completely new form of reality that is somehow both real and not real and, at the same time, neither simply one nor the other.

Like the virtual, the concept of the "cyborg" has been defined and characterized as a "third term" that integrates what had been traditionally differentiated and opposed. The word "cyborg" is itself a synthesis of the words "cybernetic" and "organism" and was initially introduced in a 1962 article on manned space flight written by Manfred Clynes and Nathan Kline. For Clynes and Kline, "cyborg" named an "exogenously extended organizational complex functioning as an integrated homeostatic system."[71] Since this introduction, the word has come to be employed to name any integration of organism and machine into a hybrid entity. As Chris Hables Gray defines it, "a cyborg is a self-regulating organism that combines the natural and the artificial together in one system."[72] Defined in this way, the cyborg, in whatever way it is configured, does not take up an appropriate position on either side of the conceptual oppositions by which we have typically parsed and organized our world. Cyborgs, as Anne Balsamo points out, "cannot be conceived as belonging wholly to either culture or nature; they are neither wholly technological nor completely organic."[73] Instead cyborgs comprise hybrids that blur the boundaries between and mix together the two terms of a traditional binary opposition, like organic/machinic and natural/artificial. The Borg of *Star Trek*, for example, are neither human nor machine. They comprise a third kind of entity that is neither one nor the other but consists in an integrated and symbiotic mixture of the two. Although this characterization appears to be an almost perfect illustration of what has been called "dialectic"—the cyborg comprising a synthetic third term that combines thesis with antithesis—the situation is more complex. Gray, for instance, recognizes and utilizes the thesis-antithesis-synthesis formula in the course of articulating a cyborg epistemology, or what he calls "cyborgology."[74] At the same time, however, he introduces an important enhancement and extension by appending to the triplicity a fourth step—prosthesis. "We wanted," Gray explains, "to keep the dynamism of the traditional dialectic and yet go beyond the binary/dualistic framework it is trapped in. Reality isn't just action and reaction, it is lumpy, we argued. . . . So we said a cyborg epistemology is: 'Thesis, antithesis, synthesis, prosthesis. And again.' The order doesn't matter. Prostheses can be attached at any stage, and lead to their own dialectical interactions. And theses are multiple, as are antitheses. And more than one synthesis can come out of a thesis-antithesis dance. Much of reality is just too complicated for simplicity, in words or images."[75] This rehabilitation of the dialectic does not contest the trinary procedure per se but enhances it by adding a fourth substantive element that can, according to Gray, be attached anywhere in the process. In this way, the new prosthetic stage constitutes a kind of prosthesis that is added onto and that is designed to supplement the dialectic. And what Gray writes about prosthesis applies equally to this particular addition: "Enhancements and replacements are never fully integrated into a new synthesis, rather they remain lumpy and semi-autonomous."[76] Gray's addition of prosthesis to the dialectic is not something that is easily integrated into the tripartite formula and, therefore, remains somewhat conspicuous and, in his words, "lumpy."

The most ambitious attempt to apply dialectic to the thinking of ICT, however, appears in Jay David Bolter and Richard Grusin's "Remediation," an essay and later a book that not only considers the special features of digital technology but also offers its insights as a general theory of media. Remediation is involved with dialectic in at least two ways. First, it is situated as the third and final term in a triplicity of logics: immediacy, hypermediacy, and remediation. The logic of immediacy is, as Bolter and Grusin explain it, the tendency of a medium to want to erase itself and to produce a transparent interface. "A transparent interface is one that erases itself, so that the user would no longer be aware of confronting a medium, but instead would stand in an immediate relationship to the contents of the medium."[77] VR technology, for example, endeavors to immerse the user in its computer-generated representations so that one confronts this content in such a way that s/he completely forgets about the apparatus by which it is created. Hypermediacy is "the opposite number" or "alter ego" of this kind of experience and therefore constitutes "a cultural counterbalance" or "historical counterpart" to the desire for immediacy. "If the logic of immediacy leads one to erase or automatize the act of representation, the logic of hypermediacy acknowledges multiple acts of representation and makes them visible. Where the logic of immediacy suggests a unified visual space, hypermediacy offers a heterogeneous space, in which representation is conceived of not as a window onto the world, but rather as 'windowed' itself—with windows opening onto other representations or other media. The logic of hypermedia calls for representations of the real that in fact multiply the signs of mediation."[78] Understood in this way, immediacy and hypermediacy are "contradictory imperatives"[79] that are situated in a dialectical relationship, whereby the one constitutes the opposite or inverse of the other. This opposition, however, is resolved or sublated in "remediation," which consists in what Bolter and Grusin call "a double logic." "Our culture wants both to multiply its media and to erase all traces of mediation: it wants to erase its media in the very act of multiplying technologies of mediation."[80] Remediation, therefore, names the combination of immediacy and hypermediacy. It is the sublation—the surpassing and preserving—of the contradiction that had been situated between and that had distinguished these two different and opposed media logics.

Second, remediation, as Bolter and Grusin characterize it, is the formalization of a remark that was recorded by McLuhan in *Understanding Media*: "The content of any medium is always another medium."[81] Remediation, therefore, names the way in which a new medium (e.g., the World Wide Web) incorporates, reuses, and recycles elements of the previous media (e.g., print, television, radio) that it is often said to be in the process of replacing. "We call," Bolter and Grusin write, "the representation of one medium in another 'remediation,' and we will argue that remediation is a defining characteristic of the new digital media. What might seem at first to be an esoteric practice is so widespread that we can identify a spectrum of different ways in which digital media remediate their predecessors, a spectrum depending upon the degree of perceived competition or rivalry between the new media and the old."[82] New media are, in both name and function, distinguished from and situated in opposition to old media. This new vs. old conflict is apparent not only in the competition for market share but also in the critical evaluations that are associated with the introduction of new media. The appearance of a new medium is almost always accompanied by statements announcing, often prematurely, the death of a previous form of media—television was supposed to have been the death of film, the Internet has been called the end of the book, and video killed the radio star. The opposition and conflict between old and new media, however, is resolved in the movement of remediation. A new medium does not simply oppose the old but takes up and preserves the characteristics of old media in the form of the new. The World Wide Web, for example, does not simply oppose the older media of print and television. Instead it combines text information and the conventions

of page layout together with the motion images and audio of television to create a new hybrid form that combines both. Although this description appears
to be perfectly Hegelian in its account of an ongoing evolution of media, Bolter
and Grusin introduce an important modification. "In the first instance we may
think of something like a historical progression, of newer media remediating
older ones and in particular of digital media remediating their predecessors.
But we are offering a genealogy of affiliations, not a linear history, and in this
genealogy, older media can also remediate newer ones. Television can and does
refashion itself in the image of the World Wide Web."[83] And in a footnote to this
passage, the authors not only explicitly recognize the similarities between "remediation" and the Hegelian *Aufhebung* but, at the same time, mark this important modification: "It is in this sense of older media remediating newer ones
that our notion of remediation can be distinguished from the Hegelian concept
of sublation ('*Aufhebung*'), in which prior historical formations (like pagan religions) are sublated or incorporated by newer formations (like Christianity)."[84]
Like the Hegelian *Aufhebung*, remediation names a process by which prior media formations are sublated or incorporated into newer ones. However, remediation, unlike Hegelian philosophy, can also move in the other direction and
incorporate newer media formations within the old. Although not all Hegelians
would agree with this particular clarification, what is not debated is the fact that
Bolter and Grusin explicitly identify their project with Hegel and define it as a
remediation of Hegelianism.

Historically, responses to the dialectic tend toward the extremes. Hegelianism is either embraced as a sophisticated means for dealing with the oppositions that have organized thinking or rejected *tout court* as an overly complicated
process that defies all common sense.[85] In any event, there are systemic features
of the dialectic that affect and influence both modes of reception. Specifically,
Hegelian philosophy, in whatever way it is characterized, constitutes a closed loop,
in which all opposition is deployed by and reinvested for the dialectical process.
In the dialectic, all modes of difference comprise a negation whereby the other,
what one might call the antithesis, is always the negative and counterpoint of
an initial positive term or thesis. Likewise all forms of differentiation, in whatever particular way they appear, are always surpassed through a negation of this
negation or what Hegel calls a "sublation" of the initial dialectical opposition.
Consequently, there can be no differentiated alterity other than the negative of a
positive, and there can be no mode of opposition other than that which is sublated
in and by the movement of *Aufheben*. This has at least two consequences. First, it
is extremely difficult, if not impossible, to escape from or to oppose Hegel. Michel
Foucault points out this particular problem in "The Discourse on Language": "To
escape Hegel involves an exact appreciation of the price we have to pay to detach
ourselves from him. It assumes that we are aware of the extent to which Hegel,
insidiously perhaps, is close to us; it implies a knowledge, in that which permits
us to think against Hegel, of that which remains Hegelian. We have to determine

the extent to which our anti-Hegelianism is possibly one of his tricks directed against us, at the end of which he stands, motionless, waiting for us."[86] In other words, opposing Hegel is difficult if not close to impossible, because any form of opposition may in fact already be made in terms of Hegelianism and therefore would not be opposed to Hegel but instead already working for and with Hegel. This rather abstract description is exemplified by Heim, whose argument for a form of balance that is situated in opposition to dialectical synthesis turns out to be perfectly Hegelian. Heim makes explicit reference to Hegelian dialectics in the process of describing virtual realism and immediately dismisses it as an inappropriate method to contend with the opposition that is situated between network idealism and naïve realism: "Hegel would have appreciated their mutual opposition while betting on an eventual synthesis. Unfortunately, no synthesis is in sight. A collision may be imminent. We are looking at an opposition of primal forces, as basic as love and death."[87] According to Heim's estimations, the opposition that is situated between the network idealist and naïve realist looks like something that would fit the Hegelian process of thesis-antithesis-synthesis. But the opposition in question is, in his opinion, too essential and primordial. Not only is no synthesis in sight, it seems forever postponed insofar as the differences between the two terms appear to be irreducible and irreconcilable. In contrast to this impossible synthetic resolution, Heim advocates virtual realism, a method that balances the two options against each other. This argument is persuasive as long as Hegelian dialectic is exclusively understood according to the Marxian formula of thesis-antithesis-synthesis. Unfortunately, the watchword of Hegelianism is not "synthesis" but *"Aufheben." Aufheben*, according to Hegel, comprises a double gesture that overcomes and preserves difference. Consequently, *Aufheben* appears to accomplish exactly what Heim has in mind with virtual realism. Virtual realism is described as a new, third term that would overcome the mere difference of network idealism and naïve realism and, at the same time, preserve their differences in a careful balancing of the one against the other. Heim's attempt to articulate something that is distinct from and opposed to Hegelian dialectic turns out to look very much like Hegelianism. This is, it should be emphasized, not because Heim is some kind of "closeted Hegelian." It is instead a component of the dialectic, which has already determined all forms of opposition to be a moment of its own process and success.

Second, because the opposed other in the process of dialectic is always the inverse or negative of the first term, difference is only figured as derivative, contradictory, and deficient. Consequently, for dialectic, as for all forms of binary opposition in general, difference is configured negatively, meaning that there can be no thinking of difference or alterity outside negation. This situation produces, as poststructuralists like Jacques Derrida, Elizabeth Grosz, Hélène Cixous and others have pointed out, binary arrangements that are not situations of equality between two terms but an a priori hierarchy and order of precedence. "In a classical philosophical opposition," Derrida explains, "we are not dealing with the peaceful coexistence of a *vis-à-vis* [literally, "face-to-face"] but rather with a violent hierarchy. One of the two terms governs the other, or has the upper hand."[88] This kind of fundamental "bias," if we can be permitted to use a word that is already somewhat biased, is operative and evident in the three examples provided above. First, in the dialectic of the virtual, the real is a privileged term. This is evident by the fact that the conceptual opposition that generates the virtual is one that is situated between the real, which is defined positively, and its other, which is defined, quite literally, as its negative—the "unreal." It is also manifest in characterizations of the "virtual." VR theorists, like Stanovsky, call the virtual a "new reality." They do not write "a new unreality" or even "a new imaginary," although this would be no less appropriate. Second, despite the fact that the cyborg constitutes a hybrid of human and machine, there remains a privileging of the human and humanist values in the writing and theorizing about cyborgs. This residue of a kind of anthropocentrism can be tracked in the way that humanist values continue, for better or worse, to inform the presentation of the cyborg in many of the theoretical writings and the images that are provided in popular culture.[89] Finally, despite the fact that remediation constitutes the sublation of immediacy and hypermediacy, it is immediacy that is situated in the privileged position. Bolter and Grusin make no bones about it: "The logic of immediacy has perhaps been dominant in Western representation, at least since the Renaissance until the coming of modernism, while hypermediacy has often had to content itself with a secondary, but nonetheless important status."[90] In the dialectic of remediation, immediacy has been the dominant term, while its other, hypermediacy, has been secondary in both sequence and status.

Poststructuralism

> Our age, whether through logic or epistemology, whether through Marx or through Nietzsche, is attempting to flee Hegel.[91]—Michel Foucault

Although dialectic had wanted to be the final word, there have been a number of different strategies to think beyond and outside the system of Hegel in particular and the structure of binary opposition in general. These different practices are often collected and organized under the general category *poststructuralism*. "While poststructuralism does not constitute," as Mark Taylor points out, "a unified movement, writers as different as Jacques Derrida, Jacques Lacan, and Michel Foucault on the one hand, and on the other Hélène Cixous, Julia Kristeva, and Michel de Certeau devise alternative tactics to subvert the grid of binary oppositions with which structuralists believe they can capture reality."[92] Since poststructuralism does not constitute a unified movement or singular method, what makes its different forms cohere is not an underlying similarity but a difference, specifically different modes of thinking difference differently. In other words, what draws the different articulations of poststructuralism together into an affiliation that may be identified with this one term is not a homogeneous method or technique "which is mechanically applied to different works and imposed on diverse objects."[93] Instead what they share is a common interest in thinking the difference customarily situated between binary opposites outside of and beyond not just the grasp of Hegelian dialectic but the entire history of Western philosophy, of which Hegelianism, on its own account, was to have been the culmination. Consequently, the different approaches that constitute poststructuralism all take aim at difference and endeavor to articulate, in very different and often incompatible ways, a kind of difference that is, for lack of a better description, radically different.

This abstract and somewhat difficult characterization can be explicated by considering a few examples.[94] Consider, for instance, Gilles Deleuze's *Difference and Repetition*, a 1968 publication that not only marked an important transition from Deleuze's earlier writings on the history of philosophy to the act of writing philosophy but also indicated, as he suggests, the direction of all his subsequent publications, including those coauthored with Félix Guattari.[95] As is immediately evident from its title, *Difference and Repetition* is concerned with the "metaphysics of difference," specifically the formulation of "a concept of difference without negation."[96] As Deleuze describes it in the text's preface, "we propose to think difference in itself independently of the forms of representation which reduce it to the Same, and the relation of different to different independently of those forms which make them pass through the negative."[97] Deleuze, therefore, proposes a "new" concept of difference that cannot be reduced to negation and, as such, necessarily exceeds comprehension by the customary philosophical understanding of difference that had persisted from Plato to at least Hegel, if not beyond. In a similar but entirely different way, Derrida's neologism *différance*, a nonconcept that is, quite literally in this case, different from difference, marks a point of contact with and differentiation from the thinking of difference that had been situated in Hegelianism. As Derrida explains, "I have attempted to distinguish *différance* (whose *a* marks, among other things, its productive and conflictual characteristics) from Hegelian difference, and have done so precisely at the point at which Hegel, in the greater *Logic*, determines difference as contradiction only in order to resolve it, to interiorize it, to lift it up (according to the syllogistic process of speculative dialectics) into the self-presence of an ontotheological or onto-teleological synthesis."[98] For Derrida, the visibly differentiated *différance* indicates a different way to think and write of a difference that remains in excess of the Hegelian concept of difference, which has been exclusively understood as negation and contradiction. And in a different but not altogether unrelated way, Emmanuel Levinas addresses difference differently by focusing attention on others. As Levinas demonstrates, the history of Western philosophy has been "engaged in reducing to the same all that is opposed to it as *other*."[99] In this way, the other, in all the diverse ways in which it makes its particular appearances, has been conceptualized as the negative counterpart of the self-same and, therefore, has been reduced to a mode or modification of it. In advancing what many have since called "a philosophy of radical otherness," a way of thinking that is attuned to the absolute exteriority of alterity, Levinas introduces a conceptualization of *the other* that remains otherwise than what belongs to and is controlled by the tradition. This other that is otherwise is, as Levinas writes, situated on "the hither side of the negativity which is always speculatively recuperable" in the movement of the dialectic.[100] Although the particular tactics employed by these different manifestations of what is called "poststructuralism" differ significantly and sometimes even collide with each other,[101] they all participate in what Foucault characterized as the "attempt to flee Hegel" and do so by advancing different ways to conceive of difference differently.

Although poststructuralism is commonly associated with continental philosophy, semiotics, and literary theory, it has been uploaded into the currents of cyberculture studies and examinations of information technology. This is evident, for instance, in Mark Taylor's work on VR and Donna Haraway's "A Cyborg Manifesto."[102] Taylor's engagement with VR, it is important to note, is not simply an application of poststructuralist methods to the object of VR. Poststructuralism, as Taylor points out, already renders the distinction between method and application problematic and questionable. Instead Taylor's text employs and engages poststructuralism in both its theory and practice. That is, his analysis of VR draws on and utilizes the theoretical insights introduced by poststructuralism and, at the same time, submits these innovations to a similar kind of investigation. "In what follows," Taylor writes, "I will attempt to think what poststructuralism leaves unthought by showing how nontotalizing structures, which nonetheless act as a whole, are beginning to emerge in the tangled networks and webs through which reality is virtualized and virtuality is realized."[103] In attempting to think what poststructuralism leaves unthought, Taylor's investigation applies lessons that have been learned from poststructuralism, namely the conceptualization of what remains outside of and beyond traditional modes of thinking, to poststructuralism. In this way, he does not so much apply poststructuralist thinking to the technology of VR but uses VR as an occasion and opportunity to apply poststructuralist thinking to itself. Consistent with the poststructuralist strategy to think difference differently, Taylor begins by "recasting differences as interfaces." "The nondialectical mean between which extremes are suspended constitutes something like an *interface*, which is the condition for the possibility and the impossibility of seemingly seamless systems and structures. When radically conceived, this interface extends beyond every margin of difference to 'contaminate' opposites that once seemed fixed."[104] For Taylor, *interface*, conceptualized at the extreme limit of its usual characterization within the field of information technology, constitutes a "strange notion or nonnotion" that does not simply "reinscribe structures of difference and systems of oppositions"[105] but makes these different opposites interact and pollute each other in a way that is entirely unexpected and thoroughly different. This operation can be seen at work, Taylor argues, in VR technology, which is, according to his own analysis, not just one mode of interface but its privileged manifestation:

> As the infosphere and dataspace steadily expand, virtual technologies become ever more pervasive. The response to these developments has been predictably mixed. For some, virtual reality is a nightmare in which isolated subjects sit in front of computer terminals, alienated from their bodies, other people, and the environment. For others, virtual reality creates the possibility of escaping the limitations of time and space, and holds the promise of realizing the ancient dream of global unity and harmony. It should be clear by now that these antithetical assessments of virtual reality share mistaken assumptions and presumptions. First, by failing to contextualize their analyses, supporters as well as critics make the mistake of representing virtual reality as a specific technology rather than an effective figure of the postmodern condition. Second, previous responses to virtual reality reinscribe oppositions like mind/body, human/machine, natural/artificial, and material/immaterial, which the long process of virtualizing reality subverts. What once seemed to be hard-and-fast oppositions now appear to be interfaces in which neither term remains the same. Virtual reality involves neither synthesis of opposites not the suppression of one term by the other but gives rise to a different order of "reality" that eludes traditional classificatory structures. When virtual reality is understood as a process rather than a product, ostensibly stable oppositions become oscillating interfaces that are constantly reconfigured.[106]

With this explanation, Taylor takes us back to where it all began. Like Heim, he finds that responses to VR have tended to be organized around two apparently opposite poles—either a dystopian nightmare of mechanized alienation and computer-mediated narcissism or a utopian dream of transcendence and global reunification. In considering these two opposed perspectives, however, Taylor focuses not on balancing their differences but on tracing their unacknowledged points of contact. That is, he concerns himself with what the two sides of the debate must share in order to take up opposing positions in the first place. In the case of VR, there are, Taylor argues, two mistaken assumptions. First, both sides assume that the various problems and challenges introduced by VR are exclusively a matter of technology. They situate their arguments in the material of computer systems and quibble about the technical details. In this way, they remain unaware of the larger context in which VR operates and in which it makes its appearance. Second, and because of this common blind spot, each side of the debate has articulated and argued for its position by mobilizing, without hesitation or question, the traditional metaphysical oppositions (i.e., mind/body, natural/artificial, human/machine, etc.) by which we have explained virtually everything. Although these metaphysical pairings have a long and venerable history, what is happening with VR is entirely otherwise. VR, Taylor argues, does not easily conform to one side or the other but, like other figures of poststructuralism, tends to disturb and to subvert oppositional structures, creating permeable interfaces between what had been differentiated elements. VR, therefore, cannot be adequately comprehended by mobilizing binary oppositions, because it dissolves such distinctions and fosters a general pollution of the one by the other. Understood according to this characterization of *interface*, VR concerns neither a choice of one term over the other, a careful balancing of two opposing viewpoints, nor a grand synthesis in some dialectical third term. Instead it constitutes a thorough contamination of binary oppositions where neither term remains as it had been and, as a result of this complete reconfiguration, "creates new interpretive and critical possibilities."[107]

The deliberate contamination of traditionally opposed terms is also the defining feature of what Haraway[108] calls "cyborg." For Haraway, whose writing on this subject matter precedes application of the modified and "lumpy dialectic" that is promulgated by Gray and associates, "cyborg" is the product of "three crucial boundary breakdowns" that foster illegitimate fusions and subvert the usual conceptual order.[109] The first concerns the differentiation of the human from the animal. This conceptual distinction, by which human beings have defined themselves in opposition to what they are not, has been fundamental to Western forms of theology, philosophy, and science. According to Haraway, however, everything is now up for grabs: "The boundary between human and animal is thoroughly breached. The last beachheads of uniqueness have been polluted if not turned into amusement parks—language, tool use, social behavior, mental events, nothing really convincingly settles the separation of human and animal."[110] The second "leaky distinction" affects the division that had been established between living organisms (human-animal) and machines. This conceptual opposition, like the one that had been situated between the human and the animal, has been and continues to be one of the fundamental means by which Western systems of knowledge come to be organized and justified. For Haraway, however, the machinery of the computer has altered everything. "Late twentieth-century machines have made thoroughly ambiguous the difference between natural and artificial, mind and body, self-developing and externally designed, and many other distinctions that used to apply to organisms and machines."[111] Not only is the human increasingly indistinguishable from its animal counterpart but the living organism, whether human or animal, is also increasingly indistinguishable from the machine. This boundary breakdown is especially evident in the science of cybernetics, where the machine and the animal were both characterized and addressed as systems of communication and control. The third boundary breakdown, which is, Haraway explains, actually a subset of the second, involves contamination across the border separating the physical from the nonphysical. As both the machine and the body of the living organism dematerialize into little more than a stream of data (binary digits in the case of the machine and DNA code in the case of a living organism) the distinction between what had been physical and what is nonphysical becomes increasingly difficult to mark, defend, and sustain. For Haraway, then, the cyborg appears and gives its unique name to this network of transgressed boundaries. Consequently, the cyborg consists in a thoroughly monstrous figure that neither maintains binary opposition as such nor seeks resolution in some dialectical third term. In a kind of affinity with what Taylor names *interface*, the cyborg resists totalizing gestures of all kinds, insists on noise and advocates pollution, and does so for the purpose of opening new and previously unheard-of possibilities. "Cyborg imagery," Haraway concludes, "can suggest a way out of the maze of dualisms in which we have explained our bodies and our tools to ourselves."[112]

The promise of what Taylor calls "new interpretive and critical possibilities" is unquestionably compelling. Any mode of thinking that can, as Haraway describes it, "suggest a way out of the maze of dualisms" that have structured and limited our knowledge of ourselves and our world sounds both attractive and liberating. There are, however, important consequences to these alternatives that may temper initial enthusiasm and that need to be taken into account. First, in order to articulate a "non-dialectical third term" that exceeds and subverts traditional binary oppositions, poststructuralists often find themselves in a difficult situation with regards to language and communication. If structuralism is right and language, any language, is a system of differences, then any alternative that is determined to escape binary opposition can only be described in and by using a vocabulary that is necessarily composed of binary oppositions. In such a situation, language must be twisted and contorted in such a way as to make that which is fundamentally binary in its structure articulate something that no longer can be and never was able to be comprehended by such arrangements. The manner by which this is accomplished, although obviously different for individual theorists, usually entails the use of two related strategies. On the one hand, a writer can employ *neologism*, inventing a brand-new word to name a new possibility or object. Examples abound. There are, for instance, the well-known and often difficult Derridian neologisms: *différance*, *deconstruction*, and *arche-trace*. But this is by no means something that is limited to Derrida. Other theorists have pursued a similar strategy: Trinh T. Minh-ha's *inappropriate/d other*, Levinas's *il y a*, and Deleuze's *le dispars*.[113] This is also the approach employed by Haraway. Although she did not invent the word "cyborg," she did resurrect and redefine this all but forgotten neologism in order to name something that exceeds the usual conceptual oppositions and the limited set of available names. On the other hand, a writer can practice what Derrida calls *paleonomy*, the use of an "old name in order to launch a new concept."[114] These "old names" can be archaic words that have almost fallen off the linguistic radar, like Derrida's use of the ancient Greek terms χώρα (chora) and φάρμακον (pharmakon) or the French *tympan* and *hymen*. Or they can be common words that are stuck with a significant difference that makes them slide away from their usual meaning and usage, like *writing, spacing, trace, supplement*, etc. Although Derrida's work supplies ample illustrations of the paleonomic strategy, this approach, like the strategy of neologism, is not something that is limited to the Derridian text. Deleuze's *Difference and Repetition*, for example, is rather economical in its use of neologism. Instead of inventing new words, Deleuze, as the text's English translator points out, "often draws upon existing words to create a terminology for concepts of his own making."[115] Likewise, Levinas takes a common word like *other* and makes it function in a way that is entirely otherwise. And Jean Baudrillard repurposes *simulation* to name the collapse of the distinction that had customarily differentiated the simulacrum from the real. This is also the strategy that is employed by Taylor in his consideration of VR. Whereas Haraway employs the strategy of neologism, Taylor uses and repurposes an old name, calling the interface of VR a "new 'reality.'" In reusing a word that is often considered to be the mere polar opposite of the virtual, Taylor finds it necessary to distinguish what he means by "reality" from the usual understanding of this word, and he does so by suspending the name of the new concept in quotation marks and by including additional qualifiers, which in this case, as in so many others, take the form of adjectival modifiers and disclaimers.

Second, because of this "communications problem," the innovations of poststructuralism always and necessarily risk becoming reappropriated into the existing binary oppositions that they work to undermine and exceed. The peculiarity of a neologism, for example, comes to be domesticated, through the actions of both advocates and critics, by making it conform to existing conceptual structures, often in the face of explicit statements to the contrary. This has, for example, been the fate of *deconstruction*. The word "deconstruction" does not mean to take apart, to un-construct, or to disassemble. It is neither a form of destructive analysis, a kind of intellectual demolition, nor a synonym for what had been called criticism. As Derrida has described it, "the de- of *de*construction signifies not the demolition of what is constructing itself, but rather what remains to be thought beyond the constructionist or destructionist schema."[116] Despite this qualification, "deconstruction" has been routinely reabsorbed by and understood according to a construction/destruction schema. For example, the practice of "deconstructive criticism," as the name implies, appropriated the term "deconstruction" to the task and project of literary criticism, turning it into a method of textual decomposition and explication. Similarly the word has been (mis)understood and employed as a synonym for analysis—the process of taking something apart in order to investigate its component elements. Physicist Brian Greene, for instance, examines the original components of the physical universe under the title "Deconstructing the Bang." Stephen P. Stich reevaluates recent developments in cognitive science by *Deconstructing the Mind*. And Lynda Weinman investigate the components of effective graphic design in *Deconstructing Web Graphics*.[117] The word has also found application outside the academy, where it has been used as another name for demolition and disassembly. Susan Morris and Associates define "deconstruction" as the process of "taking a building apart in a manner that achieves safe removal and disposal of hazardous materials and maximum salvage and recycling of materials."[118] And Iron Chefs Bobby Flay and Mario Batalli (dis)assemble "deconstructed salads" by arranging separate piles of greens, vegetables, and dressing on a plate. In all these cases, the neologism is domesticated and regulated through a misappropriation that makes "deconstruction" just another name for criticism, a synonym for analysis, a new term for dismantlement, or the mere opposite of assembly and construction. Paleonomy is exposed to a similar difficulty and is often easier to domesticate, because it does not take much interpretive work to make an "old name" function in the old way. *Writing*, for example, which for Derrida comes to be used to name something beyond and prior to the speech/writing opposition that is operative in and definitive of Western metaphysics, has often been simply resituated within the context of that particular conceptual pair. Consequently, critics like Walter Ong and John Ellis have taken Derrida to task for simply inverting the speech/writing hierarchy and, in the face of what appears to be overwhelming empirical evidence to the contrary, situating writing in the position of priority.[119] All of this is perpetrated in direct opposition to or in complete ignorance of carefully worded explanations that have been specifically designed to preempt and protect against such misunderstandings. Consequently, poststructuralism, whether employing the strategy of neologism, paleonomy, or a mixture of both, always runs the risk of having its innovations reappropriated into the binary oppositions in which and on which it supposedly works. This exposure to reappropriation and misunderstanding, however, is not the result of an individual critic who has it in for poststructuralism, even if critics have often exploited this situation for their own purposes. Instead it is a systemic necessity and unavoidable by-product of logic and language. It is caused by the fact that poststructuralism cannot conceptualize or articulate its innovations without employing a terminology that is already and inescapably organized in terms of binary oppositions.

Finally, due to the fact that "the hierarchy of dual oppositions always reestablishes itself,"[120] there neither is nor can be finality. "Leading poststructuralists," as Taylor explains, "realize that, since they remain unavoidably entangled in the systems and structures they resist, the task of criticism is endless."[121] Because the poststructuralist intervention in binary opposition necessarily and unavoidably runs the risk of falling back into binary opposition, there is always the need for additional work to address the newly reestablished hierarchy. For this reason, a poststructuralist investigation is not, strictly speaking, able to finish its work or complete its examination. The task is, as Derrida has described it, something of "an interminable analysis,"[122] a never-ending engagement that must continually submit its own innovations, movements, and conclusions to further scrutiny. Poststructuralism, therefore, does not conform to a concept of "science" understood and imagined as linear progress. This is not to say, however, that poststructuralism is not "scientific." It all depends on how one defines "science." In fact, by taking the form of an interminable engagement, poststructuralism dissimulates (with at least one crucial difference) the "speculative science" that is the hallmark of Hegelian thought. Here again, we encounter a difficulty imposed by the limitations of available terminology. For Hegel, "speculative" is not, as is often the case in colloquial discourse, a pejorative term meaning groundless consideration or idle review of something that is often inconclusive. Instead, Hegel understands and utilizes "speculative" in its original and strict etymological sense, which is derived from the Latin noun *speculum*, meaning mirror. For Hegel, a "speculative science" is a form of self-reflective knowing. That is, it is a manner of cognition that makes its own cognizing an object of its consideration. Like the speculative science that is described by Hegel, poststructuralism constitutes a thoroughly self-reflective undertaking that continually submits its own operations and innovations to investigation. However, unlike the Hegelian system, which has a definite teleological orientation and exit strategy, poststructuralism is caught in the vortex of what can only appear to be an infinite regress of endless self-reflection and auto-affective inquiry. Poststructuralism, therefore, does not conform to traditional models of knowledge production and representation. Its investigations do not and cannot supply anything like a definitive answer or conclusive solution, in the usual sense of the words. Instead its different queries, no matter what angle or aspect is pursued, entail an endless reproduction of questioning that becomes increasingly involved with the complexity of its own problematic. Although this is something that clearly cuts against the grain of common sense, it is necessary if the projects of poststructuralism are to be at all successful, consistent, and rigorously applied. At the same time, however, this particular form of endless self-involvement has engendered important ethical questions and political concerns. "The growing self-reflexivity of theory," Taylor writes, "seems to entail an aestheticizing of politics that makes cultural analysis and criticism increasingly irrelevant."[123] In other words, what's the matter with poststructuralism is that as it becomes more and more involved in its own questions and problematic, it appears to be increasingly cut off from the real questions and issues that matter. "Instead of engaging the 'real,' theory seems caught in a hall of mirrors from which 'reality' is 'systematically' excluded."[124] Critics of poststructuralism, therefore, find the insistence on an "interminable analysis" to be solipsistic at best and a potentially dangerous kind of intellectual narcissism at worst. At the same time, however, poststructuralism already has a response to this criticism, which, it rightfully points out, necessarily mobilizes and relies on one of the classic logical oppositions (the real vs. the unreal) that poststructural analysis had put in question in the first place.

Conclusion

> We invoke one dualism only in order to challenge
> another. . . . Each time, mental correctives are
> necessary to undo the dualisms we had no wish
> to construct but through which we pass.[125]
> —Gilles Deleuze and Félix Guattari

The digital computer processes and stores data by employing just two variables, zero and one. This binary logic not only comprises the technical operations of the information processor but also characterizes much of its critical reception. Like zero and one, which represent an electrical circuit that is either off or on, critical investigations of the computer and related digital information systems tend to be organized in terms of conceptual oppositions, where one term is situated and defined as the opposite of the other. There are, as we have seen, at least four different ways for addressing and responding to these binary oppositions or conceptual dualisms. One, the either/or approach, is not so much a method for dispensing with binary opposition as it is the condition for their possibility. Either/or constitutes the logical structure of opposition as such; one term is set in conflict with and excludes another. This approach, therefore, does not challenge or question dichotomy but organizes, confirms, and perpetuates its structure. The other three approaches—balance, dialectic, and poststructuralism—constitute increasingly sophisticated ways to think binary oppositions otherwise. In generally, they all endeavor to define alternative transactions that complicate dualisms, dichotomies, and binary oppositions. Balance seeks to define the middle ground that lies between two opposing terms, finding some kind of compromise or equilibrium. In doing so, however, it remains defined by and the property of the binary opposition that it had wanted to interrupt. Dialectic adds a dynamic dimension to this undertaking by submitting conceptual opposition to the movement of *Aufhebung*, sublating difference in a new or third term. This third term, however, immediately passes over into self-differentiation and consequently establishes a new dialectical conflict. And poststructuralism, which takes aim at this restricted conceptualization of difference and its inherent negativity, endeavors to proceed otherwise by defining a "non-dialectical third term" that both exceeds comprehension by and reconceptualizes the two terms that comprise binary opposition. All of this engenders a set of questions that have accompanied the investigation but have not yet been explicitly articulated as such. If binary opposition already defines the structure of logic and language, then why even question it? Especially if, as Deleuze and Guattari point out, any challenge to the system of binary oppositions necessarily entails the use of and a passage through binary opposition. In other words, if binary opposition is something that is, for whatever reason, inevitable, inescapable, and necessary, what is the point of questioning or opposing it? Why, as Derrida asks, "engage in the work of deconstruction, rather than leave things the way they are?"[126] Why bother thinking otherwise? There are at least three responses to this line of questioning.

First, there are epistemological reasons. Conceptual oppositions tend to organize and to package debate by pushing things toward the extremes. In binary mode, any given phenomenon is assumed to be reducible to either x or its opposite, *not-x*. Although this kind of exclusivity has a certain functionality and logical attraction, it often is not entirely in touch with the complexity and exigency of things on the ground. In other words, binary oppositions necessarily arrange polemics where there may be something that is less contentious, not so easily bifurcated, and significantly more noisy. A good example can be found in the critical reception of VR. The main debate surrounding this technology, as Heim, Taylor, and Stanovsky have all pointed out, has been organized in terms of a discrete, logical dichotomy. On the one hand, advocates describe a utopian scenario where human beings transcend the limitations of the body, physical distance and delay are negligible, and our world becomes reprogrammed in the image of paradise. On the other hand, detractors warn of a techo-dystopia akin to what is imagined in *The Matrix* trilogy, a nightmare situation where human beings are wired into and controlled by computer-generated fictions that cut them off from each other, the world, and anything that could be called real. As compelling as this debate initially appears to be, the issues and concerns are often not as dramatic or pronounced. The majority of individuals involved in designing VR hardware and software are not trying either to recreate paradise or to enslave the human race in service to the machines. In fact, most VR systems have been designed and are used for much more mundane (relatively speaking) operations and tasks, like helping homeowners redesign a kitchen, assisting commercial pilots in maintaining their flight rating, and entertaining teenagers and young adults with interactive games. Although the critical debates about VR usually involve extraordinary forms of apocalyptic thinking, the technology and its employments are more often than not involved in what appears to be rather ordinary concerns. A similar problem has become evident with the *digital divide*, a concept that takes account of the social problems resulting from the unequal distribution of computer equipment and differences in access to information networks like the Internet. Discussion of the digital divide, although crucial to understanding the social and economic impact and costs of ICT, tends to segregate populations into either "information haves" or "information have-nots." As with VR, this either/or duality tends to restrict understanding by disregarding the fact that ICTs and access to the data they supply are often much more diverse and complex and not so easily separated into just one thing or another. To operate in accordance with this or any other binary opposition is to accept, whether explicitly recognized or not, the terms and conditions of a polemic without any critical hesitation or questioning. Thinking otherwise, therefore, actively challenges and inquires about the epistemological limitations that are part and parcel of any kind of binary arrangement.

The second reason is, for lack of a better word, metaphysical. Many of the logical oppositions that are employed to organize and comprehend new technology are old, very old. Plato's *Phaedrus*, for example, concludes with what is arguably the first recorded debate about new media—a debate that both is recorded in writing and addresses the new (during Plato's time) recording technology of writing. The conflict is composed of two opposed positions, which Plato has Socrates attribute to an ancient source. On the one side, there is the technologist, Theuth, who presents the new invention of writing with the promise of vast social and individual improvements. On the other side, there is Thamus the king, who remains skeptical of these claims and argues that such an invention will actually foster the exact opposite of what had been attributed to it by the technologist.[127] The terms and conditions of this particular polemic have instituted a precedent for understanding new technology that has been successfully applied to subsequent developments and innovations. Walter Ong, for instance, finds that the same arguments which had been made in the face of writing during Plato's time are in fact already operative in and shape contemporary responses to the computer.[128] Like the ancient debate about writing, the computer is determined either to enhance the powers of the intellect or to create debilitating dependencies that foster self-delusion, alienation, and social decay. In this way then, a new technology, no matter how innovative it appears to be, comes to be domesticated by the tradition and to take its appropriate position on one side or the other of an old and well-established conceptual opposition. There is, at least in the abstract, nothing wrong with this particular operation. Conformity with an ancient and reputable precedent has the obvious advantage of providing current and future examinations with a tested and secure foundation that is considered to be correct, proven, and unquestionable. As long as the understanding of a new technology conforms to this arrangement, one already knows what debates are possible, what questions should be asked of it, and what answers will count as appropriate. At the same time, however, proceeding in this fashion neither challenges the hegemony of the ancient dualism nor examines the way in which a new technology might question and reconfigure traditional ways of thinking. Consequently, instead of simply comprehending the new by means of the old, which is of course just one more oppositional pair, it is also possible to foster an arrangement where the new is permitted to question and challenge the established structures and assumptions, providing alternative ways to look at and consider the tradition itself. This is only possible when the customary binary oppositions are not simply employed without question but are themselves submitted to some kind of thinking that is and remains oriented otherwise.

Finally, and perhaps most importantly, there are ethical concerns. Conceptual oppositions, despite initial appearances, are never neutral. They do not divide up the world in a way that is equitable and indifferent. They institute difference, and these differences always make a difference. In any conceptual opposition, as Derrida and others have pointed out, one of the two terms is inevitably privileged and the other is defined as its negative or derived counterpart. In the classic gender distinction situated between the two terms "male" and "female," for example, it is the male who is, from Genesis to Hegel and beyond, considered to be the original form of the human species. The female, who is *his* other, has been characterized as a derivative and negative counterpart. That is, she has typically been described by what it is she lacks in comparison to the male. This hierarchical arrangement, whether it is explicitly recognized as such or not, has real and potentially devastating consequences for others. As Donna Haraway argues, "certain dualisms have been persistent in Western traditions; they have been systemic to the logics and practices of domination of women, people of color, nature, workers, animals—in short, domination of all constituted others, whose task it is to mirror the self. Chief among these troubling dualisms are self/ other, mind/body, culture/nature, male/female, civilized/primitive, reality/ap-pearance, whole/part, agent/resource, maker/made, active/passive, right/wrong, truth/illusion, total/partial, God/man."[129] Conceptual oppositions, therefore, do not institute an equitable division between two terms that are on equal footing and of comparable status. They are always and already hierarchical arrangements that are structurally biased. And it is this hierarchical order, as many poststructuralists, feminists, and postcolonial theorists argue, that installs, underwrites, and justifies systems of inequality, domination, and prejudice. There is, then, a moral reason to question the system of binary oppositions and to attempt to think in excess of and outside the usual conceptual arrangement. Thinking otherwise is necessary for ethics, especially an ethics that is attentive to the moral consequences of the structures and exigencies that have ordinarily organized both thinking and acting.

Chapter Two

What's the Matter with Books?

Ceci tuera cela.—Victor Hugo

The question "what's the matter with books?"[1] may be understood on multiple registers. Taken colloquially, it asks about print technology and its product. Such a query usually denotes a worry or concern over something that has perhaps gone wrong, become a problem, or deviated from accepted practices or anticipated outcomes. At the same time, however, the question may also be understood in a more literal and material sense. In this way, it inquiries about printing's matter, questioning both the subject matter of print and the materiality of its product. This question which is traced in many places and in innumerable ways, is perhaps the query most appropriate at this time, in the era that is commonly called "the late age of print." It especially matters when, for example, the computer is purported to replace the printed book as the depository and definition of human knowledge. The question, then, is palpable at this point in time when we read so much about the end of the book, the death of literature, or its remediation in digital form.[2]

The following does not necessarily provide an answer to the question "what's the matter with books?" but endeavors to position this inquiry in such a way that its polysemia resonates and becomes *material*, as the jurist would say, for the subject matter and material of books.[3] It does so by engaging a quotation from Victor Hugo's *Notre-Dame de Paris*, "Ceci tuera cela [This will destroy that]."[4] The statement is voiced by the archdeacon Frollo and constitutes his assessment of the impact of Gutenberg's technological innovation. Looking up from a printed book on his table to the stone edifice of the gothic cathedral visible through the window of his cell, Frollo laments, "alas, this will destroy that." The anecdote has been recounted several times in examinations of the history of the technology of moveable type.[5] Recently, however, the episode has been employed to address another form of technological transformation. Jay David Bolter's *Writing Space*, which begins with Hugo's text, provides a good illustration of this practice, if not the precedent. "Today we are living in the late age of print. The evidence of senescence, if not senility, is all around us. And as we look up from our computer keyboards to the books on our shelves, we must ask ourselves whether 'this will this destroy that.'"[6] "Destroy" is perhaps too strong a word, and Bolter, following Hugo, is careful to delimit its meaning. Obviously, the book did not (literally) raze the gothic cathedral. It merely displaced its function as the principal mode of human expression and the repository of memory. Similarly, the computer will not put an end to writing and the publication of books. "The issue," Bolter writes, "is not whether print technology will completely disappear; books may long continue to be printed for certain kinds of texts and for luxury consumption. But the idea and ideal of the book will change: print will no longer define the organization and presentation of knowledge, as it has for the past five centuries."[7]

Questioning whether the computer will destroy or displace the book is not something that is unique to Bolter's *Writing Space*. In fact, Father Frollo's apocalyptic statement has been invoked, in one way or another, in virtually every publication addressing computers and the future of print technology and culture. As Geoffrey Nunberg characterizes it, "no conference or collection of essays on the future of the book would be complete without someone citing these words."[8] The shelves of libraries and bookstores, in fact, are now crowded with books that investigate whether the computer will destroy or replace print. A brief review of titles makes this immediately evident: Sven Birkerts's *The Gutenberg Elegies*, Eugene Provenzo's *Beyond the Gutenberg Galaxy*, Nicholas Negroponte's *Being Digital*, James O'Donnell's *Avatars of the Word*, Alvin Kernan's *Death of Literature*, George Landow's *Hypertext*, Frank Ogden's *The Last Book You Will Ever Read*, Charles Meadow's *Ink into Bits*, Roger Chartier's *Forms and Meanings: Texts, Performances, and Audiences from Codex to Computer*, etc. The examination of this matter will not, at least directly, engage the particulars involved in this transformation of information technology. It will not ask or attempt to address the question, "Will the computer destroy the book?" It will not even assess whether this alteration is beneficial or detrimental. These may yet be important and fecund avenues of investigation. I am, instead, interested in a much more mundane and materialistic question. As we look up from our computer keyboards to the books on our shelves, the question is not "Will this destroy that?" but "Why do so many of the books ask or address this question?" What does it mean to examine this matter in a book? And how do these publications explain, manage, and contend with the problems and incongruities this material necessarily entails? Such an inquiry is not concerned with the equipment and exigencies of technology per se. Its object is neither the hardware and software of computers nor the intricacies of print. Instead, it is, following the example of Friedrich Kittler's *Gramophone,*

Film, Typewriter, interested in how these so-called "post-print" technologies have come to inscribe themselves in the paper of books[9] and, more importantly, what they do to contend with this matter.

The Paradox of a Book

> One of the ironies of our culture's fascination with virtual technologies is its fondness for consuming books and articles that proclaim the death of print culture—or its disappearance into the matrix.[10]
> —Robert Markley

Publications addressing computer technology and the fate of print culture, whether celebrating the utopian possibilities of a new technology or bemoaning the passing of a rich tradition, are involved in a curious, if not contradictory, situation. There is a disjunction between what these books state about their subject matter and the material in which these statements appear. This tension is evident in many publications that treat the development of computer technology and the fate of print media. In some cases, it is explicitly identified as such. Nicholas Negroponte's *Being Digital*, for example, argues that we are witnessing a revolutionary change in the way information is created, stored, and distributed. Until recently, information was produced, accumulated, and exchanged solely in the form of atoms, in the material of books, magazines, newspapers, videocassettes, and compact disks. This situation, Negroponte asserts, is being irrevocably altered by the rapid development of digital technology and computer networks. Information now takes the form of immaterial bits of digital data that are circulated at (or near) the speed of light. Consequently, what the book states about the exciting new culture and economy of bits is abraded by the fact that this information has been delivered in the slow and outdated form of atoms. Negroponte calls this friction "the paradox of a book," and he addresses it directly in the preface. "So why an old-fashioned book, Negroponte, especially one without a single illustration? Why is Vintage shipping *Being Digital* as atoms instead of bits, when these pages . . . can be so easily rendered into digital form, from whence they came?"[11]

Vilém Flusser describes a similar paradox operative in his examination of the future of writing. Flusser's book, called simply *Die Schrift*, begins with the stunning proclamation that "writing, in the sense of the lining-up of letters and other writing signs, seems to have no future or almost none." The investigation of this matter, Flusser admits, would require a "voluminous book." "The only catch," he adds, "is that such a book would be a book."[12] Likewise Mark Taylor and Esa Saarinen, in the Telewriting section of *Imagologies*, identify and question a cascade of paradoxes that befall the subject matter of their undertaking and the material in which it necessarily appears (figure 2).

Esa - -

By extending our project from the
global classroom to the book, we
encounter paradox after paradox. How
can we write a printed work that
reflects and embodies the criticism
of print culture our enterprise
presupposes? If an electronic text
can be published in printed form, is
it really electronic? The
alternative would be to give up print
and publish an electronic text. But
the technology necessary for
accessing electronic texts is still
rather limited. Furthermore, most of
the people we want to reach remain
committed to print. There is no
sense preaching to the converted.
Our dilemma is that we are living at
the moment of transition from print
to electronic culture. It is too
late for printed books and too early
for electronic texts. Along this
boundary we must write our work.

Figure 2
Taylor and Saarinen's reflection on the paradoxes
encountered in the material of their project.[13]

This passage, although recorded in a book, clearly attempts to dissimulate
the form of an email message sent from Mark Taylor to Esa Saarinen. This is indicated not only by the personal address with which the text begins but also by
the monospaced font that is emblematic of the ASCII character set used in early
forms of computer-mediated communication. In this printed dissimulation of
an email message, Taylor deliberately calls attention to the paradoxical problems
that immediately confront *Imagologies*. In writing a book about electronic text
that is critical of print technology, the subject matter seems to be opposed to the
material in which it appears. The alternative, Taylor suggests, would be to abandon print altogether and publish an electronic text. This option, however, is not
currently feasible. Taylor recognizes, on the one hand, that the presently available technology for accessing electronic text remains limited and cumbersome
and, on the other hand, that there is still a sizable audience committed to print.
The dilemma facing any project addressing computer technology and the fate of
print culture is that one currently finds oneself in the middle of a technological
transformation. The printed book is already on the way out but not quite gone,
and the new forms of electronic text are not yet conveniently available. "The

old," as Antonio Gramsci once described it in another context, "is dying and the new cannot be born."[14] Writing during this *Zwischenzeit* or *interregnum* requires that one engage in seemingly contradictory activities, employing print to address a technology that surpasses it and renders it effectively obsolete. Similar forms of critical self-reflection have been situated at the beginning of Michael Heim's *Electric Language*, David Bell's *An Introduction to Cybercultures*, and Peter Lunenfeld's *The Digital Dialectic*. For Heim, whose book comprises a philosophical study of word processing technology, "there is an irony in reflecting on digital writing in a publishing medium that is still committed . . . to the preservation and maintenance of writing in printed books in a culture where books are still a major source for the exchange of information and ideas."[15] David Bell begins his book-length introduction to cybercultures by identifying a similar conflict: "Sitting here, at my computer, pondering how to start this book, how to introduce my own 'walkabout' in cyberspace, I find myself struggling. Maybe it's because I've just been reading and writing about hyperlinks and the web as text—as text, moreover, that is open and infinite, that has no beginning or end. But a book is still a linear thing, decidedly non-hypertexty. . . . So I have to abide by the logic of the book, even if it seems increasingly contradictory in the digital age to do so."[16] And Peter Lunenfeld finds the introduction to his critical anthology on new media, *The Digital Dialectic*, to be "as appropriate a place as any to deal with the inevitable question: 'Why publish a book dealing with the culture of an era that has supposedly transcended the printed page?'"[17]

Books that consider the paradox of a book or question the irony of publishing books about technologies that challenge the dominance of print are, in the words of Frank Hartmann, "conscious of their own form of presentation."[18] In other cases, publications are not "conscious" of this matter, and this tension between the book's subject matter and material is never identified as such. In these situations, the disjunction only becomes evident in the course of a reading that exposes and demonstrates the discrepancy. A segment of Michael Benedikt's introduction to *Cyberspace: First Steps* provides adequate material. "Cyberspace," Benedikt writes, is "the realm of pure information, filling like a lake, siphoning the jangle of messages transfiguring the physical world, decontaminating the natural and urban landscapes, redeeming them, saving them from the chain-dragging bulldozers of the paper industry, from the diesel smoke of courier and post office trucks, from the jet fumes and clogged airports . . . from all the inefficiencies, pollutions (chemical and informational), and corruptions attendant to the process of moving information attached to *things*—from paper to brains—across, over, and under the vast and bumpy surface of the earth rather than letting it fly free in the soft hail of electrons in cyberspace."[19] According to Benedikt, cyberspace comprises a mode of pure information exchange that is uncorrupted by the various inefficiencies, pollutants, and contaminants of ink and paper. This statement, however, is nevertheless communicated through the mediation of the very corruption it criticizes. Nowhere does Benedikt confront or even identify this tension whereby the information that is presented is already at variance with and opposed to the means of its presentation. Because the publication is not "conscious of its own mode of presentation," this difficulty only becomes evident through a reading that attends to the tension between what the text explicitly states and the material it employs to make this statement.[20]

In summary, books addressing new forms of information technology and the future of print are involved in what appears to be contradictory matters. What is stated in these books about the limitations, obsolescence, or even termination of print is opposed by the material in which these statements have been created and distributed. In some instances, the conflict is explicitly identified as such and termed a paradox, an irony, or contradiction. In others, it is not identified and only becomes evident in the process of a reading that attends to and demonstrates the terms of the disjunction. In either case, what's the matter with books is that the proclaimed "death of the book," which is the subject matter of so many publications in the so-called "late age of print," appears to be contrary to and undermined by the very material in which these claims have been made. Whether the computer will, following the pronouncement of Hugo's archdeacon, destroy the book is a question that is literally put in question by the seemingly incessant appearance of this material in books. Consequently, it would, on the one hand, be impetuous to decide that these publications simply condemn or denounce print. To do so would, indeed, be contradictory. On the other hand, it would be just as careless to discount these books as contradictory. To do so would, in fact, be impetuous. Whereas the former does not make enough of the tension between subject matter and material, the latter makes too much of it. In either case, the disjunction is written off as *immaterial*. What is needed, therefore, is another mode of inquiry, one that does not dismiss but is attentive to the intricacies of this curious situation. Jacques Derrida's examination of this matter in Plato's *Phaedrus* provides useful direction. In a procedure that is structurally similar to the ones we are concerned with here, Plato indicts writing in writing. Derrida not only rejects the simple interpretation, namely that Plato condemns writing, as insensitive but also resists the tendency to judge Plato's writing as merely contradictory. Instead, he asks what institutes and regulates this tension, which is commonly identified as "contradictory." "What law governs this 'contradiction,' this opposition to itself of what is said against writing, of a dictum that pronounces itself against itself as soon as it finds its way into writing, as soon as it writes down its self-identity and carries away what is proper to it against this ground of writing?"[21] The critical issue, then, is not whether there is a contradiction between the subject matter and the material of books addressing computer technology and the fate of print. The question is, "How have these books understood, explained, and/or managed this tension, which cannot help but appear to be contradictory?" What regulates and justifies these explanations and maneuvers? And what does this indicate about computer technology, the book, and terms of their relationship?

Signs of Print

> It is not surprising that this is a book
> and not a computer program.[22]
> —Rob Wittig

As we have seen, books addressing computer technology and/or the future of the book are involved in what Negroponte calls "the paradox of a book." What these publications state about their subject matter is all too often inconsistent with the material in which these statements have been made. This apparent "contradiction" is not an accidental or contingent matter. It is programmed and regulated by the classically determined structure of the sign. First, whether it is determined in the course of a metaphysics, the science of linguistics or semiotics, or in what is commonly called, perhaps incorrectly, "everyday language," a sign is always the sign of something. "The signification 'sign,'" Derrida writes in the essay "Structure, Sign, and Play," "has always been understood and determined, in its meaning, as sign-of, a signifier referring to a signified, a signifier different from its signified."[23] A sign, in order to be a sign, indicates something else. Accordingly, one distinguishes the signifier from the signified. The signifier indicates or points to the signified, but it remains differentiated from the signified. In explaining this, Derrida's sentence is already involved in performing what is described. The word "sign" (in quotation marks) is employed to indicate and explain this form of indication. "Sign" is utilized as a signifier of the structure of signification. This structure, although marked with different names in different contexts, remains remarkably consistent from Aristotle to, at least, Charles Sanders Peirce. In *De interpretatione*, Aristotle distinguishes spoken and written signs from the things to which they refer: "Spoken words are the signs [σημεῖα] of mental experience and written words are the signs of spoken words. Just as all men have not the same writing, so all men have not the same speech sounds, but the mental experiences, of which these are the primary signs [σημεῖα πρώτος] are the same for all, as also are those things of which our experiences are the images."[24] For Peirce, the founder of the American tradition of semiotics, the sign is differentiated from the object it designates: "A sign is something which stands to somebody for something in some respect or capacity . . . the sign stands for something, *its object*."[25] Consequently, despite variations in terminology, what one might call, according to the logic described here, different "signifiers," the structure of signification that is indicated remains remarkably consistent.

Second, in referring to something else, the sign takes place by taking the place of another. "The sign," Derrida explains in the essay "Différance," "is usually said to be put in the place of the thing itself, the present thing, 'thing' here standing equally for meaning or referent. The sign represents the present in its absence. It takes the place of the present. When we cannot grasp or show the thing, state the present, the being-present, when the present cannot be presented, we signify, we go through the detour of the sign."[26] As the sign of something, a sign is commonly understood as a kind of delegate of or substitute for something else. It is put in the place of something when that thing is unable to be present as such. It is a detour that becomes necessary when something that should be present remains, for whatever reason, absent or inaccessible. The sign re-presents the present when it is not present. In this way, the classically determined structure of the sign constitutes what Derrida calls "deferred presence," *defer* being understood in the double sense of "to delegate to something else" and "to postpone." The sign defers to something else in its deferred presence.

Finally, defined as a form of deferred presence, the sign is situated in the interval separating two presents. "This structure," Derrida continues, "presupposes that the sign, which defers presence, is conceivable only on the basis of the presence that it defers and moving toward the deferred presence that it aims to re-appropriate. According to this classical semiology, the substitution of the sign for the thing itself is both *secondary* and *provisional:* secondary due to an original and lost presence from which the sign thus derives; provisional as concerns this final and missing presence toward which the sign in this sense is a movement of mediation."[27] A sign, as Geoffrey Bennington succinctly describes it, "stands between two presents."[28] On the one hand, a sign, as the surrogate of something else, is only possible on the basis of an originally present thing from which it has been derived and to which it defers. On the other hand, a sign functions as a kind of promissory note, pointing towards the eventual reappropriation and future presentation of this now absent and deferred thing. Situated in the interval between something that was but is no longer and the promise of something that is not yet, a sign is considered to be both secondary and provisional. It is secondary, because it is derived from and defers to an original presence. It is provisional, because it stands in for something for the time being, guaranteeing the presence of that which is now absent.

It is this "classical semiology" that has been employed to explain and justify the paradox of a book. In the first edition of *Writing Space*, for example, Jay David Bolter addresses this matter in one concise sentence, explicating what many books leave unexplained. "This printed book can be about, but cannot be, an electronic book."[29] The printed book, *Writing Space*, is concerned with or refers to an electronic book but necessarily remains otherwise than an electronic book. The print publication can characterize, explain, and even question the features, structure, and function of the electronic book, but it clearly is not that which it indicates. Understood in this way, *Writing Space*, quite literally, stands between two presents. On the one hand, the printed book has been derived from an original hypertext that was present only in the mind of the author. The first line of Bolter's book refers to this original but now absent hypertext: "Because the subject of this printed book is the coming of the electronic book, I have found it particularly difficult to organize my text in an appropriate manner—appropriate, that is, to the printed page. In my mind the argument kept trying to cast itself intertextually or 'hypertextually.'"[30] The printed book, Bolter tells us, is a derived and highly constrained manifestation of what had originally presented itself in hypertextual form. The book stands in for this original hypertext, which could not present itself as itself because of the demands and requirements of print. On the other hand, *Writing Space* is also a promissory note. It points to a hypertext that is not yet but may be present. The last page of the book addresses this matter directly. "At the end of this printed book, the reader has the opportunity to begin again—by working through the text on a computer diskette that can be obtained by sending in the order form enclosed in the book. The diskette, which runs on Macintosh computers, contains a hypertextual rewriting of this book. The hypertext shadows the printed version, presenting paragraphs that appear in print and offering hypertextual notes that expand particular ideas. These elaborations could not be included in the printed version because of limited space or because a particular digression did not seem appropriate to the linearity of print."[31] *Writing Space* ends by pointing the reader to the electronic text that the book indicates but could not be. The printed text, therefore, not only refers to an absent hypertext that existed in the mind of the author but also promises a hypertext that can, at the end of the book, be made present for an additional $9.95 plus $2.00 shipping and handling (figure 3).

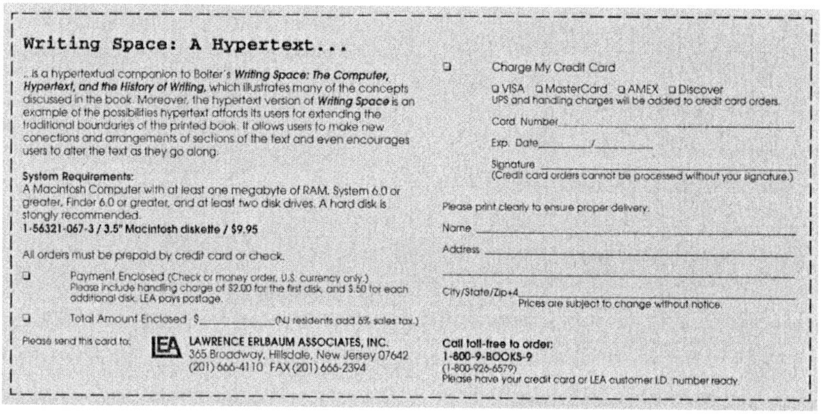
Writing Space: A Hypertext...

...is a hypertextual companion to Bolter's ***Writing Space: The Computer, Hypertext, and the History of Writing,*** which illustrates many of the concepts discussed in the book. Moreover, the hypertext version of ***Writing Space*** is an example of the possibilities hypertext affords its users for extending the traditional boundaries of the printed book. It allows users to make new conections and arrangements of sections of the text and even encourages users to alter the text as they go along.

System Requirements:
A Macintosh Computer with at least one megabyte of RAM. System 6.0 or greater, Finder 6.0 or greater, and at least two disk drives. A hard disk is stongly recommended.
1-56321-067-3 / 3.5" Macintosh diskette / $9.95

All orders must be prepaid by credit card or check.

❑ Payment Enclosed (Check or money order. U.S. currency only.)
Please include handling charge of $2.00 for the first disk, and $.50 for each additional disk. LEA pays postage.

❑ Total Amount Enclosed $______ (NJ residents add 6% sales tax.)

Please send this card to: LEA **LAWRENCE ERLBAUM ASSOCIATES, INC.**
365 Broadway, Hillsdale, New Jersey 07642
(201) 666-4110 FAX (201) 666-2394

❑ Charge My Credit Card

❑ VISA ❑ MasterCard ❑ AMEX ❑ Discover
UPS and handling charges will be added to credit card orders.

Card Number ______

Exp. Date ____ / ____

Signature ______
(Credit card orders cannot be processed without your signature.)

Please print clearly to ensure proper delivery.

Name ______

Address ______

City/State/Zip+4 ______
Prices are subject to change without notice.

Call toll-free to order:
1-800-9-BOOKS-9
(1-800-926-6579)
Please have your credit card or LEA customer I.D. number ready.

Figure 3
The order form included with the first edition of *Writing Space* (1991).

In describing his publication in this fashion, Bolter, whether he explicitly recognizes it or not, defines *Writing Space* in accordance with the classically determined structure of the sign. He distinguishes a signifier, the printed book, from its signified, an electronic book, and he situates it in the interval between two presents, a hypertext that was but now is not and a hypertext that is not currently present but will be.

This sign structure, although applied to a different object, is reiterated in the second edition of *Writing Space*. The second edition, which is shorter than the first by some 10,000 words, recasts the argument of the original publication in order to take into account changes that have occurred in "the writing space offered by electronic technology."[32] "Those changes," as Bolter (2001) points out in the new preface, "are due almost entirely to the development of the World Wide Web," which now provides the definition and privileged example of hypertext.[33] In reworking *Writing Space* to take the Web into account, Bolter revises both the preface and introduction and concludes by pointing the reader not to a diskette containing a "stand-alone hypertext," but to a website, which incidentally does not exist at the published URL (http://www.lcc.gatech.edu/~bolter/writingspace/). In this web-oriented remix, the subject matter of the printed book is not the electronic book but the remediation of print that is effected by digital technology. This shift in the object of the investigation—a shift that could be characterized as a change from a nominal to verbal object—is announced by the text's new subtitle, "Computers, Hypertext, and the Remediation of Print." As Bolter describes it, "this edition of *Writing Space* is meant . . . to show how hypertext and other forms of electronic writing refashion or 'remediate' the forms and genres of print."[34] Likewise, the website, referenced at the end of the book, is described as remediating the book itself. "If the hypertext diskette for the first edition was meant to provide a shadow text, a metaphoric replacement of the printed text, the Web site is instead an extension, and a remediation of the printed text."[35] The concept of *remediation*, as it is described by Bolter, is a remarkable reiteration of Marshall McLuhan's understanding of the process of technological transformation. According to McLuhan, a new medium does not simply replace an old medium; the content of any new medium is the old medium it is said to be replacing.[36] Likewise, "remediation," as we have seen in the previous chapter, describes the shift from one form of information technology to another, "in the sense that a newer medium takes the place of an older one, borrowing and reorganizing the characteristics of the writing in the older medium and reformulating its cultural space."[37] Consequently, the goal of the second edition of *Writing Space* is to describe the remediation of print by digital technology, and the website that is referenced at the end of the book provides an example of this remediation, performing what is indicated. This reformulation of *Writing Space*, or what one might be tempted to call its remediation, still operates according to the classically determined structure of the sign. The printed text is *about* the remediation of print by digital media. In being about the process of remediation, the book not only refers to something else but stands between two presents. It refers to a remediation of print that is already underway in the technology of the World Wide Web, and it anticipates a website (which seems to be endlessly postponed) that remediates the printed book, which presents this information. In occupying the interval between these two remediations, *Writing Space* is a sign of the remediation of print in print.

   In defining both editions of *Writing Space* in accordance with the classically determined structure of the sign, Bolter effectively circumvents the complications inherent in the "paradox of a book" and avoids the potential charge of self-contradiction. In distinguishing signifier from signified, the subject matter to which the book refers is detached and insulated from the material in which it appears. And in occupying the interval between two presents or what Bolter calls in the first edition "this period of transition,"[38] the printed book is and remains effectively immaterial. In providing an account of this matter, Bolter explicates what appears to be obvious and virtually beyond question. Whether it is explicitly demarcated in a statement like "this book is about . . ." or remains implicit in the course of its undertaking, a book is about something. In being *about*, it defers and refers to something else. And in being referred elsewhere, the material of the book is considered to be secondary and provisional. It does not and should not matter, or, if it matters, it does not matter much. What is of primary and lasting importance is what the book indicates about its subject matter. Accordingly, the material of the book recedes from view and becomes virtually transparent. In fact, the more transparent the signifier is, the better it functions as the delegate of the signified. In *Remediation*, the book coauthored with Richard Grusin, Bolter and Grusin describe the features of this kind of transparent intermediary: "A transparent interface would be one that erases itself, so that the user is no longer aware of confronting a medium, but instead stands in an immediate relationship to the contents of that medium."[39] This transparency, which is achieved through deliberate self-erasure, has also been the ideal of the ideal book. "The purpose of the book," Mark Taylor writes in *Erring*, "is to render present the discourse of the world by bringing about the absolute proximity or perfect transparency of object to subject. Though not always obvious, this aim implies the self-negation of the book. In the course of approximating its goal, the book inscribes a paradoxical 'progression' toward its own self-effacement."[40] It is because of this programmed auto-erasure and resulting transparency that so many books about virtual reality, cyberspace, the Internet, and computer technology not only ignore the material of print but say little or nothing about this process. As the means of providing information about something else, the actual material of these books is effectively invalidated, taken for granted, and not made the explicit object of investigation.

There are, of course, exceptions to this programmed transparency—books where the structure of signification becomes, in one way or another, increasingly opaque and questionable. In these cases, the issue is explicitly identified and described in the course of handling the "paradox of a book." Negroponte, for example, not only makes explicit identification of the paradox but supplies several responses to the question "Why an old-fashioned book?" "First there are just not enough digital media in the hands of executives, politicians, parents, and all those who most need to understand this radical new culture. Even where computers are omnipresent, the current interface is primitive—clumsy at best, and hardly something with which you might wish to curl up in bed. A second reason, is my monthly column in *Wired* magazine. The rapid and astonishing success of *Wired* has shown that there is a large audience for information about digital life-styles and people, not just theory and equipment. I received so much thoughtful feedback from my (text only) column that I decided to repurpose many of the early themes, because a great deal has changed even in the short time since those stories were written."[41] The principal reason *Being Digital* is a book and not a computer program or multimedia presentation is that, despite everything that is stated about the advantages of being digital, there are at least two problems with digital technology. On the one hand, it is scarce. There simply is not enough of it to go around. Although constituting the foundation of a new culture, the technology Negroponte considers is, in his opinion, not yet widely available to the individuals who most need to understand it. On the other hand, even when the technology is available, it is not easy to use. The interface, which is a combination of both hardware and software elements, is inconvenient, cumbersome, and certainly not user-friendly. Print, by contrast, is not only widely available and easy to use but has, as is evidenced by the remarkable success of magazines like *Wired*, a considerable and attentive audience. Even though digital technology marks the end of the circulation of information in the form of "dead-tree" atoms, magazines and books persist. They remain popular and are not yet passé. *Being Digital* is an old-fashioned book, because 1) digital technology is not able to present itself as such; it either is not present or, if present, is ostensibly inaccessible. And 2) print remains accessible, convenient, and not yet obsolete. It is because digital technology is not yet able to present itself as such that Negroponte has recourse to printed signs. These signs, which are still widely available and popular, are employed to stand in for this technology, which remains absent or inaccessible. The printed book, therefore, takes the place of that which is not, at the present, able to be present, re-presenting what should be present in its absence.

In this way, *Being Digital* stands between two presents. On the one hand, the descriptions of digital technology that are provided in the book have, it is assumed, been derived from an original encounter with the things that are represented in the text. On the other hand, this technology, although not currently present, will be present and widely available in the near future. In *Being Digital*, this situation is substantiated and authorized by the figure of the author. As Douglas Adams succinctly describes it in an endorsement for the book, "Nicholas Negroponte writes about the future with the authority of someone who has spent a lot of time there."[42] What authorizes Negroponte to make signs of a not yet available technology is that he has had access to it. Digital technologies, although not currently available to everyone, have at least been made present to Negroponte, who has either participated in their development or experienced them firsthand at places like MIT's Media Lab. Without this unique access to technology, Negroponte's signs would be nothing but conjecture and groundless speculation—a kind of science fiction. Likewise, the technology Negroponte describes in the book will not always be absent; its presentation is merely delayed.

It either is just beginning to be made available or will be available at some point in the future. Consequently, the representations provided in *Being Digital* are the result of and authorized by a previous encounter with what will be the future. This situation is neither particularly strange nor disturbing; it is nothing less than the temporality of the sign.

The "paradox of a book" is explained, if not resolved, by enlisting the classically determined structure of the sign. In being about computers and new technology, the book is understood as a surrogate for something else from which it is originally derived and to which it ultimately refers. The printed signifier, therefore, is considered to be both secondary and provisional in relation to the primacy of the signified. And for this reason, the tension between the book's material and its subject matter is rendered effectively *immaterial*. There is, however, at least one difficulty with this explanation. Critiques of this classical semiology, from the work of Charles Sanders Peirce and Ferdinand de Saussure to that of Umberto Eco, Julia Kristeva, and Jacques Derrida, have demonstrated that this formulation of the sign is a metaphysical fantasy. Most notably, signs do not refer to something that transcends and exists outside the order of signs. In fact, signs only refer to other signs. Bolter explains this by employing the familiar example of the dictionary.

> For the dictionary has always been the classic example of the semiotic principle that signs refer only to other signs. . . . We can only define a sign in terms of other signs of the same nature. This lesson is known to every child who discovers that fundamental paradox of the dictionary: that if you do not know what some words mean you can never use the dictionary to learn what other words mean. The definition of any word, if pursued far enough through the dictionary, will lead you in circles. This paradox is the foundation of semiotics. A sign system is a set of rules for relating elements. The rules are arbitrary, and the system they generate is self-contained. There is no way to get "outside" the system to the world represented, because, as in the dictionary, signs can only lead you elsewhere in the same system.[43]

According to the "semiotic principle" identified by Bolter, signs do not refer to things that exist outside the system of signs; signs refer only to other signs. The dictionary provides the classic illustration. In a dictionary, words are defined by other words. Consequently, one remains inside the system of linguistic signifiers and never gets outside language to the referent or what semioticians call the "transcendental signified."[44] For Bolter, this formulation is not merely a theoretical possibility. It is exemplified in and embodied by the technology of computer-based hypertext.

> The new view of signs is embodied unambiguously in electronic hypertext. Here the writer and reader know that there is no transcendence, because they know that the topical elements they create are arbitrary sequences

of bits made meaningful only by their interconnecting links. . . . The fact that electronic signs only refer to other signs is the fundamental characteristic of the medium, made apparent in every act of electronic writing. . . . Electronic readers and writers have finally arrived at the land promised (or threatened) by post-modern theory for two-decades: the world of pure signs. While traditional humanists and deconstructionists have been battling over the arbitrary, self-referential character of writing, computer specialists, oblivious to this struggle, have been building a world of electronic signs in which the battle is over.[45]

According to Bolter, the critique of classical semiology materializes in hypertext. That is, hypertext demonstrates the seemingly infinite self-referential character of the sign that has been espoused in recent theory.[46] This insight, Bolter argues, is unmistakably evident in every act of electronic writing. Mark Amerika's *Hypertextual Consciousness*, "a companion theory guide" to his award-winning *Grammatron*, for instance, provides an illustration of Bolter's position. *Hypertextual Consciousness* is unique in that it presents hypertext theory in the form of hypertext. Unlike Landow's *Hypertext*, Lanham's *Electric Word*, or even Bolter's *Writing Space*, Amerika's examination of hypertext is situated in and takes place as hypertext. "Not," Amerika points out, "because its words can't be printed and bound by traditional book-contained media,"[47] but because the subject matter of the work calls into question the assumptions and material of traditional forms of reading and writing. By appearing in this manner, *Hypertextual Consciousness* does what it says and says what it does. "I link therefore I am," states one of the initial pages, where the word "link" is a hypertext link to be activated by the reader/participant (figure 4). "Link," however, literally refers the reader/participant to other signs situated elsewhere in the hypertextual system, and a simple JavaScript function embedded in the page randomly changes the link's destination. Like the words listed in a dictionary, the signifier "link" does not have a stable referent situated outside the hypertextual document in which it appears. It is made meaningful only by its interconnecting links.[48]

But if Bolter is correct about this matter, then the material of his own project becomes questionable, if not contradictory. On the one hand, Bolter's book employs the classically determined structure of the sign, situating *Writing Space* as a sign of either the electronic book or the hypertextual remediation of print. In this way, he explains and even resolves the apparent contradictions involved with the paradox of a book. The various determinations that are published in the material of the book point to and are about something else. On the other hand, Bolter endorses the standard critique of this structure of signification. He not only affirms the original absence of a "transcendental signified" and the hypothesis that signs refer only to other signs, but he also claims that electronic hypertext illustrates and embodies this fundamental semiotic principle. Consequently, it appears that Bolter's book cannot function as it has been determined. *Writing Space* requires a transcendental signified in order for it to

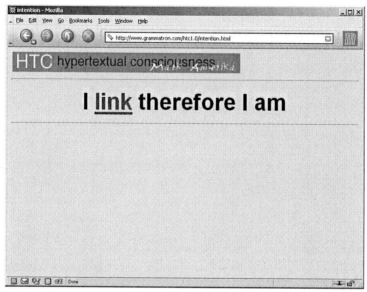

Figure 4
Mark Amerika's *Hypertextual Consciousness.*

deflect the charge of self-contradiction and to resolve the paradox of a book, but the signified, computer-based hypertext, already demonstrates the impossibility of there ever being such a thing.

Sign Matters

> The world does not exist outside its expressions.[49]
> —Gilles Deleuze

In the end, what's the matter with books is that the subject matter of so many print publications in the so-called "late age of print" disputes the material in which it necessarily appears. In book after book we read about how the computer, the Internet, virtual reality, and other forms of ICT will eventually replace the "civilization of the book" with the wired and now wireless civilization of computer-mediated communication. *Ceci tuera cela.* Books have dealt this with matter by mobilizing the classically determined structure of the sign. Whether explicitly acknowledged or not, print publications have resolved this "paradox of a book" by distinguishing between the printed signifier and its signified. As the sign of something else, to which it refers and ultimately defers, the material of the book is rendered immaterial and the tension between its material and subject matter is apparently resolved. This classical semiology, however, is not without significant complications. For at least half a century semioticians, linguists, literary theorists, and philosophers of language have questioned its validity and applicability. The signifier, they argue in one way or another, does not simply refer to a "transcendental signified" but makes reference to other signifiers. Although there remains considerable debate as to the actual consequences of this insight, what is not debated is the fact that the "classically determined structure of the sign," although useful in certain contexts, is too simple an explanation. This conclusion renders classical semiology questionable and, as a consequence, impedes resolution of the "paradox of a book," which had relied on it. If signs refer to other signs and the existence of a "transcendental signified" is suspended or, at least, questionable, then the material of the book can no longer be written off as virtually transparent and effectively immaterial. The signifier matters, and the subject matter of the book cannot be insulated from the effects of its own material. Or as Paul Taylor and Jan Harris describe it in another context, "communication and information must be understood as an im/material performance in which none of the factors involved can be privileged over the other; medium and message must be approached as a single im/material complex."[50] This has at least three consequences that affect how we read and understand books about technology.

First, "there is," to deploy one of Derrida's more controversial statements, "nothing outside the text."[51] If there is no "transcendental signified" outside the system of signs, then a book about computer technology refers not to computer technology per se but to other signs in the system of what could be called, for lack of another word, "literature." This does not mean, of course, that there is no actual or even virtual technology. Certainly the computer, hypertext, interactive multimedia, and virtual reality systems exist. What this does mean, however, is that this technology, although extant, does not constitute a transcendental signified that would anchor and substantiate the classically determined structure of the sign that is deployed in books about technology. This is evident in the material of books that purport to be about the computer. *Writing Space*, for example, does not, strictly speaking, refer to technological equipment. Like the dictionary, its signifiers signify other signifiers. Bolter explicitly marks this in the preface to the second edition: "In revising this book, as I have noted, I have depended on the published work of many colleagues in literary hypertext and computer science, as the references indicate. In addition to drawing on their printed and electronic publications, I have also been privileged to know many, perhaps most, of the important figures in the field. I have benefitted from attending their conference papers and from e-mail discussions and private conversations."[52] *Writing Space*, as its extensive list of references indicates, refers not to actual hardware and software but to other published works, conference papers, email discussions, and even private conversations. This statement does not imply that the technology of hypertext and the computer does not exist outside these various texts. What it does mean, however, is that the assumed transparency of literature, which is the standard operating presumption of publications addressing technology, is at least questionable, if not a fiction. The same is true with Negroponte's *Being Digital*, a book that appears to be, by all accounts, all about technology. Like *Writing Space*, *Being Digital* does not refer to technology but to all kinds of other signifiers and signifying events: films, conversations, presentations, demonstrations, Congressional hearings, etc. A book addressing technology, therefore, is not, technically speaking, about technology, if the word "about" is understood in its prepositional form as pointing to a transcendental signified that exists beyond the system of signs. Instead, a book about technology actually takes place in the seemingly endless play of signifiers and can be said to be "about technology" if "about" is understood in its adverbial sense as "circling around" and "indirect."[53]

Second, material matters. If there is nothing outside the text, that is, if the existence of the "transcendental signified" is questionable and everything is already involved in the play of signifiers, then the way we address and investigate technology has to change. The words, descriptions, and metaphors used to examine or question a new technology can no longer be perceived as transparent instruments for the sake of conveying information about something else that exists outside the system of signification. It is not the case that there either is or will be a new technology that is then represented in the convenient and, at least for now, accessible forms of print media. Instead, what a new technology is and what it will become is itself a product of the print media it is said to challenge and to be in the process of replacing. Consequently, one would need to submit McLuhan's statement concerning technological change to the kind of inversion for which he is famous: The content of a particular medium is the "new medium" that supposedly will replace it. William Gibson's *Neuromancer*, the book that introduced the neologism "cyberspace," provides the proverbial example.[54] Technically speaking, cyberspace is not a matter of technology. It is a fiction fabricated in a work of science fiction. Consequently, cyberspace is not the result of innovations in computer hardware and software, but is the product of the play and circulation of signs that commences with Gibson's imaginative novel, which was, we are often reminded, composed not on an Internet-connected PC but on a manual typewriter. This does not mean that something similar to what Gibson describes does not exist outside the various fiction and nonfiction texts that address themselves to the subject matter of cyberspace. It means that cyberspace—what it is and how we understand what it is—is not something that is found empirically in some object existing in the world. It is something that is continually manufactured, mediated, and supported by a complex network of signifiers that include science fiction novels, television programs, films, magazines, academic studies, technical papers, conferences, trade shows, comic books, websites, threaded discussions, blogs, etc. This approach is not simply anti-empirical or idealistic. It is, on the contrary, honest about the necessary restrictions and requirements of what would be a strict and serious form of empiricism. If we are honest with ourselves, we would have to admit that information technology has never been immediately present in and of itself such that we could justify the stance of a naïve empiricism. Instead, what we know about information technology is always already mediated by other forms of information technology. If we are to address and investigate ICT, we cannot ignore this situation, which constitutes the very possibility of an experience with technology. We need to make it the foundation of our endeavors.

Such an approach would institute something like a "rhetoric of technology"—a method of examination that is attentive to the various ways technology has been situated in the material of discourse. This would be the case if and only if "rhetoric" is understood outside its classical opposition to philosophy. Because what is described reiterates the inaugural gesture of the first and exemplar philosopher. "It is," John Sallis writes, "in the *Phaedo* that Socrates, recounting his own history, tells of that decisive turn by which he was set once and for all on his way."[55] In this crucial scene, situated on the eve of his execution, Socrates describes how he began his practice by following the way of his predecessors, seeking, as he characterizes it, "the kind of wisdom that they call investigation of nature."[56] Socrates recounts how this attempt to grasp the immediate, sensible things continually led him adrift and how, in the face of this disappointing failure, he began anew, having recourse to these things in discourse. "So I thought I must have recourse to λόγους and examine in them the truth of things."[57] Consequently, the inaugural gesture of philosophy, as described by its principal practitioner, consists in a turn away from a direct and immediate investigation of the nature of things toward an investigation situated in and attentive to λόγος. A similar turn or course adjustment is necessary with regards to the investigation of ICT. Like Socrates, one has recourse to discourse and examines in it the truth of things.

Third, because of this, the examination of ICT must be a self-reflective endeavor or what Hegel calls a "speculative science."[58] If what we know about technology is always already mediated by other forms of technology, then the object of investigation is already implicated and involved in the method of its investigation. Just as there is no transcendental signified outside the play of signifiers, there is also no privileged position of observation situated outside of and insulated from the material of the investigation. This situation, despite initial appearances, is not some kind of circular reasoning that would either neutralize the investigation or be at odds with what is commonly called "objective science." "It characterizes," as Briankle Chang has argued, "the epistemic quandary of writers from diverse fields in which the act of the investigation is itself implicated in the object of inquiry."[59] The crucial task in all such situations is not to break free of the circularity to substantiate what Chang calls the "naive empiricist picture"[60] but to recognize the necessity of the circularity and to learn to enter into and to work through it in a way that is attentive to its structure.

What matters, then, are examinations like that posed by Adilkno, the Foundation for the Advancement of Illegal Knowledge. Adilkno begins their book *Media Archive* with a remarkable question that puts everything on the line in one line: "To write about media is to ask the question what gives writing the right to speak for other media."[61] The first line of the book asks about writing a book and the presumptions involved in such an activity. This book about media, therefore, begins with a question about its own form of mediation that puts in question what it does as it does it. Although this kind of inquiry seems hopelessly self-involved, it is only by addressing itself to this question that Adilkno's text addresses its subject matter in a way that matters and takes its own matter seriously. A similar gesture can be found at the beginning of Derrida's "Signature Event Context." Derrida begins this essay on communication by questioning the very possibility of that in which he is engaged. "Is it certain that to the word communication corresponds a concept that is unique, univocal, rigorously controllable, and transmittable: in a word, communicable?"[62] Finally, the same can and must be said of this entire investigation. In asking the question "What's the matter with books?" the material of the text is already and unavoidably involved in the subject matter it addresses. Consequently, whatever comes to be written about the self-referential character of the signifier must be applied to and put into practice by the text that makes this statement. This has, in fact, been the case insofar as this investigation, from the beginning, refers only to other texts and addresses nothing other than the apparent failure of signification, that is, the antagonism of subject matter and material that is evident in these texts. In other words, what this text "says" about the self-referential quality of text necessarily affects and has already determined how it operates.

What is illustrated in these three cases is a kind of interminable, if not confusing, self-reflection, where the subject matter addressed in the investigation is mirrored in the material of the investigation and vice versa. But if such self-reflection is interminable, then it seems that the investigations will never get on with the matter; they will never be able to say anything about the subject matter that matters. The real danger, however, is that if we get on with matter too quickly, that is, at the expense of recognizing and dealing with the way the subject matter is already embedded and implicated in this material, we will forget and pass over a great deal that matters. If we continue to write and read books about technology, then the crucial questions—the questions that matter—will not be about computer technology and the fate of print media. These inquiries, which claim to target the actual material of hardware and software and even address wider social and political matters, move quickly, perhaps too quickly into the subject matter and often ignore the material in which they appear. Instead the critical questions, the ones that are material for any publication about information technology, are the ones that take these matters seriously. Such inquiries, from the beginning, recognize that the subject matter addressed and the material in which it is addressed are already implicated in and necessarily involve each other. Furthermore, this kind of critical self-reflectivity is not something that is or can be restricted to the material of print technology but inevitably concerns and affects, as will be apparent in the chapters that follow, virtually every aspect of ICT. Consequently, the question that matters is not, for example, "Will the computer replace or even destroy the book?" but "How and why does this question materialize in books?" What are the effects of this particular matter on the subject matter that is addressed? What's the matter with books?

Chapter Three

Second Thoughts

Toward a Critique of the Digital Divide

> Significant differences seem to prevail among
> social groups within nations and among nations in
> the access to and utilization of new ICTs. This is
> generally understood as the "digital divide" and the
> term has quickly become so popular as to serve as a short-
> hand for any disparity associated with digital networks.[1]
> —Sinikka Sassi

The term "digital divide" has come to occupy a privileged position in recent debates about the Internet, computer technology, and access to information systems. It has surfaced, in one way or another, in scholarly studies and investigations, professional meetings and conferences, political speeches and policy analysis, and the popular press and media.[2] This attention to disparity in access to and use of information technology appears to be an obvious advance over the euphoric cyberbole that characterized much of the rhetoric of computer technology since the mid-1980s. In these initial explanations and investigations, ICT was routinely celebrated for creating a new world of limitless opportunity that was liberated from problematic sociocultural determinants, like race, gender, age, and geography.[3] The digital divide supplies a much needed critique of these often unquestioned presumptions, showing that this utopian rhetoric remains oblivious to the fact that access to technology is limited by specific circumstances and should not be assumed to be automatic or universally applicable.

But the critical standpoint introduced by the digital divide, no matter how informative, is not simply insulated from critique. It also has a perspective, and this has been defined by various decisions that delimit its focus and scope. Critical examinations of the digital divide, however, appear to be in short supply. The few commentaries that have been published are little more than reactions and editorials, which argue, mainly through anecdotal evidence and personal opinion, that the divide is a myth, political hyperbole, bunk, nonexistent, or rubbish.[4] What is needed, therefore, is neither uncritical adherence to nor simple reaction against the digital divide but a *critique* that exposes and investigates the problems inherent in both. "Critique," however, is a word that is not without significant ambiguity. In colloquial usage, it has a negative definition, indicating a form of judgmental evaluation or rudimentary fault-finding. It is only under this denotation that many of the current commentaries and editorials may be called "critiques." There is, however, a more precise definition that is rooted in the tradition of critical philosophy. "A critique of any theoretical system," as Barbara Johnson characterizes it, "is not an examination of its flaws and imperfections. It is not a set of criticisms designed to make the system better. It is an analysis that focuses on the grounds of that system's possibility. The critique reads backwards from what seems natural, obvious, self-evident, or universal, in order to show that these things have their history, their reasons for being the way they are, their effects on what follows from them, and that the starting point is not a given but a construct, usually blind to itself."[5] The following investigation comprises this kind of operation. As such, the analysis does not target flaws and imperfections. It does not attempt to point out problems and difficulties. And it does not aim to provide solutions. Instead, it examines the terminology, structure, and form that make articulation of the problem of the digital divide possible. Such an investigation will attend to the necessary but often unexpressed preconditions of the digital divide, trace their history and rationale, and project the direction of their future examination.

Terminology

> The "digital divide" is one of the most discussed social phenomena of our era. It is also one of the most unclear and confusing.[6]
> —Mark Warschauer

The origin of the term "digital divide" remains uncertain and ambiguous. Recent publications and studies routinely reference *Falling Through the Net: Defining the Digital Divide*, the third in a series of reports published by the U.S. Department of Commerce's National Telecommunications and Information Administration (NTIA). NTIA, however, did not originate this expression. Larry Irving, who was the Department of Commerce's assistant secretary for Communications and Information at the time of the report's composition and publication, provided a candid explanation of this in a post to the Benton Foundation's digital divide discussion list:

I am certain I stole the term, but I am not certain who I stole it from. Jonathan Webber of the *Industry Standard* makes a compelling case that somewhere back around 1995 he and Amy Harmon (when both were with the *LA Times*) invented the term to describe the social division between those who were very involved in technology and those who were not. I believe I first heard the term in the late '95 early '96 time frame at a conference in a Western State, Montana, North Dakota or South Dakota. We did not formally use the term at NTIA until months later, and the term did not gain the ubiquity it enjoys today until the release of the third *Falling Through the Net* report in July '99. I hope that helps. The fairest thing to say is that no one at NTIA invented the term, digital divide. NTIA's reports were, however, the catalysts for the popularity, ubiquity and redefinition (from the *LA Times* original usage) of the term.[7]

According to Irving, the "digital divide" was appropriated from an unknown source and redefined by the NTIA in the process of preparing the third *Falling Through the Net* report. The best guess Irving has for the term's origin is the *LA Times*'s Jonathan Webber and Amy Harmon, who began using it in 1996 to name differences in opinion about new technology.[8] But this assignment is not without complication. Andy Carvin of the Benton Foundation agrees that Harmon may have been one of the first journalists to use the term publicly, but argues, in a response to Irving's comment, that 1996 is "a little too recent for her to have actually coined it."[9] Carvin's research indicates that the expression was already being used to name a gap in educational opportunities by the Clinton-Gore administration, Massachusetts Congressman Ed Markey, and *New York Times* reporter Gary Andrew Poole. He also cites Dinty Moore's *The Emperor's Virtual Clothes* as containing one of the earliest occurrences of the phrase.[10]

The definition of the term in these and subsequent places has not been homogeneous or univocal. Moore, for example, employed "digital divide" to distinguish between advocates and detractors in debates about the value of information technology.[11] Harmon used the expression to name a similar concern in her "Daily Life's Digital Divide," a story published in the 29 July 1996 edition of the *LA Times*. Although Harmon's story makes passing reference to the "deepening divide between rich and poor," the digital divide in the headline refers not to the gap between information haves and have-nots but to a "voluntary partition . . . galvanized by strongly held views about whether today's technology is a force for progress or destruction."[12] For Harmon, as for Moore, the digital divide names the difference of opinion that exists between those who are "deeply suspicious of a new generation of engineering solutions to the world's problems" and those who "insist that, this time around, the enlightenment promise of better living through rationality and science will be realized."[13] At roughly the same time, the term was also employed to name the unequal distribution of information technology in American public schools. It appears, for example, on 29 May 1996 in a speech delivered by then vice-president Al Gore, who used "digital divide" to name the gap between the information haves and information have-not in K–12 education.[14] Beginning in 1996, the Clinton-Gore administration employed the trope of the digital divide to justify various educational initiatives and policies, and press coverage of these events popularized this particular understanding and use of the term. This denotation, however, probably did not originate with the Clinton-Gore White House. Just as it is doubtful that Gore invented the Internet or even the term "information superhighway,"[15] evidence suggests that the Clinton administration most likely appropriated the "digital divide" from other sources. In particular, the term had already been used in the context of education by Congressman Markey in a 10 April 1996 press release addressing the proposed E-Rate and by two journalists, Howard Wolinsky of the *Chicago Sun-Times* and Gary Andrew Poole of the *New York Times*. On 17 March 1996, Wolinsky published "The Digital Divide," which examined how "unequal computer access for students is creating tomorrow's haves and have nots."[16] Two months earlier, a *New York Times* article considered what Poole termed "A New Gulf in American Education, the Digital Divide."[17]

Subsequent usage does not conform to either precedent but adds further denotations to the term's already complicated definition. Beginning in 1997, "digital divide" was used in a number of contexts to describe not differences of opinion about digital technology or inequalities in educational opportunity but technical incompatibilities. Shawn Steward, for example, used the expression to name interoperability problems between analog and digital cellphone networks. For Steward, "digital divide," indicated differences between the Time Division Multiple Access (TDMA) and Code Division Multiple Access (CDMA) digital technologies and the Advanced Mobile Phone Service (AMPS) analog system.[18] The term has also been used to name similar incompatibles in analog and digital television, satellite transmission, and film and filmless radiology.[19] In 1998, the *San Francisco Chronicle* added yet one more denotation. Between May and August of that year, the *Chronicle* published several stories investigating racial diversity in the high-tech industries of Silicon Valley. The series began with Julia Angwin and Laura Castaneda's study "The Digital Divide: High-tech Boom a Bust for Blacks, Latinos," which concluded that "employment records for 33 of the leading Silicon Valley firms show that their Bay Area staffs, on average, are about 4 percent black and 7 percent Latino—even though blacks and Latinos make up 8 and 14 percent of the Bay Area labor force respectively."[20] For Angwin and Castaneda, "digital divide" identifies a form of racial discrimination situated in the unequal distribution of employment opportunities. Similar usage occurs in Art Perio's investigation of "institutionalized racism and employment patterns in the computer industry."[21]

It is not until 1999 that the term appears in the NTIA's *Falling Through the Net: Defining the Digital Divide*. In this report, "digital divide" is defined as "the divide between those with access to new technologies and those without."[22] In this way, "digital divide" names a form of socioeconomic inequality demarcated by the level of *access* one has to information technology. "Digital divide," therefore, functions as another name for a problem that had previously been identified by a number of other expressions—information haves and have-nots, the question of access, and universal service. But even within this particular usage of the term there is considerable equivocation. First, the NTIA has not been consistent. The meaning of "digital divide" has changed from study to study. "In the original iteration of the NTIA surveys," Benjamin Compaine points out, "it meant primarily personal computer ownership. More recently it has come to incorporate Internet access. The latest noises is that it further delineates those with high speed (broadband) access from slower dial-up modem access."[23] Second, the Benton Foundation's Digital Divide Network, which comprises one of the largest databases concerning digital divide issues, has modified the NTIA's definition. For the Benton Foundation (2001), the digital divide names the "gap between those who can effectively *use* new information and communication tools, such as the Internet, and those who cannot."[24] According to this characterization, access to technology is not the only or even most important determination. Beyond access to equipment, individuals need to know how to employ it.

In the end, the digital divide clearly has changing denotations and is, as Compaine advises, "a moving target."[25] It not only names different kinds of technological and social differences but, even when it appears to refer to the same object, does so differently at different times and in different contexts. This complexity does not derive from some univocal origin that subtends and anchors the multiplicity. It is not some form of terminological confusion that has subsequently come to afflict what had initially been a pure and homogeneous concept. Instead, the "digital divide" is originally and persistently plural. This plurality has at least two consequences. First, there is not one digital divide; there is a constellation of different and intersecting social, economic, and technological differences, all of which are properly named "digital divide." Although these various inequalities and discrepancies may be related to one another, it would be hasty and inaccurate to conclude that they are simply identical. This means, on the one hand, that studies of the "digital divide" need to learn how the various problems marked by this appellation relate to, interact with, and influence each other. Employment discrimination in high-tech industry, for example, is certainly related to discrepancies in educational opportunities and access to technology. On the other hand, these different issues should not be conflated. The problem of employment discrimination cannot be reduced to differences in access to technology or adequately addressed by the singular effort to wire all American schools to the Internet. The situation is more complex and involves a number of different variables that need to be taken into account.

Second, lexical multiplicity, despite the value placed on consistent and precise use of terminology, is not necessarily a deficiency. It is not always a semantic problem to be resolved by prescribing, even provisionally, a univocal and noiseless definition. Because information technology has evolved at historically unprecedented rates, the various problems that are associated with it also experience accelerated change. This is one reason for the variability in the NTIA reports. The changing definition of the digital divide is not the result of capriciousness or an inability to be precise. It has varied because the technology in question has changed considerably. For example, the NTIA's first report, *Falling Through the Net: A Survey of the "Have-Nots" in Rural and Urban America*, was published in July of 1995 and relied on data collected by the U.S. Bureau of the Census in 1994. At this time, the Internet was still considered the specialized domain of academics, defense contractors, and computer enthusiasts. For this reason, the first report does not address differences in Internet access and usage but limits its investigation to telephone service and computer and modem ownership. By the time the third report was published in July 1999, however, the Internet was recognized as one of the fundamental technologies comprising the nation's information infrastructure. As a result, the third report addresses "which American households have access to telephones, computers, and the Internet and which do not."[26] In this way, the locus and object of the "digital divide" was updated from the time of the first report to adapt to changes in technology. What is necessary in this situation is not the application of some rigid and univocal definition but a flexible characterization that can respond to and function in this protean environment. Because the problems of the digital divide have been and will probably continue to be moving targets, the term's definition should be similarly mobile.[27]

Structure

> Someone once wittily remarked that the world
> is divided into those who divide people into two
> types, and those who don't.[28]—Daniel Chandler

No matter how it is defined, the digital divide organizes things into two dialectically opposed types. The NTIA segregates American households into those who have access to information technology and those who do not. The Benton Foundation draws a similar distinction, dividing between those who are able to use technology and those who cannot. Harmon and Moore, like Stanovsky and Heim in chapter 1, differentiate between techno-utopians, who celebrate the wonders of digital technology, and techno-dystopians, who remain skeptical of any technological solution. And the Clinton-Gore administration, Congressman Markey, and Poole address the gap that exists between information haves and information have-nots in K–12 education. Consequently, the digital divide, despite apparent variation in its referent, is articulated in digital form. It represents its problematic according to a binary logic, dividing things into one of two types, where the one option is nominally defined as the negative or antithesis of the other. This dichotomized structure, although useful for describing the limits of various social and technological inequalities, is not without significant complications and difficulties. By taking the form of a dichotomy, the digital divide participates in what Daniel Chandler calls "great divide theories."[29] According to Chandler, these theories became prominent during the 1960s with the publication of a number of studies[30] addressing the differences between literate and non-literate cultures. "Such theories," Chandler argues, "tend to suggest radical, deep, and basic differences between modes of thinking in non-literate and literate societies. They are often associated with attempts to develop grand theories of social organization and development."[31] The difficulty with the "great literacy divide," Chandler and others argue, rests in the incompatibility between the seemingly rigid and often simplistic binary representation and its referent, which is usually perceived as being a complex continuum. The binary form literate/non-literate, for example, has been perceived as an exaggeration and even a false dichotomy. Subsequent studies of literacy, as Warschauer points out, have revealed that there is not one, but many types of literacy, that the meaning and value of literacy is not homogeneous but varies according to social circumstances, and that these different literacies exist on a continuum and do not take the form of a simple binary opposition.[32] Consequently, the "all or nothing" scenario that is presented by great divide theories often does not adequately represent the actual state of affairs. Or as Harvey Graff describes it, "none of these polar opposites usefully describe actual circumstances; all of them, in fact, preclude contextual understanding."[33]

Similar criticism has been applied to the various dichotomies that compose the "digital divide." The dialectically opposed perspectives of techno-utopia and techno-dystopia, for example, are not usually experienced as an either/or option. Instead, they delimit a continuum that contains many intervening possibilities for how one understands ICT and its social effects. Andrew Shapiro's *The Control Revolution*, for example, contests the extremes that define the current debate about the Internet and advocates a more nuanced understanding. "Technology," he argues, "is not like anchovies, which some people can love and others hate, nor is it like the right to abortion, which some are for and others are against. Rather, it is an indelible feature of our cultural environment—one we must strive to understand in all its gray-shaded complexity."[34] Similarly, access to and use of information technology is not something that is easily encoded in binary form. Although the digital divide is often characterized as the gap between the information haves and have-nots, it is not the case that one either possesses information or does not. Instead, there is significant variability in the forms of information one possesses and the modes of its access and use. Warschauer provides an instructive illustration: "Compare, for example, a professor at UCLA with a high-speed connection in her office, a student in Seoul who occasionally uses a cyber café, and a rural activist in Indonesia who has no computer or phone line but whose colleagues in the nongovernmental organization (NGO) with whom she is working download and print out information for her. This example illustrates just three degrees of possible access a person can have to online material. The notion of a binary divide between haves and have-nots is thus inaccurate and can even be patronizing because it fails to value the social resources that diverse groups bring to the table."[35]

Although the dichotomies of the digital divide have been expedient for describing sociotechnological differences, the binary form, as was demonstrated in the first chapter, necessarily risks oversimplifying the situation and neglecting the important variations that exist in the object of study. Because of this, it appears that what is necessary is an alternative formulation—one that does not distinguish between two, opposed alternatives but becomes capable of perceiving and articulating fine gradations within complex conglomerates. According to Chandler, the alternatives to great divide theories are sometimes called "continuity theories." These theories "stress a 'continuum' rather than a radical discontinuity" and "an on-going dynamic interaction between various media" instead of a mutually exclusive, either/or opposition.[36] Warschauer, for instance, argues that the digital divide should be redefined as a problem of "social stratification," which "indicates that the 'divide' is not really a binary division at all, but rather a continuum based on different degrees of access to information technology."[37] A similar point is made by Jan A. G. M. van Dijk, who takes issue with the term *divide*, because it "suggests a simple division between two clearly divided groups with a yawning gap between them." For van Dijk, the situation is much more complex and nuanced. "In contemporary society," he writes, "we may observe an increasingly complex social, economic, and cultural differentiation. The image of an extended spectrum of positions stretching across populations might be more appropriate."[38] Some of the empirical studies, most notably the third, fourth, and fifth NTIA reports, have attempted to distinguish varying degrees of Internet use based on where one accesses the network and the kind of equipment that is employed.[39] Such approaches, which are consistent with the development of alternative strategies in the study of literacy, appear to provide a mode of inquiry that is not limited by the restrictive and reductive logic of either/or.

The problem with such binary logic, however, is not simply the inability of a linguistic dichotomy to represent a complex state of affairs. It is not a discrepancy between the sign and the signified. Instead, the difficulty resides in the binary structure itself. The distinction between the "information haves" and "information have-nots," for example, is articulated in such a way that the latter is both segregated from and defined in opposition to the former. These two possibilities, as in any binary arrangement, are not on equal footing. They are always and already, as Derrida and others have pointed out, involved in a violent and asymmetrical hierarchy.[40] The "information haves" are not only characterized positively but are presumed to be in the desirable position. The "information have-nots" are defined, quite literally, by what they lack in comparison to the "information haves." They comprise the negative counterpart and undesirable version of their positively defined other. This formulation, although useful for calling attention to extant technological and social inequalities, has potentially disquieting ethical consequences, especially when applied in a global context. In distinguishing "information haves" from "information have-nots," the technologically privileged situate their experiences with technology as normative, so that those without access to similar systems and capabilities become perceived as deficient and lacking. This evaluation, which establishes an asymmetrical hierarchy, is not substantially modified by including intervening stages in the binary structure, for the other would still be defined negatively by what she lacks in comparison to the technologically privileged. Defining others as existing in various states of deficiency, however, can be interpreted as arrogant and paternalistic. The Internet, although potentially useful in some highly specific sociocultural situations, is not an unqualified and unquestioned human good. Unlike clean water, nutritious food, and adequate shelter, the value of this technology has been determined by unique circumstances that are only applicable to a small fraction of the world's population. In defining others as deficient, one does not simply provide a neutral expression of inequality. The very technique by which the discrepancy is articulated necessarily employs an asymmetrical logic that already warrants the position of a privileged minority and depreciates and simplifies the situation of others.

Given this structural difficulty, the task of criticism might appear to be to escape or to avoid all forms of binary logic, replacing the dichotomies of the digital divide with something that is less decisive and derisive. This proposal would be fantastic if not impossible. The binary structure that is evident in the concept of the digital divide is neither unique nor voluntary. In fact, such logic organizes and informs the entire event-horizon of the Western episteme, up to and including that by which one would describe and/or criticize this tradition as such. Binary logic, as poststructuralists have demonstrated, underlies, organizes, and animates all possible modes of knowing—scientific, mathematical, critical, and even everyday language. As Mark Dery explains it: "Western systems of meaning are underwritten by binary oppositions, which include, among others: self/other, mind/body, culture/nature, male/female, civilized/primitive, reality/appearance, whole/part, agent/resource, maker/made, active/passive, right/wrong, truth/illusion, totality/partiality."[41] If all meaningful discourse is generated in and by using such binary terms, then there is, strictly speaking, nothing of significance outside this system. In other words, it may not be possible to think, speak, or reason otherwise. What is required, therefore, is a procedure that not only recognizes this requirement but learns how to operate in this curious and complex situation.

This insight furnishes at least three conclusions useful for understanding the digital divide and directing its critical investigation. First, the examination of the divide needs to develop a sense of self-reflectivity. Although empirical studies adequately diagnose and quantify the gap that currently exists, for example, between information haves and have-nots, they do not explicitly recognize how

this apparently altruistic endeavor might also entail significant ethical complications. In structuring its problematic in the form of a binary opposition—a
structure that is logically necessary and not merely optional—the digital divide
does not simply identify a kind of sociotechnological discrimination but already entails evaluative decisions that encompass potentially disturbing forms
of prejudice. Consequently, the structure of the problem may itself be a problem.
Second, the examination of this binary opposition cannot take place except by
employing what is investigated. Because binary logic underwrites all possible
modes of meaning, it also governs any and all attempts to question and criticize
this structure as such. Or as Chandler cleverly demonstrates, one is compelled
to employ binary logic even when questioning and describing the limits of such
logic.[42] The binary structure of the digital divide, therefore, is not something
one can surpass, overcome, or even avoid. It delimits both the articulation of the
problem and the parameters of any meaningful critique. Consequently, the task
of criticism is not to break out of this logic but to learn how to use it to question
its own limits and exigencies. Finally, and as a result of this situation, there neither is nor can be finality. Critics must realize, as Mark Taylor points out, "that
since they remain unavoidably entangled in the systems and structures they resist, the task of criticism is endless."[43] Criticism of the digital divide, therefore, is
not some singular undertaking having definite goals and a conclusive solution. It
is and remains an ongoing project—one that must, following the example provided by poststructuralism, continually submit its own findings to the process
of critical inquiry.

Form

> Despite the media's penchant for beating to death anything
> to do with the Internet, a new phrase has recently entered
> the public's online lexicon, one that actually carries signifi-
> cant societal ramifications: the "digital divide."[44]
> —Andy Carvin

The digital divide is concerned not so much with technology as with its "significant societal ramifications." The effect of technology in the social sphere has
often been posed in the terms of *technological determinism*. "The technological
determinist view," according to Chandler, "is a *technology-led* theory of social
change: technology is seen as the 'prime mover' in history. According to technological determinists, particular technical developments, communication technologies or media, or, most broadly, technology in general are the sole or prime
antecedent cause of change in society, and technology is seen as the fundamental condition underlying the pattern of social organization."[45] This particular
formulation of a causal connection between technology and society is usually
credited to American sociologist Thorstein Veblen.[46] It becomes an influential

theory in the sociology of communication through the work of individuals like Charles Horton Cooley, who argued that "we understand nothing rightly unless we perceive the manner in which the revolution in communication has made a new world for us."[47] And it plays a constitutive role in the fields of technology and media studies.[48] Since its introduction at the turn of the last century, technological determinism has developed into two subsets, generally called "hard" and "soft determinism." Hard determinism makes technology the *sufficient* or *necessary* condition for social change, while soft determinism understands technology to be a key factor that *may facilitate* change. Although these two modes are distinguished from one another, the boundary between them is often blurry and flexible. As Ruth Finnegan points out, "it is easy to slide from one to another without realizing where one is being led."[49]

Despite several decades of healthy skepticism,[50] technological determinism figures prominently in the rhetoric of computers, information technology, and the Internet. Jay David Bolter's *Turing's Man*, for instance, argues that the computer redefines "man's role in relation to nature," producing "a change in the way men and women in the electronic age think about themselves and the world around them."[51] In his 1995 best-seller, *Being Digital*, Nicholas Negroponte distinguishes bits from atoms and argues that bits of digital information introduce revolutionary changes in communication, education, politics, entertainment, and human communities.[52] And the work of Alvin Toffler, which figures prominently in the ideology of techno-libertarians, divides history into three distinct "waves," which are primarily defined by the technological innovations of agriculture, industrial production, and information systems.[53] The reports, texts, and discussions of the digital divide do not question this prevailing technological determinism but exploit it. First, the digital divide, no matter how it has been defined, assumes radical and persistent differences between distinct socioeconomic forms and defines these differences technologically. The discourse of the digital divide employs the distinctions between digital and analog technology, the "new digital economy" of e-commerce and the "old economy" of industrialized production, the Information Age and the Industrial Age, and the opportunities enjoyed by those individuals who are able to participate in the "digital revolution" and the unfortunate experiences of those who (for whatever reason) cannot. Indicative of this form of technological determinism is the U.S. Department of Commerce's *The Emerging Digital Economy* reports, which complement the NTIA's *Digital Divide* studies.[54] In the introduction to the first *Emerging Digital Economy* publication (April 1998), the authors differentiate between two socioeconomic revolutions, each of which is defined and propelled by technological innovations—the Industrial Revolution, which "was powered by the steam engine, invented in 1712, and electricity, first harnessed in 1831," and the digital revolution, driven by information technology and "the harnessing of light for nearly instantaneous communication."[55] In the discussions and debates concerning the digital divide, the computer and the Internet are not just another convenience. They are often assumed to be epoch-defining technologies that determine radically new socio-economic opportunities for individuals and institutions.

Second, in the rhetoric of the various digital divide studies and reports one finds both hard and soft forms of technological determinism. The gap between the information haves and have-nots, for example, is not just another socioeconomic division. As Compaine points out, the question concerning access to information technology is approached as a unique disparity that is not on par with other kinds of technological inequalities, like that existing between individuals who have access to automobile transportation and those who do not.[56] Instead, the digital divide is perceived to be a definitive social issue. It is characterized as such, because the technology in question is assumed to effect socioeconomic opportunity and success. This understanding often takes the form of hard determinism. This is especially evident in political speeches, where ICT is presented as the sufficient cause of social change. Former vice-president of the United States Al Gore is probably best known for this kind of rhetoric: "We meet today to break down walls. At each critical point in our nation's history, we have acted on our duty to give every citizen the chance to live out the American Dream. In the Agricultural Age, we ensured that land went not only to the privileged few, but to the common yeoman farmer. In the Industrial Age, we focused on making sure that all Americans—and not just the industrial barons—had access to capital. Today in the Information Age, connecting all people to a universe of knowledge and learning is the key to ensuring a lifetime of success."[57] Other times the demonstration employs a softer approach, suggesting that information technology may contribute to social transformation. Compaine, for instance, finds that "access to the information available from networked devices may be critical in the education process—for both teachers and students." "But," he asks, "will the stakes be as high as some prognosticators proclaim?"[58] And sometimes the rhetoric of the digital divide drifts, as Finnegan explains, from one form of determinism to the other. The third NITA report, for example, begins with Irving's proclamation that the digital divide "is now one of America's leading economic and civil rights issues." It ends, however, with a more modest and measured assessment: "To be connected today increasingly means to have access to telephones, computers, *and* the Internet. While these items may not be necessary for survival, arguably in today's emerging digital economy they are necessary for success."[59]

Discussion of the digital divide regularly employs elements of technological determinism. This is a potential difficulty not only because technological determinism, as a general theory of social change, remains controversial, but because there are specific problems with the technological determinist perspective as it applies to computer technology. First, the theory of technological determinism is refuted by two other theories concerning the relationship between technology and society—*sociocultural determinism* and *volunteerism*. According to Chandler, the former "presents technologies and media as entirely subordinate to their development and use in particular socio-political, historical, and culturally specific contexts." The latter "emphasizes individual control over the tools which they see themselves as 'choosing' to use."[60] Both alternatives complicate the technological determinist perspective. Although the various empirical studies and reports addressing the digital divide[61] employ forms of technological determinism in constructing their hypotheses and conclusions, they often support the theory of sociocultural determinism in the course of their investigations. In the diagnostic phase, these different studies find that access to and use of information technology is dependent on social and economic conditions. The first NTIA report (1995), for example, discovers that geography is an important factor in defining the divide between information haves and have-nots. The third report demonstrates that race is a significant element and argues that the digital divide is actually a "racial ravine."[62] And the 2000 Forrester brief, penned by Ekaterina Walsh, discovers that it is personal income that makes up the primary and determining factor. Although there is still significant debate over the exact cause of the digital discrepancy, survey research demonstrates that social, cultural, and economic opportunities play a constitutive role in determining the level of one's access to and ability to use information technology. In other words, access to and use of technology appears to be a symptom and not the cause of socioeconomic opportunity. What the empirical studies demonstrates, therefore, is that the theory of technological determinism, although persuasively deployed in the rhetoric of the digital divide, remains an inadequate explanation of the problem and risks oversimplifying a situation that is obviously more complex and nuanced.

The perspective of volunteerism introduces additional complications. In modern philosophy, volunteerism, which emphasizes an active agent's individual freedom to choose between competing alternatives, is traditionally opposed to determinism, which proposes what is often described as a mechanistic model of causation. For this reason, volunteerism has been employed by humanists, existentialists, and other individuals who "insist that people are active agents and not helpless automatons" that are determined by sociocultural or technological circumstances.[63] In *The Labyrinths of Literacy*, for example, Graff (1987) counters the technological determinist perspective in literacy studies by employing a volunteerist argument. According to Graff, "neither writing nor printing alone is an 'agent of change'; their impacts are determined by the manner in which human agency exploits them in a specific setting."[64] Similar arguments have been made for studies of the digital divide. Compaine, for instance, argues that the almost undocumented existence of voluntary nonusers significantly complicates the statistics:

> In the statistics on nonsubscribers to telephone, cable service, PC ownership or Internet connectivity there has been scant attention paid to voluntary nonusers. There is both anecdotal evidence and increasing statistical verification that large numbers of individuals are voluntary non-participants.... The Cheskin Research study of Hispanic households found that

the second most voiced reason for not owning a computer, nearly 40%, was "don't need." Another six percent had similar reasons—"too old" or "not interested." This is generally consistent with the NPR/Kaiser Foundation/Kennedy School survey. . . . Of those characterizing themselves as being "left behind" in computers, barely 20% blamed cost. A third were just not interested.[65]

Studies of the digital divide, therefore, appear to overemphasize sociotechnological factors at the expense of individual volition. Consequently, critics of current digital divide studies point out that the world is not simply divided into information haves and have-nots. There are also information want-nots and even Internet drop-outs—those who had access at one time and decide, for various reasons, against continued use.[66] Accordingly, studies of the digital divide have been denounced for being too deterministic and neglecting these important voluntary aspects affecting access to and use of new technology.

Second, the social impact of computer technology is contested and inconclusive. Citing a study conducted by Carnegie-Mellon University, Hubert Dreyfus concludes that the Internet has not provided the kind of social improvement that is espoused in the technical, academic, and popular presses: "We are told that, given its new way of linking and accessing information, the Internet will bring a new era of economic prosperity, lead to the development of intelligent search engines that will deliver to us just the information we desire, solve the problems of mass education, put us in touch with all of reality, allow us to have even more flexible identities than we already have and thereby add new dimensions of meaning to our lives. But, compared with the relative success of e-commerce, the other areas where a new and more fulfilling form of life has been promised have produced a great deal of talk but few happy results."[67] Similar disappointments with the social promise of computer technology have been registered by Zillah Eisenstein, Gordon Graham, and Kevin Robins and Frank Webster.[68] Although the digital divide studies situate computer technology as a force for positive social change, this assumption is neither universally accepted nor without considerable debate. In fact, one must remember that the determinist perspective can be and has been employed to explain both positive and negative social transformation. Jacques Ellul, for instance, argues that technology is not necessarily a progressive force but also produces new sociocultural conflicts and uncertainties.[69] Determinism, whether hard or soft, cuts both ways.

Complicating this insight is the fact that technology is often employed in ways that deviate from its intended or projected use. "The street," as William Gibson points out, "finds its own use for things—uses the manufacturers never imagined."[70] This is especially true for the Internet, which was initially developed by the U.S. Department of Defense (DOD) for the purposes of telecomputing and research but was actually utilized by participants as a medium of communication.[71] The digital divide reports position the Internet as a tool for lifelong learning, job improvement, and democratic participation. Data concerning actual use, however, contest this. Both the 1998 and 1999 NTIA surveys and the Forrester brief, find that users employ the Internet for purposes other than the projected social and political improvements. "The surveys," Compaine points out, "have found that services such as chat rooms (sex is popular), sports, and game playing top the list of activities. It is wonderful having access to news and finance and diverse opinions from providers who would never have a world wide audience pre-Internet. But as the research presented in this volume and elsewhere repeatedly confirms, once digitally enabled, all groups—by income, ethnicity, gender and education—fall into almost identical patterns of usage."[72] ICT, despite assurance to the contrary, is not necessarily experienced as "a leading economic and civil rights issues." Although the Internet may provide some minor improvements in education, career development, and retail shopping, there remains significant dissonance between the socioeconomic liberation promised in the rhetoric of the Internet and the actual patterns of use discovered in the empirical surveys.

Finally, history is against us here. The sociocultural opportunities promoted in the technological determinist rhetoric of the Internet is nothing new. Similar promises have been made for other forms of information technology. Electric telegraphy, for example, was introduced with a kind of messianic narrative. According to James Carey, "this new technology entered American discussions not as a mundane fact but as divinely inspired for the purposes of spreading the Christian message farther and faster, eclipsing time and transcending space, saving the heathen, bringing closer and making more probable the day of salvation."[73] Similar assurances were associated with radio during the first three decades of its development and commercial expansion. As Martin Spinelli demonstrates in his "Radio Lessons for the Internet," wireless technology was "instilled with the hopes of initiating utopian democracy, providing for universal and equal education, and bringing a sense of belonging and community."[74] These promises, which bear an uncanny resemblance to the current rhetoric of ICT, were espoused by industry leaders like David Sarnoff, government officials and agencies like Herbert Hoover[75] and the FCC, and cultural critics like Hans Magnus Enzensberger, Rudolf Arnheim, and Bertolt Brecht. The history of telegraphy and radio, however, demonstrate that both forms of information technology were unable to effect these fantastic social promises. The telegraphic network, for instance, did not hasten the coming of the kingdom of heaven but either fed the desire for mundane gossip, as Henry David Thoreau had argued,[76] or supported nationalist aggression and empire building.[77] "The messages that passed through these far-flung communications links were," as Steven Lubar points out, "messages not of peace and unity but of unprecedented technological warfare."[78] Radio also failed to deliver on its projected social transformations. The technology of wireless communication, although initially associated with idealistic pretensions, actually evolved to serve military purposes and the profit motives of corporations.[79] One would in fact be hard-pressed to find any trace of the utopian ideals that were initially associated with broadcasting in the current spectrum of seemingly infinite varieties of classic rock, contemporary country, and talk radio. There is, therefore, significant dissonance between the projected social impact attributed to a particular technology and the actual effects that are observed to follow from its development and proliferation. If telegraph and radio failed to fulfill the promises of participatory democracy, new economic opportunities, and social improvement, one should be skeptical of similar technological determinist rhetoric when applied to the Internet. In stating this, I am not arguing that the Internet will necessarily follow the historical precedent established by other forms of media, especially broadcast communication. Such a position amounts to a kind of naive "historical determinism" and would not be attentive to the important qualitative differences that exist between these technologies. Instead, the issue is the theory of technological determinism and the way it has functioned in the history of ICT. Like the Internet, telegraph and radio were at one time new technologies that were introduced and associated with the promise of sociocultural liberation. Unfortunately, neither technology delivered on what was promised. The history of telegraphy and radio, therefore, do not prescribe some fated destiny for the Internet but merely indicate that there are good reasons to be skeptical of technological determinism whenever it is deployed.

Conclusion

> Anyone who practices the art of cultural criticism must endure being asked, What is the solution to the problems you describe?[80]
> —Neil Postman

Critique of the digital divide does not identify difficulties in order to correct them but aims to articulate the necessary and often unexamined preconditions that organize and underlie its discussions, debates, reports, and examinations. This form of investigation does not contest the data that has been collected, dispute the analyses that have been published, or undermine the work that has been and continues to be done. On the contrary, the purpose of critique is to assist these and future endeavors by making evident their starting points, stakes, and consequences. To have second thoughts about the digital divide is not to question the validity or importance of the different social and technological issues that are identified by this term. "Second thoughts" means rethinking the problematic of the digital divide, exposing its assumptions, and explicating how such preconditions authorize and regulate its examination and proposed reparation.

At the end, then, what we have are not conclusive solutions to specific problems but guidelines for understanding and questioning the issues of the digital divide. First, the term "digital divide" is originally equivocal, irreducibly plural, and constantly flexible. It names not one problem but a changing constellation of different and not always related concerns. Unfortunately, "digital divide" is something that has been used far too casually in industry, government, and the academy. The goal of criticism is not to formalize a rigid and univocal definition. The fact is, the phrase will probably continue to be plural and multifaceted. Instead, the task is to help delimit the range of possible denotations and to assist digital divide discourse in understanding the complexity and nuances of the various problems that have been collected under this appellation. What is needed, therefore, is not a precise and exclusive definition but an understanding of the essential polysemia that already characterizes the term "digital divide." Such understanding will not only help abate terminological equivocation but will foster a more discerning conceptualization of the digital divide's fundamental plurality.

Second, no matter what socioeconomic or technological differences the term "digital divide" identifies, it projects a binary structure. It describes its various concerns by differentiating between two variables, where one comprises the negation or antithesis of the other. This binary opposition not only is unable to represent something that essentially resists division into a simple either/ or dichotomy but also institutes an asymmetrical hierarchy. The issue, then, is not just the inability of the linguistic sign to describe a complex state of affairs but the implicit value judgments that are already encoded in the structure of a dichotomy where the two terms are not on equal footing. The task of criticism is not to break out of this binary logic, which would be nonsense, but to learn to use it to develop self-reflection. The task, therefore, is to question the terms and conditions by which studies of the digital divide define their own mode of questioning. Doing so will help ensure that examinations of the digital divide do not proceed blindly but understand the structure and consequences necessarily imposed by their own problematic. This approach, as we will discover in the chapters that follow, is not something that is limited to the digital divide but constitutes a general strategy that is applicable to any binary structure.

Third, the examinations and discussions of the digital divide, whether executed in government reports, popular media, or academic analyses, rely on and deploy elements of technological determinism. In fact, it is through the common and often unacknowledged assumption of this perspective that the problem of the "digital divide" becomes something worth studying, discussing, and debating. Technological determinism is a persuasive position—socioeconomic problems are reduced to technological issues so that investment in technology is directly associated with social and economic improvement. The issues, however, are more complex. The purpose of critique is not to overturn or repair technological determinism, but to expose and make explicit the way this particular theory organizes the definition of the problem of the digital divide and the range of its possible reparations. In formulating this position, other theories of social change, like sociocultural determinism and volunteerism, although no less controversial, can provide critical foils for questioning and investigating digital divide rhetoric. It is, then, not a matter of finding the "right" theory and applying it consistently but of using theory dynamically to open the "digital divide" to critical reflection and a mode of thinking that is otherwise. Understanding how the theory of technological determinism participates in shaping the problematic of the digital divide is indispensable for anyone interested in evaluating the studies, reports, and proposals addressing this important sociotechnological issue.

Chapter Four

VRx: Media Technology, Drugs, and Codependency

Drugs and media are equal partners.[1]—Adilkno

The debates and decisions surrounding "new media technology" (e.g., virtual reality, cyberspace, the Internet, and other forms of ICT) have been, like so much reasoning within the Western tradition, organized around antinomies. One of the principal concerns involves a tension between the real world and the computer-generated representations that appear to threaten it. As Peter Horsfield describes it, the question is "whether the essential characteristics of virtual reality as a reality in which the frustrations and disappointments of the actual world do not exist, will inevitably lead to a diminishing desire to live in the actual world. So, instead of learning the disciplines of living with or changing one's individual or communal environment, one finds it easier to escape into a reality where these practicalities do not exist."[2] This concern, despite the future tense that is employed by Horsfield, is not just some speculative possibility; it is in fact already happening. In his empirical investigation of virtual worlds, economist Edward Castronova found that "Norrath," a computer-generated virtual reality situated in the massive multiplayer online role-playing game (MMORPG) *Ever-Quest*, possesses a gross national product (GNP) per capita that "easily exceeds that of dozens of countries, including India and China," supports an hourly wage of approximately USD 3.42, and has been identified as "the principle place of residence" for some 12,000 individuals.[3] According to Castronova's findings, MMORPGs are not just fun and games, but represent a real alternative and challenge to what used to be called reality.

This conflict, and the numerous metaphysical and ethical considerations it entails, is perhaps best dramatized in a pivotal scene from *The Matrix*, the first episode of a cinematic trilogy written and directed by Andy and Larry Wachowski. In this scene, the leader of the opposition, Morpheus, presents the protagonist, Neo, with a decisive choice between two alternatives. "This is your last chance," Morpheus says stoically. "After this, there is no going back. You take the blue pill and the story ends. You wake in your bed and you believe whatever you want to believe. You take the red pill and you stay in Wonderland and I show you how deep the rabbit hole goes. Remember all I am offering is the truth. Nothing more."[4] What Morpheus offers Neo in the form of two pills is a choice between two very different and opposed possibilities. To select the blue pill is to decide not only to live in an immaterial, computer-generated fantasy but to remain ignorant of the mechanisms of this simulation. This fantastic virtual world is, if not perfect, at least vastly superior to the post-apocalyptic, real world that exists outside the space of the Matrix. To select the red pill is to choose the truth no matter how disturbing and difficult the "desert of the real" might turn out to be. It is a decision to live in the real world that exists and persists outside the fictional experiences created and sustained by the computer. Consequently, what Morpheus offers Neo in the form of two pills is nothing less than a choice between real truth and computer-generated artifice.

Without exception, critical investigations of and commentaries addressing this scene immediately focus on and examine the protagonist's choice of one pill over the other. In essay after essay, philosophers, film scholars, theologians, and critics of all varieties target and investigate Neo's decision to take the red pill. And this interest is not without justification. In taking the red pill, Neo decides in favor of the real and the true in opposition to the virtuality of computer-generated simulation. This decision, as is demonstrated in the numerous texts that have addressed it,[5] clearly has metaphysical, epistemological, and ethical consequences that have repercussions reaching far beyond the narrative of the *Matrix*. As tempting as it is to add yet another layer to the examination of this pivotal decision, I hesitate to do so. In fact, I want to purposefully delay an explicit consideration of Neo's decision[6] and ask about another decision, one which is prior to and situated outside of the decision that is presented within the space and time of this particular film's narrative. Instead of asking about the selection of one pill over the other, I want to inquire about the terms and conditions of this particular choice. I am, therefore, interested not in Neo's decision, which is portrayed within the space and time of the film, but in the prior decision that was made to define and confine his actions to these two particular options. Before Neo decides between the truth of the real world and the computer-generated fiction of the Matrix, it was already decided that this decision should consist in a choice between two different pills. My concern, therefore, is not (at least for now) with Neo's choice, however crucial that may turn out to be, but with the prior determination that already makes this choice dependent on drugs. This situation, we will discover, is not something that is unique to *The Matrix*. In fact, the two pills that are cradled in Morpheus's hands constitute, quite literally, the form in which all media technology, from writing to full-immersion virtual reality (VR), have been understood, developed, and evaluated. Whenever it is a matter of distinguishing or deciding between what is called, not without some difficulty, "real truth" and "mediated artifice," the difference is presented, packaged, and explicated in the form of drugs. As Adilkno succinctly describes it, drugs and media are equal partners, and this codependency has quite a lineage.

Connecting the Dots

> If the literature of electronic culture can be located in the works of Philip K. Dick or William Gibson, in the imaginings of a cyberpunk projection, or a reserve of virtual reality, then it is probable that electronic culture shares a crucial project with drug culture.[7]
> —Avital Ronell

From the beginning, cyberspace has been associated with and described in terms of drugs. In William Gibson's *Neuromancer*, the proto-cyberpunk novel that introduced the neologism, cyberspace is officially described as a "consensual hallucination,"[8] and its functioning is articulated by employing obvious drug references and rhetoric.[9] Case, the protagonist of the novel, is a cyberspace junky and his data fix is presented, within the context of the narrative, as both a liberating ecstasy and a crippling dependency. When jacked into the matrix, Case is carried away into another realm, and the experience is emotionally liberating. "Disk beginning to rotate, faster, becoming a sphere of paler gray. Expanding—And flowed, flowered for him, fluid neon origami trick, the unfolding of his distanceless home, his country, transparent 3D chessboard extending to infinity. Inner eye opening to the stepped scarlet pyramid of the Eastern Seaboard Fission Authority burning beyond the green cubes of Mitsubishi Bank of America, and high and very far away he saw the spiral arms of military systems, forever beyond his reach. And somewhere he was laughing, in a white-painted loft, distant fingers caressing the deck, tears of release streaking his face."[10] But when this cyberspace cowboy is unable to jack into this electronic euphoria, he not only suffers from withdrawal symptoms but also turns to pharmaceuticals. In fact, *Neuromancer* begins at the bottom. When the reader first encounters Case, he has been poisoned with a "wartime Russian mycotoxin" that has damaged his nervous system.[11] As a result, Case is physiologically unable to access the computer matrix and, until he can find an antidote, is reduced to getting his fix by taking speed and other chemical stimulants. For Case, then, it is not a matter of either being on drugs or not. It is a question of which drug—either the computer-generated hallucinations of the cyberspace matrix or the chemically induced high caused by ingesting amphetamines. The former consists in a dazzling spectacle of "bright lattices of logic," where one's disembodied consciousness circulates through virtual space at the speed of light.[12] The later is associated with the dark and decaying streets of a polluted and postindustrial urban environment called Chiba City.

Like the term "cyberspace," which quickly made its way into both academic and popular writings on information technology, this "drug ethos" was also immediately appropriated and elaborated by researchers, critics, and journalists. In fact, throughout the 1990s, writings about ICT seemed to have developed quite a dependency on drugs. In 1990, for example, the *Wall Street Journal* published an article on VR under the now-famous headline "Electronic LSD." The exact source of this phrase has never been fully settled and the credit or blame is still debated. As Chris Chesher points out, the VR industry, which for better or worse caught a buzz off this connection to the hallucinogenic drug of the 1960s counterculture, often tried to assign the phrase to media hyperbole in order to solidify commercial legitimacy. The association of VR with LSD (lysergic acid diethylamide) was, Robert Jacobson argued during a speech at "Virtual Reality '92," an unfortunate accident resulting from "a popular press that is lazy, inaccurate, and sensation-seeking."[13] Likewise Jaron Lanier, the individual who is credited with coining the term "virtual reality" and who was one of the subjects of the *Journal's* article, has continually and consistently resisted the confluence. According to Lanier, the VR experience is "not anything like what you'd associate with a psychedelic drug. A drug, because it's operating directly on your brain, is changing your subjective perception, whereas Virtual Reality only happens outside your sense organs, so it only directly addresses what you objectively perceive."[14] For Lanier, the crucial difference between VR and LSD has to do with the boundary between the inside and outside of sensation. The drug is ingested into the body and changes perception subjectively by working on the brain from the inside. VR, on the contrary, only affects perception from the outside. Therefore, it is encountered like any other object that is presented to and has an effect on our senses.

Despite this argument, the connection between VR and LSD remained part and parcel of high-tech R&D (research and development). According to Benjamin Woolley, "the link with LSD was established early on in the history of virtual reality,"[15] and it can be traced in the experiences of many of the influential players. Stewart Brand, for example, who was one of Ken Kesey's Merry Pranksters and the originator of the "Trips Festivals" of 1966, organized the seminal Cyberthon at SIGGRAPH 1990 and penned *The Media Lab: Inventing the Future at MIT*, a book that, Woolley claims, contains one of the first published references to "virtual reality."[16] In 1989, John Walker's Autodesk, one of the first companies involved in the commercialization of VR software, selected Timothy Leary, the principal spokesperson for psychedelic experimentation, to be the on-screen narrator for its promotional films.[17] Leary, who in the last years of his life became a stanch advocate of everything virtual, revised his original psychedelic mantra "turn on, tune in, drop out" with the updated cyber-slogan "turn on, boot up, jack in" and argued that "the PC was the LSD of the 90's."[18] All of this is synthesized in Leary's 1994 "psybernetic" magnum opus *Chaos and Cyberculture*, which exhibits the connection between psychedelic drugs and cyberspace both in its content and its design: the front cover has the deliberate look and feel of a Peter Max painting, a page from *Oracle* magazine, or a Grateful Dead album (figure 5).

Figure 5
Brian Groppe's cover for Timothy Leary's *Chaos & Cyberculture*. Copyright 1994 Timothy Leary. From *Chaos & Cyber Culture*, Ronin Publishing, by permission of Ronin Publishing, Berekely, CA. All rights reserved. (www.roninpub.com)

This connection with the Dead is not coincidental. John Perry Barlow, one-time lyricist for the band and founding father of the Electronic Frontier Foundation, recounts how he turned Jerry Garcia on to the high-tech trip.

Knowing that Garcia is a sucker for anything which might make a person question all he knows, I gave him a call not long after my first cyberspace demo. Hell yes, he was interested. . . . He adapted to it quicker than anyone I'd watched other than my 4 year old daughter Anna (who came home and told her sisters matter-of-factly that she had been to a neat "place" that afternoon.) By the time he crossed back over to our side of the Reality Horizon, he was pretty kid-like himself. "Well," he finally said, "they outlawed LSD. It'll be interesting to see what they do with this." Which brings me to a point which makes Jaron Lanier very uncomfortable. The closest analog to Virtual Reality in my experience is psychedelic, and, in fact, cyberspace is already crawling with delighted acid heads.[19]

Observing the experience of Garcia in cyberspace, Barlow was compelled to affirm the association between LSD and VR that was reported in the *Wall Street Journal* and that has been emphatically resisted by Lanier and other "serious" researchers. According to Barlow, the effect and experience of computer-generated simulation is analogous to that produced by chemical hallucinogens, and for this reason, cyberspace attracts and is already populated by "heads."

The correspondence between the experience of hallucinogenic drugs and the rather new technology of VR and cyberspace is not something that is restricted to the insights and musings of former acid-heads. It has also been marked in the work of computer graphics designers and media theorists. Nicole Stenger's "Mind Is a Leaking Rainbow," for example, not only evokes the atmosphere of 1960s psychedelia in its title but begins by marking a precise correlation between the descriptions of chemically induced hallucinations and computer graphics practices. "The French poet Henri Michaux, in *Connaissance par les Gouffres* (1988), has left us descriptions of his (provoked) experiences with hallucination, experiences that have, strangely enough, found their exact replicas in the generating patterns of computer animation."[20] According to Stenger, Michaux's drug-induced poetry provides descriptions of "alterations of vision that strikingly resemble the properties of imaging software" and creates "images that are today all familiar scenes to the computer specialist."[21] For Stenger computer-generated graphics have a look and feel that closely resembles, if not exactly replicates, the experiences of chemically induced hallucinations. A similar correlation is documented by journalist Douglas Rushkoff in his chronicle of late-twentieth-century subcultures, *Cyberia*. Like Stenger, Rushkoff charts the convergence of psychedelic drugs, computer technology, and the complex graphical patterns produced by fractal geometry. In fact, *Cyberia* begins and is initially defined with a description of this convergence in the experience of two university students who drop acid while experimenting with computer-generated graphics: "The boys just don't think this, they feel it—and in many ways at once: their consciousness is being drawn into an intense psychedelic trip, their computer picture is about to shift into a new multidimensional representation of an equation, and their world is changing around them faster than they can articulate or even imagine. And these are the people who grok this turf. Welcome to Cyberia."[22] Likewise media philosophers Mark Taylor and Esa Saarinen find inescapable parallels between the experience of psychedelic drugs and electronic media. "Hallucinogenic drugs . . . electronics . . . all-at-onceness . . . all-at-oneness. Fibers link these disparate points. Virtual reality is the LSD of the electronic age."[23] These various affiliations are marked, quite literally, by Michael Horowitz's neologism *cyberdelic*,[24] a concatenation of the prefix "cyber-" and the word "psychedelic" that, according to Mark Dery, "reconciles the transcendentalist impulses of the sixties counterculture with the infomania of the nineties."[25] Because of this affiliation, one needs to rethink the popular conception of the sixties counterculture. "The distance," Taylor and Saarinen write, "between Haight Ashbury and Silicon Valley is not as great as it initially appears. The counter-culture's technophobia always harbored a technophilia that promised to transform the chemico-religious prosthesis into the electronic prosthesis."[26] A similar insight is provided by Dery in *Escape Velocity*: "Analyses of sixties counterculture that characterize it as intractably antitechnological neglect the cyberdelic motifs that counterpointed its back-to-the-land primitivism: the perception of psychedelics as liberatory technologies and of electronic media as mind-expanding psychedelics."[27] Like Taylor and Saarinen, Dery finds the distance between the hippies/yippies of Haight Ashbury and the cybernauts of Silicon Valley to be almost negligible. Psychedelic drugs were already understood as technologies of liberation and electronic media were experienced as mind-expanding pharmaceuticals.

This essential connection between the chemical and electronic prosthesis was already noted by Marshall McLuhan, the 1960s media guru who became the later-day patron saint of the *Wired* world, in his now-famous *Playboy* interview.

> The upsurge in drug taking is intimately related to the impact of the electric media. Look at the metaphor for getting high: turning on. One turns on his consciousness through drugs just as he opens up all his senses to a total depth involvement by turning on the TV dial. Drug taking is stimulated by today's pervasive environment of instant information, with its feedback mechanism of the inner trip. The inner trip is not the sole prerogative of the LSD traveler; it's the universal experience of TV watchers. LSD is a way of miming the invisible electronic world; it releases a person from acquired verbal and visual habits and reactions, and gives the potential of instant and total involvement, both all-at-onceness and all-at-oneness, which are the basic needs of people translated by electric extensions of their central nervous systems out of the old rational, sequential value system. The attraction to hallucinogenic drugs is a means of achieving empathy with our penetrating electric environment, an environment that in itself is a drugless inner trip.[28]

For McLuhan, who during the same interview affirmed that he is only an observer of drug usage and not a participant, there is a fundamental connection between the experience of electronic technology, which for him consisted mainly of television, and drugs, especially LSD. Both substances, he argues, alter consciousness by opening the user's senses to a total depth involvement in instantaneous information and by challenging established ways of seeing and thinking. LSD is electronic media *sans* apparatus, and media technologies constitute forms of electronic LSD.

Whatever the origin and accuracy of the phrase "electronic LSD," this confluence of drugs and media technology has led to a pair of differing and somewhat predictable interpretations. On the one hand, the computer, VR, and cyberspace are understood as a kind of "smart drug" or medicine that promises what can only be described as beneficial, mind-altering possibilities. In this way, ICT has been situated as another technique to achieve what 1960s counterculture often called "mind expansion" or "altered consciousness." Rushkoff, for example, suggests that "psychedelic tripsters" and "computer hackers" share common experiences and are involved in "groping towards the same thing."[29] Both, he argues, "appear to be a way to crack open our civilization's close-mindedness" and to empower users with "a sense of authorship over reality itself."[30] Barlow, who essentially agrees with this position, goes one step further and claims that the technology of the computer provides a more effective means for achieving these lofty goals. "The problem," he writes, "is the same today as it was in the 60s: How can consciousness be changed? We had the right vision but the wrong stuff. It's not acid and Buddhism but computers and cyberspace."[31] For the counterculture of the 1960s, experimentation with psychedelic drugs was not, at least in the official rhetoric (and countercultures have always been somewhat proprietary about their own rhetoric), a matter of solipsistic hedonism. In fact, "dropping acid" was not simply for personal pleasure or even individual gain; it was a social responsibility, the obverse of political activism. As Mark Taylor describes it:

> The psychedelic revolution was, of course, part of a broader social upheaval that continues to shape the political and cultural landscape. . . . Though ostensibly disorganized, in retrospect it is clear that the counterculture was centered on two distinct poles. While sharing a commitment to social change, youthful critics differed on how best to accomplish it. One camp argued that social renewal presupposes an alteration of human consciousness, and the other insisted that society had to be transformed before consciousness would change. . . . For the later-day mystics of the 1960s, the preferred vehicles for transforming consciousness were non-Western religions and drugs. From this idealistic perspective, to see differently is to be different; *seeing is believing and believing is being.*[32]

In the parlance of the counterculture, experimentation with psychedelic drugs was, along with Buddhism and other non-Western religions, not only part of an antiestablishment practice but had the lofty goals of social transformation on a global scale. One supposedly took acid and practiced transcendental meditation not to escape from society and "real-world" problems but to learn to think and to act differently in the world. Consequently, the counterculture, as Rushkoff describes it, "saw drugs less as a form of entertainment than a method of entrainment: preparation and practice for the stresses of shepherding humanity to its next evolutionary level."[33] The same pretensions have been constitutive of all forms of "electronic LSD." Virtual reality, cyberspace, and the personal computer, despite their associations with computer gaming, are not just fun and games. They too participate in grand social, political, and even religious undertakings. At the time of its introduction, for example, VR was promoted not simply as another form of personal entertainment, an instrument for working more efficiently, or a means to escape the status quo. For individuals like Jaron Lanier, VR was a "new emergent social consciousness." "People imagine Virtual Reality as being an escapist thing where people will be ever more removed from the real world and ever more insensitive. I think it's exactly the opposite; it will make us intensely aware of what it is to be human in the physical world, which we take for granted now because we're so immersed in it."[34] According to Lanier's early musings[35] on the subject, VR was not another alienating technology that separated human beings from the natural world. Instead, it was determined to rehabilitate our awareness of the real world, to "reunite us with the flow of nature," and to "allow us to not wish we could behave like gods but actually to behave like gods, albeit in a simulation."[36] Like the rhetoric associated with psychedelic drugs, VR was promoted as a revolutionary technology that would affect our very being in the world.

Similar claims have been made for the other forms of ICT that are often associated with psychedelics. The Internet, for instance, has been promoted as a technology that transcends distance and difference, creating that feeling of all-at-oneness/all-at-onceness that McLuhan celebrated in both electronic media and LSD. On the Internet, users are said to be able to foreclose both geophysical distance and duration by extending their conscious minds over the entire globe and eradicating space and time as determining factors in human communication and community participation. For McLuhan, as for Howard Rheingold, Esther Dyson, William Mitchell, Nicholas Negroponte[37] and other proponents of what is now routinely called "virtual community," the technology of the Internet is not just a curious plaything or instrumental convenience. It is a world-altering technology that enhances human interaction, shrinks the effective size of the globe to a village, and concerns, as McLuhan described it, "the ultimate harmony of all being."[38] At the same time, users of such distance-shattering technology operate in an environment that is declared to be liberated from the debilitating prejudices and bigotries that have marked and marred human history. As Mark Dery described it, "on line, users can float free of biological and sociocultural determinants,"[39] and interact with each other in a virtually equitable world where participants "communicate mind to mind," as was once promoted in a television advertisement for MCI. This utopian vision also finds its way into popular conceptions of cyberspace. Despite and in direct opposition to the dystopian elements that were initially presented in Gibson's proto-cyberpunk novel, cyberspace has been saturated with utopian ideas.[40] As Stenger exclaims with that kind of unabashed enthusiasm that characterized so much of the early writings on this subject, "cyberspace will feel like Paradise!"[41] And this "paradise" has been described by theorists, practitioners, and users of technology by deploying religious rhetoric derived from both the East and West.[42] This curious confluence of technology, drugs, and world religions is illustrated with remarkable precision in the *Matrix* trilogy, which draws on and mixes computer technology, Christian imagery, Eastern mysticism, and pharmaceuticals in the construction and presentation of its narrative. Although some commentators and critics have found this confluence to be confused and inconsistent,[43] it is entirely consistent with the rhetorical practices of new media technology, which deploy and mix all these elements in the construction of its discourse.

On the other hand, any drug, no matter how beneficial, may always be abused, entangling the user in a potentially dangerous and self-destructive dependency. If virtual reality and cyberspace are, from the beginning, associated with drugs, this involvement is not limited to the positive experiences of mind expansion, altered consciousness, and social revolution. It also takes the form of habitual dependency and addiction.[44] According to Ann Weinstone, the connections between virtual reality and drug addiction are unavoidable and obvious. "From advertisements to scholarly texts," she writes, "it is difficult to find any writing about VR that does not engage in and . . . rely upon the rhetorics of addiction."[45] But this involvement goes beyond discursive practices. New media are not just described in and engaged with the rhetorics of addiction, they are experienced as addictive. In the same text that celebrates the "world-changing" possibilities of VR that are exuberantly projected by individuals like Garcia, Lanier, and Barlow, Howard Rheingold also cautions readers against the correlate "potential for trance, intoxication, ecstasy, or mind control."[46] Similarly Taylor and Saarinen warn of the Internet's dangerously addictive qualities. "The net," they write, "is something of a narcotic. It is addictive—terribly addictive. Surely it is possible to O.D. on the net."[47] And in his 1962 *Summa Technologica* Stanisław Lem predicted that machines for generating artificial realities would eventually pose serious competition to pharmacological substance abuse. "One can," Lem wrote, "therefore expect in this last decade of our millennium a veritable deluge of products for generating synthetic reality. It will turn out to be no small competition to drug consumption, so extraordinarily harmful to the social and medical health of society."[48] Lem's prediction is proven, at least anecdotally, in a story related by Rheingold in his 1993 publication about virtual communities. The story concerns an individual named Blair Newman, a one-time cocaine abuser cum Internet addict. "Years after he kicked his cocaine habit, he claimed, somebody put a line of the substance next to Blair's computer while he was logged on. It dawned on him, several hours later, that the white crystals were still there, and he had known about them, but had not mustered the energy necessary to sniff them. It wasn't a moral decision but a battle of obsessions, Blair explained—he could not tear his hands from the keyboard and his eyes from the screen of his current, deeper addiction long enough to ingest the cocaine."[49] Like Case in Gibson's *Neuromancer*, the net-addict, when presented with a choice, would rather jack into cyberspace than ingest amphetamines.

Similar experiences with technological substance abuse have been documented with computer games. Sue Barnes provides a typical account of this problem in her consideration of compulsive behavior with Multiple User Dimensions (MUD)—a simple text-based virtual world accessible over the Internet. "A typical story about Internet dependency describes a student who enters college and discovers MUDs. The student spends almost all of his or her free time mudding, and the MUD becomes the student's social life. As a result of the time spent online, the student does poorly in school. It is common for people to lose track of time when they are involved in CMC, and there are stories about students who have spent 24–48 hours nonstop connected to a MUD without properly eating or sleeping."[50] Comparable accounts have been documented with MMORPGs. Players of Sony Online Entertainment's *EverQuest*, for example, have been reported to indulge in 80-hour-per-week benders, forsaking not just sleep and food but career and relationships. The game has even been blamed for the death of Shawn Woolley, an avid player who took his own life while logged into the system. Because *EverQuest* has been considered to be as addictive as crack cocaine,[51] many players now refer to it by its street name—*EverCrack*. Another MMORPG, *Achaea*, has even introduced a designer drug into its game space. The virtual drug, which is called "gleam," is cheap and highly addictive, and once a character becomes hooked on the stuff, there is no going back. By incorporating an addictive drug, *Achaea* reproduces inside the virtual space of the game the substance abuse that is so often ascribed to these games, permitting a player's character to become hooked on the stuff in a way that mirrors the player's own obsession. Experiences like these have led to an explosion of research, studies, and publications addressing what is now called Internet dependency, Internet addiction, or computer abuse. The first empirical studies of the phenomenon began to appear in journals of psychology, medicine, and the social sciences in the early 1990s. By the end of the decade, "internet addiction" was classified as a "clinical disorder," and its symptoms and effects were debated in both the academic and popular presses.[52] Today Internet Addiction Disorder (IAD) has its own line of self-help books, online resources, and support groups that meet both on- and offline.[53]

Dropping electronic acid is either promoted as the gateway to a fantastic world of mind-expanding alternatives or maligned as an energy-sapping narcotic and mind-numbing addiction. Like the two pills Morpheus offers Neo, there is a tension and opposition between two very different possibilities, and each option is associated with and described in terms of drugs. This particular formulation, however, is not unique to electronic media, digital information systems, or cyberpunk science fiction. It is part and parcel of an old story. If drug culture and electronic culture, as Avital Ronell suggests, share a crucial project, it is not simply because former acid-heads, computer graphics designers, and media theorists find the experiences of various forms of electronic media to be remarkably similar to the acid trips of the psychedelic sixties or because substance abusers and addiction experts find inescapable parallels between the compulsive engagement with technology and the consumption of narcotics. These experiences are not the cause of the confluence of ICT and drugs. Instead, they are symptoms resulting from a very ancient prescription and codependency. According to Ronell, "there is a structure already in place, prior to the production of that materiality we call drugs, including virtual reality or cyberprojections."[54] This "structure," although evident in a number of places (Ronell cites modern literature and Flaubert's *Madame Bovary* in particular), receives its initial articulation in the oldest philosophical consideration of the oldest form of information technology—writing. In the concluding pages of Plato's *Phaedrus*, Socrates and Phaedrus investigate the art or τέχνη of writing and do so in pharmacological terms. If, as Walter Ong writes, "most persons are surprised, and many distressed, to learn that essentially the same objections commonly urged today against computers were urged by Plato in the *Phaedrus* . . . against writing,"[55] then what is even more surprising, and perhaps equally distressing, is that these objections were originally formulated in terms of drugs.

Plato On Drugs

> Who will ever relate the whole history of narcotica?—It is almost the history of "culture," of our so-called high culture.[56]
> —Friedrich Nietzsche

The *Phaedrus* is a dialogue on drugs. It begins with an intoxicating book by which the youthful Phaedrus succeeds in luring Socrates away from his proper place. "You see," Socrates admits, "I am fond of learning. Now the country places and the trees won't teach me anything, and the people in the city do. But you seem to have found a drug [φάρμακον] to bring me out. For as people lead hungry animals by shaking in front of them a branch of leaves or some fruit, just so, I think, you, by holding before me discourse in books, will lead me all over Attica and wherever else you please."[57] At the beginning of the dialogue, Phaedrus gets Socrates hooked on a book, and Socrates, something of a discourse junky, will do anything to get a fix. He will even leave the walls of the city and venture into what he considers a "bad neighborhood." This initial association between the written text and drugs, or what Socrates calls in his native tongue φάρμακον (a word in which one can already perceive the etymological connections to the English words "pharmacy," "pharmacology," and "pharmaceutical") receives explicit investigation towards the dialogue's end, where Socrates and Phaedrus discuss the art or technique of writing. This investigation commences with Socrates recounting an ancient myth he has heard concerning two Egyptian gods.

> I heard, then, that at Naucratis, in Egypt, was one of the ancient gods of that country, the one whose sacred bird is called the ibis, and the name of the god himself was Theuth. He it was who invented numbers and arithmetic and geometry and astronomy, also draughts and dice, and most important of all, letters. Now the king of all Egypt at that time was the god Thamus, who lived in the great city of the upper region, which the Greeks call the Egyptian Thebes, and they call the god himself Ammon. To him came Theuth to show his inventions, saying that they ought to be imparted to the other Egyptians. But Thamus asked what use there was in each, and as Theuth enumerated their uses, expressed praise or blame, according as he approved or disapproved. The story goes that Thamus said many things to Theuth in praise or blame of the various arts [τέχνης], which it would take too long to repeat; but when they came to letters, "This invention, O king," said Theuth, "will make the Egyptians wiser and will improve their memories; for it is a drug [φάρμακον] of memory and wisdom that I have discovered. But Thamus replied, "Most ingenious Theuth, one man has the ability to beget arts, but the ability to judge of their usefulness or harmfulness to their users belongs to another; and now you, who are the father of letters, have been led by your affection to ascribe to them a power the opposite of that which they really possess. For this invention will produce forgetfulness in the minds of those who learn to use it, because they will not practice their memory. You have invented a drug [φάρμακον] not of memory, but of reminding; and you offer your pupils the external appearance of wisdom, not true wisdom, for they will read many things without instruction and will therefore seem to know many things, when they are for the most part ignorant and hard to get along with, since they are not wise, but only appear wise.[58]

According to this ancient text—an old story that refers to an even older story—writing will either make the user wise beyond compare or foster forgetfulness and provide users with nothing but the appearance of wisdom. The inventor of this art [τέχνη], Theuth, advocates the former. Thamus, the king, the one who is according to his own account in the position to evaluate the usefulness or harmfulness of such an invention, argues the latter. This debate has at least three related consequences. First, in the way the narrative is constructed, writing is understood and presented as a technology. In the account provided by Socrates, writing is a τέχνη that has been invented by Theuth and that is subsequently presented to Thamus for judgment. The word τέχνη, which is usually translated as "art" and denotes "a system or method of making or doing,"[59] is the etymological root of the word *technology*. However, writing's status as a technology is not simply a matter of etymology. According to Walter Ong, who follows the precedent of Eric Havelock and other scholars of literacy in this regard, it is in the *Phaedrus* that Plato explicitly conceives of writing as a technology. "Plato was thinking of writing as an external, alien technology, as many people today think of the computer. Because we have by today so deeply interiorized writing, made it so much a part of ourselves, as Plato's age had not yet made it fully a part of itself, we find it difficult to consider writing to be a technology as we commonly assume printing and the computer to be. Yet writing (and especially alphabetic writing) is a technology, calling for the use of tools and other equipment: styli or brushes or pens, carefully prepared surfaces, such as paper, animal skins, strips of wood, as well as inks and paints, and much more. . . . By contrast with natural, oral speech, writing is completely artificial."[60] According to Ong, Plato considered writing a technology, because the Platonic text describes it as an artificial and external apparatus that is distinguished from the natural and internal powers of memory and speech. During Plato's time, Ong reminds us, writing was "new media." We often miss this fact because the technology of writing has become not just common but "interiorized," that is, the technical device has been made so much a part of ourselves that we no longer recognize it as external, artificial, and technical. Jay David Bolter explains it this way: "Every technological skill is internalized by its users, until it at last becomes 'second nature,' an ability that the expert exercises without conscious or labored effort. And as the skill becomes nature, the technological device itself seems to become part of the user."[61] According to this line of reasoning, we usually do not consider writing to be a technology, as Plato did in the *Phaedrus*, because this external and artificial technique as well as its various apparatuses have become so thoroughly "internalized" that they are now considered to be "second nature." Despite this interiorization and naturalization, Ong and Bolter conclude, writing is still, technically speaking, a technology. "Writing with pen and paper," Bolter writes, "is no more natural, no less technological than writing at a computer screen."[62]

These arguments all proceed by deploying two related gestures. They begin by defining technology as an external and artificial apparatus that is distinguished from the internal and natural capacities of the user. They then demonstrate that this definition applies to and characterizes the activity of writing as it was described in the *Phaedrus*, drawing the conclusion that Plato understood writing as a technology. This maneuver, however correct it might be, has at least one complication. It comprehends writing by deploying a set of criteria that are first introduced and articulated in and by writing. "It is," Jacques Derrida writes, "not enough to say that writing is conceived out of this or that series of oppositions. Plato thinks of writing, and tries to comprehend it, to dominate it, on the basis of opposition as such. In order for these contrary values (good/evil, true/false, essence/appearance, inside/outside, etc.) to be in opposition, each of the terms must be simply *external* to the other, which means that one of these oppositions (the opposition between inside and outside) must already be accredited as the matrix of all possible opposition." And writing, "far from being governed by these oppositions, opens up their very possibility without letting itself be comprehended by them."[63] In other words, the difference between inside and outside, the difference that, according to Derrida, underwrites all the other logical oppositions and possible differences that could be used to distinguish writing, originates in and by writing. What is demonstrated in the *Phaedrus*, therefore, is not that writing is understood as an external and artificial apparatus but that it is in a confrontation with writing that Plato, through the pronouncement of Thamus, originally differentiates trust in artificial and external devices from the natural and internal powers of the mind. If we are no longer able to perceive writing as a technology, it is not simply because writing has become so thoroughly internalized and seemingly natural that it no longer appears to be external and artificial. Instead, it is because writing, at least in this particular dialogue, initially describes, structures, and regulates the very distinction between the metaphysical couples—internal/external and natural/artificial—that is subsequently used to define what is called "technology." In this way, then, the *Phaedrus* does not so much define writing *as* a technology as it initiates and describes what becomes, for Ong and others, the very definition of technology, from which one would then attempt to characterize writing as such. Consequently, writing is not just one technology among others but literally constitutes what is considered to be technology. And it is for this reason that whatever is currently determined about computers and other forms of ICT had already been ascribed to and prescribed by the *Phaedrus* with writing.

Second, the consideration of the technology of writing that is presented in this parable is initiated and proceeds entirely in terms of drugs. Despite their disagreement about the different effects on the user's memory, writing is, for both the inventor and the king, evaluated and described in terms of a pharmaceutical substance. Both participants, echoing Socrates's initial statement, call writing φάρμακον. In doing so, the *Phaedrus* not only situates writing as technology but authorizes the codependency of technology and drugs that is operative in so much of the contemporary discussions and debates about ICT. When it comes to technology, the *Phaedrus* prescribes—quite literally insofar as "pre-scribe" designates a kind of writing that is determinative—drugs. Furthermore, the word φάρμακον, as Derrida demonstrates in his extended analysis of this subject, has (not unlike the equivocal English word "drug") two opposed and seemingly irreconcilable denotations. On the one hand, φάρμακον is properly defined and understood as a medicine or remedy. According to Theuth's estimations of his own invention, "this medicine is beneficial; it repairs and produces, accumulates and remedies, increases knowledge and reduces forgetfulness."[64] For Theuth, the φάρμακον of writing is interpreted as a medication that will enhance the memory, repair the deleterious effects of forgetfulness, and improve the power of the mind. On the other hand, φάρμακον can be and has also been defined as a dangerous and potentially fatal toxin. In this way, writing's effect on the memory is determined to be the exact opposite of that assigned to it by its inventor. "It can worsen the ill instead of remedy it."[65] According to Thamus's evaluation, the φάρμακον of

writing is interpreted as a powerful and dangerous narcotic that not only anes-
thetizes the memory but creates hazardous self-deceptions, leading users to believe that they possess something that they do not. Consequently, the *Phaedrus*
not only associates the technology of writing with drugs but, on the basis of this
association, articulates two alternatives, where one is positioned as the opposite
or inverse of the other. If the current interpretations of ICT tend to congregate
around two poles—a "smart drug" that will enhance consciousness and increase
knowledge or a dangerous and addictive narcotic that will cause debilitating dependencies in its users—it is because the *Phaedrus* had already assigned these
two possibilities to writing. And the participants involved in these debates have
also remained remarkably consistent. On the one hand, inventors and advocates
of information technology, like Theuth, promote their products by deploying
rhetoric and marketing strategies that, often in medicinal terms, describe the
ways that these innovations remedy social ills, repair individual deficiencies,
and make life qualitatively better. On the other hand, politicians, civic leaders,
and social activists on both the left and right worry about and enact legislation
to protect against what are perceived to be the debilitating and sometimes toxic
effects of the same. For these individuals, ICTs are, as Thamus initially demonstrates, always to be regarded with some suspicion, for technology can often
exacerbate instead of repair social ills.

Third, in the face of these two competing interpretations of the φάρμακον
of writing, Phaedrus makes a decision, and he sides with the king: "I think the
Theban is right in what he says about letters."[66] In making a decision between the
two alternatives presented in the parable, Phaedrus does not simply select one
option over the other but confirms a metaphysical and ethical system that is, as
Derrida points out, organized around a set of "simple, clear cut oppositions: good
and evil, inside and outside, true and false, essence and appearance."[67] According to the evaluation offered by Thamus, writing is a problem because it employs
external characters at the expense of the internal power of the mind, produces
ignorance instead of true knowledge, and substitutes the appearance of wisdom
for actual wisdom. In siding with the king, then, Phaedrus does not simply select
one possible interpretation/translation of the φάρμακον over another, but, more
importantly, makes a decision that favors truth as opposed to falsity, knowledge
instead of ignorance, and the real in opposition to mere appearances. This determination, which sets up a series of "simple, clear cut oppositions" is not unique
to this one episode but constitutes the fundamental decision that comprises
Western philosophy, or what is often called, sometimes pejoratively, "Platonism."
Even when it does not take the form of a choice that involves drugs, philosophy
and everything that goes by the name "science" consistently decides for truth,
knowledge, and the real in opposition to falsity, ignorance, and appearances. In
making this decision, however, the *Phaedrus* does not simply proscribe writing.
To do so would be problematic. As Derrida points out, "only a blind or grossly
insensitive reading could indeed have spread the rumor that Plato was *simply*

condemning the writer's activity."[68] Instead the value of this particular technology is assigned according to the decision that is instituted by Phaedrus. This is made clear in the Socratic summary that immediately follows: "He who thinks, then, that he has left behind him any art in writing, and he who receives it in the belief that anything in writing will be clear and certain, would be an utterly simple person, and in truth ignorant of the prophecy of Ammon, if he thinks written words are of any use except to remind him who knows the matter about which they are written."[69] As long as writing serves the interest of real truth and is used as an instrument to remind someone who already knows the truth of the matter, it is perfectly acceptable and useful. It only becomes a problem when it takes the place of real knowledge of the truth. Consequently, Phaedrus's decision does not simply resolve the polysemia of the φάρμακον but reassigns and regulates its two competing denotations according to this system. The φάρμακον of writing is properly understood as a medicine or remedy as long as it serves to assist truth. It becomes pernicious and poisonous when it threatens to replace or to take the place of real truth.

This determination applies not just to writing but to everything that has been situated under the term φάρμακον. Drugs, for example, are usually considered to be useful as long as they assist in fostering the health of the body. They become a problem when they are abused. The main problem with drug abuse and addiction, however, is not simply the adverse physiological effects it has on the user's body. It is the threat that it poses to the body politic. "What do we hold against the drug addict?" Derrida asks. "Something we never, at least to the same degree, hold against the alcoholic or the smoker: that he cuts himself off from the world, in exile from reality, far from the objective reality and the real life of the city and community; that he escapes into a world of simulacrum and fiction. . . . We do not object to the drug user's pleasure per se, but to the pleasure taken in an experience without truth."[70] The problem with drug use, Derrida suggests, is not the individual pleasure one takes in the experience of getting high. The problem rests in the way the user achieves this pleasure. The junkie, acid-head, coke fiend, or stoner seeks pleasure by cutting him/herself off from the real life of the community and escaping into a chemically induced world of simulacrum and fiction. The problem, therefore, is not the experience of individual pleasure per se but the way the drug user abandons him/herself to artificial experiences that are neither real nor true. For this reason, the question of drugs is, as Derrida points out, "the question—the great question—of truth. No more no less."[71] The same concern informs the evaluation and consideration of ICT. What is questionable about VR, the Internet, cyberspace, television, and even literature is not the pleasurable experience facilitated by the use of a technical artifice but the possibility that such use could lead one to escape from the world of objective reality, to abandon the real life of his/her community, and to take pleasure in experiences without truth. One text that embodies this concern particularly well is James Brook and Iain Boal's *Resisting the Virtual Life*, a book that is, as evident in its title, a "just say no" campaign for virtual substance abuse. Although Brook and Boal argue that ICTs are potentially detrimental to human life, they do not simply demonize technology. "Our 'complaint' is not against virtuality per se and is not made in the name of a 'natural' life, stripped to a savage state that could exist only in fantasy; in fact, we recognize the merits of relationships at a remove whether these are conducted by letter, telephone, or email. But virtual technologies are pernicious when their simulacra of relationships are deployed societywide as substitutes for face-to-face interactions, which are inherently richer than mediated interactions."[72] For Brook and Boal the problem is not virtual technology per se but the overly enthusiastic and seemingly ubiquitous substitution of computer-simulated relationships for real, face-to-face encounters. As with drug use, ICTs become a problem when they promote an escape into a simulacrum of experience that displaces and undermines the real world of social relationships. What is worrisome, therefore, is not the pleasure that one can derive from consuming information technology, which in the case of literature, television, and even computer games can always be recuperated in terms of recuperation and entertainment, but the fact that these substances deal in potentially hazardous simulations that threaten to replace real truth with fiction, artifice, and mere appearance.

Concluding Prescriptions

The computer recycles ancient Platonism.[73]
—Michael Heim

Drugs and media are equal partners, and this codependency has been prescribed and programmed by the oldest consideration of the oldest form of information technology. This conclusion has several consequences. First, despite this obvious involvement, the codependency of drugs and technology has not been an explicit theme or subject in new media or ICT scholarship. Although researchers and journalists have done an adequate job of connecting the dots by documenting the common experiences of users, tracing the similar interests of developers and promoters, and identifying analogous rhetorical maneuvers, there has been little or no investigation into why or how these connections become possible in the first place. In other words, we seem to recognize the signs of a drug habit but have done little or nothing to address it. This has not, it should be noted, been the case with other disciplines. Literary scholars in particular have realized, as Ronell describes it, that "literature is on drugs and about drugs,"[74] and there has been in recent years a good number of publications that investigate the features and consequences of this seemingly inescapable involvement.[75] Something similar needs to be instituted in the field of ICT and cyberstudies. In particular, scholars of information technology need to acknowledge and explore, following the indications supplied by Adilkno, Derrida, Ronell, and others, that

drugs and media technology share a common project, are determined to produce similar results, and often suffer, as Ronell puts it, "analogous crackdowns
before the law."[76] To continue to operate without acknowledging and investigating this codependency is not, as one might initially think, "to say no to drugs"
but to remain under their influence without explicitly recognizing or admitting
it as such. As any former user will tell you, the first step always involves taking
responsibility for your own drug use and dependency. And it is high time that
ICT come clean about its own involvements.

Second, in considering this codependency, it is obvious that we are looking at a very old and established habit. The drug influence that has been documented in the popular, technical, and academic literature concerning ICT is not
the result of recent innovations, new developments, or a posteriori interactions.
In particular, it is not a consequence of the empirical proximity of hippie counterculture and cyberpunk science fiction, the interests of acid-heads and the
"mind-altering" possibilities afforded by computer technology, or the common
experiences of compulsive Internet users and drug addicts. Instead all of these
connections and associations are first possible because drugs and media have
been inextricably involved with each other from the very beginning. There is,
as Ronell has suggested, a structure already in place that predates and predeter-
mines both the chemical and electronic prosthesis.[77] Historically, this structure
is first articulated in and programmed by Plato's *Phaedrus*. In contending with
what was, during Plato's time, the new media of writing, the *Phaedrus* not only
defines the technology of writing in terms of drugs (or φάρμακον) but offers two
different interpretations: a medicine that is determined to repair, accumulate,
and remedy and a narcotic that is said to poison the user and exacerbate existing
deficiencies. These two alternatives, as we have discovered, are not limited to the
technology of writing but also structure debate concerning subsequent forms of
information technology and communication media. Arguments about cyberspace, the Internet, virtual reality, and the computer often mobilize, whether
explicitly recognized or not, the pharmacology that had been prescribed in the
Phaedrus. All of this is collected and illustrated in the *Matrix* trilogy, where the
association of drugs and technology and the two alternatives of medicine and
poison are visually represented in the form of a red pill and a blue pill. Consequently, the choice that is presented to Neo in the initial *Matrix* film is not merely
a clever cinematic device. It is a technical and philosophical necessity that is determined, regulated, and justified by this ancient prescription.

Third, in dealing with these two alternatives, the *Phaedrus* prescribes a
metaphysics and an ethics that applies equally to the current "war on drugs,"
our understanding and evaluation of ICT, and the decision that is made by Neo
at the beginning of *The Matrix*. In the face of the two different interpretations
of φάρμακον—what could be, as in *The Matrix*, illustrated as two different pharmaceuticals or pills—Phaedrus makes a choice, and his decision sides with truth
as opposed to falsity, being as opposed to appearances, and the real as opposed

to artifice. This decision, which was originally described in writing and about writing, defines how the Western tradition has contended with and regulated both drugs and media. As long as they serve and enhance what is considered to be real and true, drugs and ICTs are determined to be entirely acceptable and appropriate. They only become a problem when their simulacrum of experience threatens to replace and undermine what really matters. Although these two alternatives are not always color-coded, as they are in *The Matrix*, everyone, from Phaedrus and Neo to advocates and critics of new media technology, decides to take what would have been a red pill. In swallowing the red pill, then, the protagonist of *The Matrix* does not make some exceptional and singular decision rooted in the strength of his unique character. The "hero of the real"[78] simply reenacts and validates one of the fundamental decisions that constitute mainstream Platonism. Conformity with Platonism has the obvious advantage of providing current and future examinations of ICT with a tested and secure foundation that is considered to be "correct," "appropriate," and "unquestionable." As long as examinations conform to this structure, we already know what debates are possible, what questions should be asked, and what answers will count as appropriate. By conforming to the "time-honored" logical oppositions that have been articulated in Plato, the critical engagement with ICT secures both a metaphysical and ethical foundation that is, for the most part, beyond question or reproach.

Finally, despite the obvious advantages that come from adhering to Platonism, there is at least one good reason to remain skeptical of this tradition and its influence. In particular, the evaluation of the technology of writing that is advanced in the *Phaedrus* is itself something that is paradoxically presented in and by writing.[79] In other words, the *Phaedrus* attempts to regulate the φάρμακον by using the very substance it tries to control. It attempts, in particular, to promote truth, knowledge, and the real through the mediation of a technology that it characterizes in terms that are exactly the opposite—deception, appearance, and fiction. Or as Derrida describes this rather curious maneuver, "Plato imitates the imitators in order to restore the truth of what they imitate: namely, truth itself."[80] For this reason, what is described in the *Phaedrus* concerning the technology of writing appears to be put in question by the way in which it provides its descriptions. This apparently contradictory circumstance, whereby the operations of the text already violate the statements made in the text and vice versa, renders much of what had been prescribed by the *Phaedrus* debatable and suspicious. In this case, Plato is like the parent who warns his teenage child against the dangers of alchohol while sipping a cocktail. The opportunity here should be obvious. Instead of simply reproducing or recycling Platonism, which would require, among other things, that one either ignore this textual difficulty or discount it as a mere "technicality," we can endeavor to proceed otherwise. Doing so, however, cannot mean simply inverting the decision that had been enacted in the *Phaedrus* and siding with deception, appearance, and simulacra. It cannot be, in the terms that have been presented in the *Matrix* films, selecting the blue pill instead of the red pill. Such a maneuver simply inverts the two terms of the conventional system and, in doing so, preserves, sustains, and reaffirms the traditional binary structure, albeit in an inverted form. And an inverted or reversed Platonism, despite what might initially appear to be a dramatic and revolutionary alteration, still operates according to and in terms of the binary oppositions that one had wanted to question and disrupt in the first place. For this reason, any critical intervention in the pharmacology that already organizes and determines the understanding and examination of ICT will need, if it is to open other possibilities and not be reducible to something that is simply more of the same, to proceed in a manner that is entirely otherwise. This chapter ends, then, like the first *Matrix* film, with the announcement of a possible "system failure" in the philosophical matrix that has structured and controlled ICT research. The significance and consequences of this systemic alteration cannot be detailed here but, like *The Matrix*, are items that will need to be addressed in one or more sequels. As Neo states at the end of the first episode, "I didn't come here to tell you how it's going to end. I came here to tell you how it's going to begin."[81]

Chapter Five

The Virtual Dialectic

Rethinking The Matrix *and Its Significance*

> Rather than designating the choice between good and evil,
> my Either/Or designates the choice by which one chooses
> good and evil or rules them out.[1]—Søren Kierkegaard

As we have seen, Neo is asked to select between two dialectically opposed alternatives, which Morpheus, like Socrates several millennia before him, presents in the form of pharmaceuticals. Should Neo decide to swallow the blue pill, he will remain within the computer-generated dream-world of the Matrix and know nothing of his decision to do so. Should he decide to swallow the red pill, he will initiate a process that is called the "awakening" and eventually come to experience the "true world" that exists outside the virtual reality that is created and sustained by the computers. Consequently, what Morpheus presents to Neo in the form of two different pills are the classic antagonisms that comprise and organize Western metaphysics—truth vs. deception, being vs. appearance, artifice vs. reality, and authenticity vs. inauthenticity. In the face of these two apparently exclusive options, Neo makes what can only appear to be the right choice. He decides to swallow the red pill and live in the real and true world. This choice matters for the film, for advocates and critics of computer systems, and for our understanding of the social position and impact of ICT.

In addressing this matter, I do not want to replay the familiar evaluations and arguments that have been publicized about this particular decision. Texts like William Irwin's *The Matrix and Philosophy* and *More Matrix and Philosophy,* Glenn Yeffeth's *Taking the Red Pill,* Christopher Grau's *Philosophers Explore The Matrix,* Karen Haber's *Exploring the Matrix,* Matt Lawrence's *Like a Splinter in*

Your Mind, and Matthew Kapell and William G. Doty's *Jacking into the Matrix Franchise* have already done an adequate job of exposing the philosophical themes involved in Neo's choice and connecting the conceptual dots in this curious hybrid of Platonic metaphysics, cyberpunk science fiction, and martial arts cinema.[2] Instead I want to submit to critical reevaluation the philosophical and technological assumptions that have been deployed in and that have informed these texts. Despite differences in methodology and interpretation, the various "critical writings" on *The Matrix* employ a set of very familiar and remarkably consistent assumptions that remain, for the most part, outside the space of critical inquiry. These assumptions go deep, and they influence not only the interpretations of this particular cinematic narrative but also our general understanding of ICT and its philosophical position and consequences. To put it in the metaphorical language of the narrative in question, the available understandings of both the *Matrix* films and information technology are already programmed and controlled by a matrix of largely unacknowledged assumptions.[3] In the face of this, there are, as was seen in the previous chapter, two customary responses. We can, on the one hand, continue to operate within this structure without question or hesitation. In doing so, we would wake in our beds and continue to believe whatever it is we have believed. On the other hand, we can opt to expose the assumptions as such and find out just how deep this rabbit hole goes. The following, like the film's protagonist, decides for the latter. But its outcome will lead in an entirely different direction, one which deliberately distorts and intentionally exceeds the either/or logic imposed by these two alternatives. To put it schematically, we can say, paraphrasing Søren Kierkegaard, that rather than being concerned with the choice between the red and blue pill, this examination is interested in that decision by which one chooses red *and* blue or rules them out.

Taking the Red Pill

> The Matrix is, at its core, a film with a moral plot.[4]
> —Iakovos Vasiliou

Morpheus presents Neo with two competing alternatives. In his left hand, there is a blue pill. It leads to illusory deception in the inauthentic artifice of technologically mediated appearances. In his right hand, there is a red pill. It leads, as Morpheus succinctly describes it, to truth, nothing more. In response to Morpheus's offer, Neo makes what can only appear (from the perspective of Platonism and the venerable history of philosophy) to be the right choice: he selects the red pill. In doing so, he becomes the hero of the narrative. In the face of seemingly impossible odds, he takes control of his life, beats the system, gets the girl, and apparently saves the human race from machinic domination. That this decision is marked, within the space of the film, as the *right choice* is perhaps best illustrated by the way Neo's actions are differentiated from that of another character—Cypher. Cypher is member of Morpheus's crew who opts to return to the computer-generated fantasies of the Matrix and does so in a way that betrays his colleagues. In a scene that functions as the antithesis of Neo's pivotal decision, Cypher makes a deal with Agent Smith while enjoying the pleasures of an artificial, computer-generated steak.

Agent Smith: Do we have a deal, Mr. Reagan?

Cypher: You know, I know that this steak doesn't exist. I know that when I put it in my mouth, the Matrix is telling my brain that it is juicy and delicious. After nine years, do you know what I've realized? . . . Ignorance is bliss.

Agent Smith: Then we have a deal?

Cypher: I don't want to remember nothing. Nothing. You understand? And I want to be rich. You know, someone important, like an actor.

Agent Smith: Whatever you want, Mr. Reagan.

Cypher: All right. You get my body back in a Power Plant, reinsert me into the Matrix, and I'll get you what you want.

Agent Smith: Access codes to the Zion mainframe.

Cypher: I told you I don't know them. But I can give you the man who does.

Agent Smith: Morpheus.[5]

In return for Morpheus and his knowledge of the access codes, Agent Smith agrees to reintegrate Cypher into the Matrix, to erase all memory of his experiences on the outside, and to give him whatever he wants. Unlike Neo, who decides for the truth, Cypher chooses deception, and he does so at all levels. He decides to deceive both his friends and himself and to live a life of deception as an actor. Cypher, therefore, freely and knowingly decides in favor of a fictional existence that is cut off from the real life of his community, and, perhaps what is worse, he does so at their expense. In being portrayed in this fashion, the character of Cypher functions as Neo's dramatic foil. If Neo is what William Gibson terms the "hero of the Real,"[6] Cypher is the opposite—the champion of fantasy, self-deception, and fraud. If Neo is interpreted as a Christ-like savior,[7] Cypher is "the Judas Iscariot of the story,"[8] the traitor who sells out his friends for the sake of selfish, bodily pleasures. If Neo's "decision to face 'the desert of the real' allows him," as Gerald Erion and Barry Smith argue, "to undertake genuine action and have genuine experiences that give his life meaning, and thus a moral value,"[9] then Cypher is the *Schauspieler* who is merely play-acting in an artificially generated fiction. He is, as Peter Boettke concludes, "choosing to not live a human life but to experience a life scripted by someone else."[10] If Neo makes what many interpreters of the film perceive as the right choice, Cypher's decision can only be judged as "wrong," "foolish," "stupid," and "immoral."[11]

In digital terms, he is the 0 to Neo's 1.[12] By counter-posing the characters of Neo and Cypher,[13] *The Matrix* conforms to a value system that equates the good with the real, truth, authenticity, self-knowledge, and free choice and identifies the bad with artifice, fantasy, inauthenticity, self-deception, and mechanistic determinism. If *The Matrix* is at its core a film with a moral plot, then the moral of the story appears to be that it is somehow morally better to face the truth than to live in an illusory world that makes us feel good.[14] And "in putting forth this message," David Weberman argues, "we get an old-fashioned Hollywood morality tale."[15]

Neo's decision is immediately recognized as "the correct one," and almost everyone, it seems, identifies with this "hero of the real." As William Irwin, editor of *The Matrix and Philosophy*, suggests, "the red pill is a new symbol of bold choice, and most people insist they would take it if they were in Neo's shoes."[16] This immediate agreement renders his decision less than surprising. In fact, there is something about his choice that is predictable and almost programmed. (And this suspicion is confirmed at the end of the second episode in the trilogy, *Reloaded*, where we learn that Neo's choice is neither unique nor unprecedented. In a kind of perverse eternal recurrence of the same, Neo has made this decision before. In fact, as far as the Architect knows, "the anomaly" has done so on at least five other occasions.[17]) Consequently, when Morpheus holds out his hands, Neo does what we all know he will do. He takes hold of and swallows the red pill. This "decision" is predictable for at least two reasons. First, it is necessitated by and for the cinematic narrative in which this scenario is presented. If Neo had for some reason not selected the red pill, there would be no "Matrix," either the one encountered by Neo within the film or the film itself that stages this encounter. Morpheus is right. You take the blue pill, and the story, quite literally in this case, ends. Had Neo decided—or better, had the Wachowski brothers, who wrote the script and directed the film, decided to have Neo decide—to swallow the blue pill, the protagonist would have been returned to the relatively uneventful and mundane computer-simulated 1990s, knowing nothing of his decision to do so. The interesting and dramatic set of events that lead Neo to Morpheus in the first place would come to an abrupt conclusion and be completely eradicated. In this way, the dramatic conflict that opens the film and motivates its narrative development would dissipate. The film too, as we know it, would have to end. Consequently, the *Matrix*, not just the Matrix that is presented within the frame of the film but *The Matrix* that is the film, requires and stipulates that Neo take the red pill. It is a dramatic necessity.

Second, Neo's choice of real truth over illusory deception is "correct," because this decision is underwritten and supported by a philosophical matrix that is some 2,500 years old. In swallowing the red pill, Neo does not make some exceptional and singular decision rooted in the moral strength of his unique character. The "hero of the real" simply reenacts and validates the fundamental decision that is at the center of Western thought. Although not always presented in the form of two pills, philosophy consistently decides for truth as opposed to falsity, being as opposed to appearances, authenticity as opposed to inauthenticity, and the real as opposed to illusion. Take, for example, Plato's "Allegory of the Cave," a curious fable situated at the center of the *Republic* that is often compared to the experience of cinema, the technology of virtual reality, and the scenario presented in *The Matrix*.[18] The allegory begins with Socrates describing a subterranean cavern inhabited by men who sit before a screen on which are projected shadow images. The men are chained in place since childhood and are unable to see anything other than these artificial projections, which constitute the only reality that is possible for them to know. At one point, one of the prisoners is released and shown the actual source of the shadows—small puppets paraded in front of a fire light. Although looking at the light that provides the illumination for the images is initially painful and disorienting, the prisoner eventually comes to understand "that what he had seen before was all a cheat and an illusion."[19] From here the newly liberated individual is dragged out of the cavern and, once his eyes become accustomed to the painfully bright sunlight, discovers the "real things" that exist outside the fictional projections encountered in the subterranean matrix. In comparing the two "realities," Socrates' prisoner sides with the real and the true, no matter how uncomfortable. If given a choice, "he would choose to endure anything rather than such a life" inside the cave.[20] The allegory, therefore, not only stages the opposition of and choice between artificial illusion and real truth but makes a decision that is remarkably similar to the one enacted by Neo.

Similar scenarios and decisions are reproduced with remarkable regularity throughout the history of Western philosophy. Robert Nozick's *Anarchy, State, and Utopia*, for example, postulates something called the "experience machine"—a computer-controlled system with electrodes that directly stimulate the user's central nervous system. Nozick's description of this machine is, as many commentators have remarked, not unlike that illustrated in *The Matrix*.[21] "Suppose," Nozick writes, "there were an experience machine that would give you any experience you desired. Super-duper neuropsychologists could stimulate your brain so that you would think and feel you were writing a great novel, or making a friend, or reading an interesting book. All the time you would be floating in a tank, with electrodes attached to your brain." Given this possibility, he then asks, "should you plug into this machine for life?"[22] In response, he argues that most people, if given such an opportunity, would not.

> First we want to do certain things, and not just have the experience of doing them. In the case of certain experiences, it is only because first we want to do the actions that we want the experiences of doing them or thinking we've done them. A second reason for not plugging in is that we want to be a certain way, to be a certain sort of person. Someone floating in a tank is an indeterminate blob. There is no answer to the question of what a person is like who has been in the tank. Is he courageous, kind,

intelligent, witty, loving? It's not merely that it's difficult to tell; there's no way he is. . . . Thirdly, plugging into an experience machine limits us to a man-made reality, to a world no deeper or more important than that which people can construct. There is no actual contact with any deeper reality, though the experience can be simulated.[23]

Like the decision made in the *Republic*, Nozick affirms the value of true experiences in the real world over illusory deception. For this reason, interpreters of *The Matrix* have used Nozick to explain the moral culpability of Cypher's decision. Lyle Zynda, for example, finds in Nozick's work a compelling case against Cypher's choice: "Would you choose to be hooked up to the Experience Machine? Nozick claims that you wouldn't, if you thought about it seriously. You don't want just the *experience* of having friends and being loved. You want to *really* have friends and be loved. It is true that if you are friendless and unloved, you might be tempted to escape reality into fantasy. (Some people use drugs for this reason.) But you would prefer real friends to imaginary ones, if you could have them. The same goes for fame, wealth, good looks, success, and so on."[24]

Neo's decision to swallow the red pill, although having the appearance of what Irwin calls "a bold choice," actually conforms to and confirms one of the fundamental values of Western thought. It is predicated on and underwritten by that general philosophical decision that Friedrich Nietzsche termed "the unconditional will to truth."[25] From Plato to Nozick and beyond—from the pre-Socratics to contemporary epistemologists, metaphysicians, ethicists, and practitioners of everything that goes by the name of science—truth is and remains of unconditioned and unquestioned value. "We see," wrote Nietzsche in *The Gay Science*, "that science also rests on a faith; there simply is no science 'without presuppositions.' The question whether *truth* is needed must not only be affirmed in advance, but affirmed to such a degree that the principle, the faith, the conviction finds expression: '*Nothing* is needed *more* than truth, and in relation to it everything else has only second-rate value.'"[26] Consequently, Neo's decision to swallow the red pill is one of those rare moments when, as Nietzsche describes it in part 1 of *Beyond Good and Evil*, "the philosopher's 'conviction' appears on the stage."[27] In this way, *The Matrix* stages the necessary and all-too-often unacknowledged decision that is the condition for the possibility of philosophy and science. Neo's choice, which takes the form of an affirmation of the "value of truth," is necessarily and unquestionably the "right" one, not simply because of some admirable moral character, but because it is the only option that makes sense. To have decided otherwise would be, from the perspective of clear and rational thinking, nothing less than sheer nonsense.

Neo is, therefore, in good company. And his decision, one that privileges the real and the true over and against artificial illusion, is something that is also valued and reproduced by ICT researchers and critics. Michael Heim, the self-proclaimed "metaphysician of virtual reality," provides a good example of the typical maneuver. His philosophical examinations of cyberspace, published in two books and many anthologized essays, point in the direction of all kinds of interesting and challenging possibilities. But when push comes to shove, Heim's investigations always fall back on rather traditional and reassuring values. For example, at the end of "The Erotic Ontology of Cyberspace," an essay included in Michael Benedikt's *Cyberspace: First Steps* and Heim's *The Metaphysics of Virtual Reality*, Heim reaffirms the principle value of truth and the real world that exists outside the Matrix. Because this essay was published almost a decade before the release of the first episode of the *Matrix* trilogy, Heim's text makes reference not to the Matrix in the Wachowski brothers' film or its antithesis, the human city of Zion, but to the cyberspace Matrix of William Gibson's *Neuromancer* and the curiously named "Zionites" who inhabit the world outside. The nominal coincidence here between the elements of the Wachowskis' cinematic narrative and Gibson's novel is anything but accidental. It not only indicates the extent to which the Wachowski brothers were influenced by Gibson's ground-breaking work but, more importantly, outlines the contours of a consistent metaphysical structure and ethical decision that underlies cyberpunk science-fiction and the science of ICT.

> Gibson leaves us the image of a human group that instinctively keeps its distance from the computer matrix. These are the Zionites, the religiously tribal folk who prefer music to computers and intuitive loyalties to calculation. The Zionites constitute a human remnant in the environmental desolation of *Neuromancer*. . . . As we suit up for the exciting future in cyberspace, we must not lose touch with the Zionites, the body people who remain rooted in the energies of the earth. They will nudge us out of our heady reverie in this new layer of reality. They will remind us of the living genesis of cyberspace, of the heartbeat behind the laboratory, of the love that still sprouts amid the broken slag and the rusty shells of oil refineries "under the poisoned silver sky."[28]

Heim concludes "The Erotic Ontology of Cyberspace" by recalling the figure of Gibson's Zionites. "We must not," he writes in the imperative, lose touch with these intuitive and tactile body people who are rooted in the energies of the earth and who abstain from the cerebral spectacles staged in the cyberspatial Matrix. According to this reading of *Neuromancer*, the Zionites are contrasted to the cyberspace cowboys who operate and lose themselves in the Matrix. Like the inhabitants of Zion in *The Matrix*, Gibson's Zionites live outside the Matrix and eschew its computer-generated fantasies. In recalling the importance and centrality of the Zionites, Heim appears to make what can only be seen as a wise and reasonable suggestion. If cyberspace has the potential to lead us into computer-generated spectacles where we can forget ourselves, the Zionites provide a kind of "reality check" that nudges us out of our heady reverie. Despite all the fantastic possibilities of cyberspace technology, Heim still advocates taking the red pill. He does so not because he is some kind of neo-luddite who has disdain for the virtual life. Rather, he advocates understanding the true reality of the situation in order to put the cyberspatial experience in proper place and perspective.[29] Neo, in fact, makes a similar decision. After selecting the red pill, he does not simply pack up his pod, move into a derelict apartment in the desert of the real, and get a job at some postapocalypse Starbucks. The choice of truth does not simply exclude interactions with illusion *tout court;* it puts illusion in its proper place and perspective. The converse, however, is not true. The choice of illusion completely eclipses and precludes truth. Anyone who decides, like Cypher, to live in a computer-generated hallucination will remember nothing. In selecting the red pill, therefore, Neo is not simply deciding to live outside the Matrix but is deciding to live in such a way that he knows what is and what is not true, what is and what is not a computer-generated artifice. It is for this reason that Neo, like the rest of Morpheus's crew, is able to enter the Matrix willfully and, once inside it, perform seemingly unreal feats. This is possible not because he has decided to live outside the Matrix. It is possible because, in selecting the red pill, in deciding for truth, Neo can interact with the artificial world of the Matrix with the self-assured knowledge that it is not real. He can, as Kenneth Rufo describes it, "see the Matrix for what it really is."[30]

The Matrix, then, is a parable that connects up with and dramatizes values that appear to be unquestioned and undeniable. Its privilege of the true and real is something that is already affirmed in the history of philosophy and is reinforced by contemporary theorists and critics of ICT. And *The Matrix* is not the only contemporary fable to entertain or to capitalize on this decision. In fact, a good number of popular films produced in the last decade of the twentieth century seem to be about similar matters. *Lawnmower Man,*[31] one of the earliest films to address the technology of VR, ends by making a similar choice. At the climax of the narrative, the protagonist terminates his ascendancy to virtual immortality and returns to the real world to save the life of his friend. As Michael Heim has interpreted it, the film ends by affirming the unmistakable importance of the "primary world" and the real human relationships that are a part of it. In this way, Heim argues, a film like *Lawnmower Man* "spells out . . . just what values should underpin virtual-worlds research."[32] A similar argument is presented in Peter Weir's *Truman Show,* which constitutes something like reality television turned up to eleven. This narrative concerns the life of Truman Burbank, who, like Plato's prisoners and the human batteries wired into the Matrix, unknowingly lives his entire life on a television set. The film concludes with the protagonist bravely exiting through the horizon of his artificial environment in order to confront the real and true world that exists outside the illusion that had constituted what he thought was reality.[33] *The Matrix,* then, is not alone. In the popular mythology of our time, we see and entertain argument after argument for taking the red pill.

The Blue Pill and Beyond

> It is less a matter of being pro- or anti-
> technology, but of developing a critical
> perspective on the ethics of virtuality.[34]
> —Arthur Kroker and Michael A. Weinstein

No one, or almost no one, it seems, advocates swallowing the blue pill. And even the small number who do do not question the metaphysical structure and values that organize the film and direct its interpretations. In fact, the few dissenting voices actually reinforce the fundamental "will to truth" that is at the core of the narrative, even though they appear to question Neo's choice and even side with Cypher. In "You Won't Know the Difference So You Can't Make the Choice," Robin Beck evaluates the two options presented to Neo and concludes that the difference between the blue and the red pills is negligible and essentially immaterial. "There are," he argues, "no rational grounds for making the decision," because "[e]pistemologically, the worlds are the same" given that either world would seem "equally real" once one pill or the other had been swallowed.[35] For Beck, it simply does not matter which pill is taken. Both lead to a "reality" that is equally true and real for the individual who encounters it. Whether he takes the blue or the red pill, Neo will live in a "reality" that will be, as far as he knows, absolutely real and unquestionably true. A similar argument is supplied by Russell Blackford in his essay "Try the *Blue* Pill." Blackford suggests that the value that has been placed on taking the red pill in the *Matrix* films and their critical commentaries may in fact be simply a matter of aesthetics, that is, a prejudice concerning the way that the trilogy has presented the material conditions of life in the virtual world. According to the presentation supplied in the first episode, life in the matrix appears to be not only less than attractive but outright disgusting. "We are shown," Blackford writes, "machines pumping a black liquid into the support capsule for a tiny human baby, and Morpheus tells Neo that the machines are feeding the humans with the liquefied tissues of the dead."[36] However, with a little imaginative tweaking or creative reengineering, things might not really be as bad as they appear. In pursuing this alternative, Blackford employs a passage from James Patrick Kelly's "Meditations on the Singular Matrix": "Kelly asks what happens if we reshuffle the deck. What if the machines had fed their human batteries 'a nice organically grown algae broth' or what if, instead of rejecting the virtual paradise that the machines originally provided them, 'the humans had accepted it and flourished?' What if they had consciously agreed to live their lives in the simulated reality of the matrix? 'Morpheus's moral crusade to wake everyone up would be at least slightly compromised, no?'"[37] Consequently, Blackford, like Beck, argues that life in the computer-generated simulation could be just as real, just as fulfilling, and just as authentic (or inauthentic, as the case may be) as life is assumed to be in so-called "real reality." For this reason, the choice between one or the other is "far from clear cut"; "it all depends," as Blackford says, "on the detail"—"What life? What simulation? What reality?"[38] And once provided with more detail (in the form of two sequels, a prequel, alternative voice-over commentaries and making-of documentaries included in all three DVD releases of the trilogy, two role-playing games, and a number of attendant texts and commentaries), it becomes increasingly difficult to draw the line. In *Reloaded*, for example, the "desert of the real" does not appear to be so deserted or desolate. Zion is not some postapocalyptic ghost-town but a sophisticated, vertically arranged metropolis (and the visual connection to Fritz Lang's film of this name is not lost on Blackford) complete with impressive cathedral-ceiling interiors, comfortable domestic spaces, a multicultural populace, orgiastic rave parties, and rockin' sounds. Conversely, the computer-generated virtual world of the Matrix does not appear to be the monotonous Microserf nightmare that is first encountered in Thomas Anderson's (a.k.a. Neo's) corporate cubicle. It also contains incredible diversity and even beauty. "In *Reloaded*," Blackford argues, "we are shown a mountainous landscape said to be five hundred (virtual) miles to the north of Neo's city. It is established that the city exists within a larger and more interesting (simulated) reality with seemingly natural elements. Indeed, the Architect (Helmut Bakaitis) shows Neo multiple images of the simulated world, making it appear just as diverse as our own."[39] Consequently, the more detail that is provided about both worlds, the more difficult it is to justify selecting one or the other pill. In fact, Blackford suggests, this apparent indecision might account for and explain the trilogy's finale.[40] *Revolutions* does not, as Slavoj Žižek also points out,[41] conclude with the ultimate victory of humanity over the machines or the validation of the real world over the computer-generated simulation of the Matrix. Instead it ends with a kind of tenuous balance and equilibrium between the two terms, one which apparently values and affirms the possibilities of both.

David Weberman, who agrees with the basic terms of this assessment, goes one step further in his "*The Matrix* Simulation and the Postmodern Age" by positing and arguing for universal values that are not negotiable or affected by this kind of relativism. Weberman agrees with Beck that the decision between blue and red is ostensibly insignificant and equivocal. But he draws an entirely different conclusion. "Of course the whole plot of the film is driven by the noble battle for liberation from the tyranny of the machines and their evil Matrix. But the film, despite itself, presents us with two worlds in a way that shows us that Cypher is the one who is right. I believe that the only sensible path is to choose the simulated world over the real one."[42] According to Weberman, if there is no appreciable difference between taking the blue or red pill, then a rational and defensible decision can be made. One should choose the option that offers the best outcome.

> The Matrix does not just offer sensual pleasures. It really encompasses much more, in fact, it gives us just about everything we could want from the shallowest to the deepest gratifications. Assuming that the machines

haven't made things unnecessarily impoverished, the virtual world gives us the opportunity to visit museums and concerts, read Shakespeare and Stephen King, fall in love, make love, raise children, form deep friendships, and so on. . . . The real world, on the other hand, is a wasteland. The libraries and theatres have been destroyed and the skies are always gray. In fact, you'd have to be out of your mind or at least seriously out to lunch to choose the real world (is that why Keanu Reeves seems so well cast in the role?). We're not talking base hedonism now, we're talking about, to use John Stuart Mill's words, "the higher faculties" and the deep and diverse types of gratifications derived from them. Such gratification is to be found more easily in the Matrix than in the "desert of the real."[43]

For Weberman, the quality of life inside the Matrix is simply better than that on the outside. And by "quality of life" he is not simply referring to the base hedonistic pleasures that have been associated with the character of Cypher. The computer-generated world can certainly provide for these "shallow gratifications," but it can also run simulations that stimulate what Weberman calls "the higher faculties," providing everything we believe makes a human life worth living. Consequently, swallowing the blue pill and living life inside the Matrix, despite the way this option has been maligned both within the film and through its various interpretations, is without question the best decision. And anyone who chooses otherwise is, Weberman believes, either out of his or her mind or "out to lunch."

A similar "quality of life" argument is made by Kevin Warwick, who finds Morpheus and his rebel colleagues to be nothing but a bunch of reactionary humanists. "Neo is kidnapped by Luddites, dinosaurs from the past when humans ruled the earth. It's not the future. We are in reality heading towards a world run by machines with an intelligence far superior to that of an individual human. But by linking into the network and becoming a Cyborg, life can appear to be even better than it is now. We really need to clamp down on the party-pooper Neos of this world and get into the future as soon as we can—a future in which we can be part of a Matrix system, which is morally far superior to our Neolithic morals of today."[44] For Warwick, being wired into the machine and becoming a component in a "Matrix system" is part of an evolutionary step by which human beings surpass the limitations of their biologically determined capabilities and become something more—what is often called a "cyborg" or "post-human." This human/machine confluence will, Warwick believes, provide a better life and will be judged to be morally superior to our current situation, which will, in retrospect, seem to be prehistoric. Consequently, to resist this evolutionary step is, in his estimations, reactionary, nostalgic, and simply unintelligible. Although Warwick's argument might appear to be somewhat extreme, his position is not unprecedented. Similar descriptions of human/machine hybridity and post-human configurations have been promoted in J.C.R. Licklider's "Man-Computer Symbiosis," Donna Haraway's "A Cyborg Manifesto," and N. Katherine Hayles's *How We Became Posthuman*.[45] Like Warwick, these scholars suggest, as Haraway succinctly describes it, that "the machine is not an it to be animated, worshipped, and dominated. The machine is us, our processes, an aspect of our embodiment."[46]

These alternative readings of *The Matrix* challenge the customary interpretations by apparently inverting the fundamental decision between the red and blue pills. I say "apparently" because these alternatives, despite their best efforts, do not even manage to effect such an inversion. If "the fundamental faith of the metaphysicians," as Nietzsche argued at the beginning of *Beyond Good and Evil*, "is the belief in opposite values,"[47] then *The Matrix* is in fact "the most philosophical film ever made"[48] insofar as its narrative is defined and motivated by a distinction between two opposed and mutually exclusive possibilities where the one is clearly valued over the other. The film and the majority of its interpretations decide, for example, in favor of the red pill over the blue pill, the immediate real world over computer-mediated simulations, and the "hero of the real," who awakens to the truth, over the anti-hero, who proclaims "ignorance is bliss." The interpretations offered by Beck, Blackford, Weberman, and Warwick seem to challenge these customary decisions by elevating the depreciated terms over and against the ones that have been customarily privileged. Such operations would be "revolutionary," because they literally "over turn" the customary value system. They would, it seems, propose an inversion of traditional metaphysics, where falsity, error, and deception would be valued over truth, and fantastic illusions would be given precedence over the real. This, in fact, *does not* occur. The substitution of the blue pill for the red pill that is suggested in these interpretations is not a revolutionary gesture. Although Beck, Blackford, Weberman, and Warwick provide alternative readings of *The Matrix*, their analyses remain bounded and structured by a metaphysical system that adheres to the assumed value of real truth. What makes the blue pill attractive, on their accounts, is not that it leads to deception, illusion, and falsity. What makes it attractive is that it too leads to a world that is just as real and true. What they dispute, then, is not the choice of truth over illusion but the fact that the decision between the two pills is presented in a way that is not entirely accurate. Despite what Morpheus says, they argue, the blue pill does not lead to something that is the opposite of true reality, but constitutes the doorway to an alternative and possibly improved reality. Consequently, the issue is not to decide between reality and deceptive illusion but to choose between two very different kinds of reality—a neo-luddite existence in the real world of the *Nebuchadnezzar* or the virtual reality created through a computer.

Even those who advocate swallowing the blue pill, then, still affirm the fundamental values of the real and the true over and against deceptive illusions. No matter how the film is interpreted, no matter who is situated as the hero of the narrative, illusion and deception are still regarded with suspicion. But why? What's the matter with illusory deceptions? Why are they so thoroughly devalued that they are, almost without question, universally maligned? Should not this absolute exclusion make us just a little apprehensive? Nietzsche is one thinker in the Western tradition who questions this seemingly universal conviction and moral prejudice. Beginning with *The Genealogy of Morals* and continuing through intervening works up to and including *Beyond Good and Evil*, Nietzsche sought not only to expose the unquestioned prejudices and unacknowledged decisions that structure Western thought but to challenge their hegemony. It is in *The Gay Science* that these misgivings are perhaps best articulated: "This unconditional will to truth—what is it? Is it the will *not to allow oneself to be deceived*? Or is it the will *not to deceive*? For the will to truth could be interpreted in the second way, too—if only the special case 'I do not want to deceive myself' is subsumed under the generalization 'I do not want to deceive.' But why not deceive?"[49] In asking these questions, Nietzsche not only exposes one of the moral prejudices of philosophy, which always decides in favor of the true, but inquires about the almost universal exclusion of deception. "Why do you not want to deceive," Nietzsche inquires provocatively, "especially if it should seem—and it does seem!—as if all of life aimed at semblance, meaning error, deception, simulation, delusion, self-delusion, and when the great sweep of life has actually always shown itself to be on the side of the most unscrupulous πολύτροποι."[50] Here, in his use of the Greek word πολύτροποι [polytropoi] Nietzsche reiterates one of the many epithets of Odysseus, whom Homer presents as the hero of "many turns," master of deceptions, disguises, and tricks.[51] According to Nietzsche, then, it is virtuosity in deception that is necessary for survival, while the "will to truth," the will to avoid deception at any cost, is a disposition that is antithetical and even hostile to life. The "will to truth," Nietzsche writes, "that might be a concealed will to death."[52] A similar form of critical reflection is situated in the context of *The Matrix* and is voiced by the only character who can occupy such a thoroughly skeptical position—Cypher: "You know, I know what you're thinking 'cause right now I'm thinking the same thing. Actually, to tell you the truth, I've been thinking the same thing ever since I got here. Why, oh why, didn't I take the blue pill!?"[53] Cypher reflects on the burden and danger of having taken the red pill. In his estimations, the "will to truth" is both a painful disappointment and a death sentence. And he not only asks the critical question, he act on it. For this reason, his character is situated as a defector and traitor. He not only "betrays Neo and his disciples,"[54] but he also betrays the unquestioned faith in and the unconditional will to truth. Consequently, Cypher is, like Nietzsche, the blasphemer of traditional metaphysics who, through a gesture that can only appear to be ethically suspect and metaphysically foolish, puts in question the seemingly irrefutable value of truth.

Cypher's actions seek and end with a reversal of Neo's affirmation of the real and the true. He questions the value of the true world, asks to be returned to the computer-generated simulations of the Matrix, and wants to live the life of an actor. Nietzsche, it seems, charts a similar course. He also questions the "will to truth," is intrigued by the actor's "delight in simulation" and "craving for appearances,"[55] and seeks to reverse the traditional value system that has defined Western philosophy. In an early notebook entry from 1870, for example, Nietzsche indicated that his research program sought to institute an inversion of the traditional values of philosophy: "My philosophy is a *reversed Platonism*. The farther removed from true beings, all the purer more beautiful and better it is. Life in illusion as goal."[56] Where the tradition of Platonism validates being, truth, and the real, this fragment proclaims the value of appearances, deceptions, and illusions. Nietzsche, however, was not satisfied with mere reversal. He knew, as both Martin Heidegger and Jacques Derrida point out, that mere inversion essentially changes nothing, because it still operates, albeit in an inverted form, on the terrain of and from the system that is supposedly effected.[57] Consequently, Nietzsche is not a mere philosophical revolutionary. He goes one step further and deliberately undermines the very logic that defines Platonic philosophy. That is, he disturbs the rules of the philosophical game, unsettling the logic by which "true being" had been opposed to illusory appearances in the first place. This is perhaps most evident in the story, included in *The Twilight of the Idols*, of "How the 'True World' Finally Became a Fable." This parable, which proceeds in several discrete steps, ends with the following remarkable statement: "The true world—we have abolished. What world has remained? The apparent one perhaps? But no! *With the true world we have also abolished the apparent one*."[58] Here, Nietzsche moves beyond a mere reversal of Platonism, undermining and collapsing the very distinction between the true world and its apparitional other. According to Mark Taylor and Esa Saarinen, "the point is not simply that truth and reality have been absorbed by illusion and appearance. Something far more subtle and unsettling is taking place. Somewhere Nietzsche suggests that when reality is effaced, appearances disappear as well. What emerges in the wake of the death of oppositions like truth/illusion and reality/appearance is something that is neither truth nor illusion, reality nor appearance but something else, something other. This other is as yet unnamed."[59] Nietzsche's questioning of the "will to truth" and his skepticism concerning the depreciation of deception do not seek to replace one term of the traditional metaphysical dichotomy with the other. Instead, he questions and undermines the entire system that opposes true being and deceptive appearances in the first place. What Nietzsche effects, therefore, is not a simple reversal of Platonism, but a *deconstruction*[60] of what is perhaps the principal binary oppositions that structure the field of philosophical thinking. This operation leaves neither truth nor illusion, reality nor appearance, but something other—something that is beyond and outside of these logical oppositions, which organize all possible modes of thinking, and that, because of this, exceeds the scope of available names.[61] That is, it ruptures the very limit of λόγος, which, in this case, can be understood as both "logic" and "word."

Technically speaking, this is also what transpires in *The Matrix*. *The Matrix* can be read as a film that not only employs but exploits the binary oppositions that define traditional metaphysics. In this way, the narrative proceeds by drawing distinctions between the red and the blue pills and deciding in favor of the one over the other. All of this, of course, is programmed and delimited by the metaphysics of opposite values—a metaphysics that not only arranges binary oppositions but determines an ethical schema by privileging one term over the other. In *The Matrix*, the blue pill, which leads to a life of self-deception in a computer-generated simulation, is both opposed and subordinated to the red pill, which leads to real knowledge of the truth. This arrangement, however, shows itself to be an artifice. If one pays attention to the structure of the narrative, the decision that Morpheus offers Neo cannot be, within the metaphysical system articulated by the film, a real alternative or choice. In other words, there is neither a blue nor a red pill. What appears as a choice between two alternatives is itself something that is simulated within the artifice of the Matrix. Neo's encounter with Morpheus takes place in a computer-generated hotel room inside the Matrix, which is, at this point in the film, the only reality Neo is capable of understanding. This situation is marked explicitly by Morpheus at the beginning of the conversation: "The Matrix is everywhere, it's all around us, here even in this room."[62] Consequently, the choice that Morpheus presents to Neo between a programmed artifice and true reality is itself an artifact in a computer-generated simulation. The decision between the blue or the red pill is something that is staged within and completely circumscribed by the Matrix. The two pills, as Peter Lloyd argues, are entirely virtual.[63] This insight is eventually confirmed in the sequel, *Reloaded*, where it becomes clear to Neo that his choice between the red and blue pill was always and already part of the Matrix's own program and operations.[64]

The task, therefore, is not a matter of simply choosing one or the other but of questioning the structure, necessity, and stakes of this particular and limited set of alternatives. It is, to paraphrase Kroker and Weinstein, less a matter of being pro- or anti-Matrix, but of developing a critical perspective on the ethics of this very choice.[65] What is at issue in such an undertaking is not deciding either for blue or red, but rather inquiring about the terms and conditions by which this either/or logic has been generated in the first place. The issue, then, is not as simple as deciding between two different pills. Instead, the task is to learn to think outside of and beyond these limited options and the customary metaphysical categories that already dictate the kinds of questions we ask, the alternatives we think we have to choose between, and the outcomes that we foresee as possible. For instance, instead of selecting between the two pills presented by Morpheus, Neo could have stood up and walked away from the entire scene. In doing so, he would have not selected either pill. He would have effectively said "no to drugs" and not consented to having his options restricted to a binary arrangement where one term is already opposed to and privileged over the other. He would, therefore, neither have awakened in the "desert of the real" nor have been returned to the anesthetized deceptions of the Matrix, where "ignorance is bliss." He would have done something entirely other, something that is neither predictable nor revolutionary, something outside of and beyond the logical op-positions of truth/falsity, reality/illusion, and good/bad.

A similar opportunity is available in ICT research. We can, of course, con-tinue to apply the usually metaphysical concepts in order to generate an under-standing of ICT and to demarcate what is considered acceptable and proper. If we do so, information technology will conform to rather predictable, calculable, and comfortable norms, becoming, as Michael Heim suggests, "Platonism as a working product."[66] If, however, the consideration of this technology extends beyond the customary categories and values, we can begin to perceive other and perhaps more interesting alternatives. This requires, above everything else, a mode of operations that both questions and eventually ruptures the limit of the conceptual system that already defines the possibility of both a metaphysics and ethics of ICT. What is needed is an entirely other kind of "metaphysics" and "ethics"—perhaps it is problematic to retain these names—that is able to inter-rupt and to operate in excess of the traditional logical distinctions that divide truth from illusion, being from appearance, and even good from evil. We can find a model for this kind of transaction by "returning to the source." It is in the concluding pages of Plato's *Phaedrus* that Socrates encodes the evaluation of the technology of writing in a binary structure, employs the figure of the φάρμακον (drug) to illustrate the two options, and limits discussion to this rather restricted binary opposition.[67] As long as evaluations of scriptural technology remain orga-nized and delimited by the two alternatives that are presented by Socrates, then writing will be understood according to a structure that has already stacked the deck against it. In other words, if writing is positioned, as it is at the end of the *Phaedrus*, as the deficient and negatively defined other of memory and speech, it can only be the wrong choice, the equivalent of swallowing a blue pill. The critical task, one taken up by writers like Stéphane Mallarmé, Roland Barthes, Maurice Blanchot, Jacques Derrida, Trinh T. Minh-ha and others, is not sim-ply to reverse the tradition, replacing the logocentric privilege of memory and speech with a revolutionary privileging of writing. This kind of simple-minded inversion changes nothing and, as Walter Ong correctly points out, would be an "uncritical literacy."[68] Instead, the task is to learn to think writing and to be able to write writing outside of and beyond the horizon of this logocentric metaphys-ics. Similarly the task before ICT theorists and practitioners is to learn to think and visualize ICT outside of and beyond the binary oppositions that have all too often been employed to structure understandings of this technology. The issue is not simply to decide between two different pills but to learn to think outside of and beyond this limited binary opposition, which already controls the field and appears to delimit the only possibilities. Indicative of this kind of alternative pro-cedure is Mark Taylor's work on VR. For Taylor, VR, like many of the technical terms introduced in poststructuralism, cannot be contained by or understood according to the customary metaphysical categories. "Previous responses to vir-tual reality," he writes, "reinscribe oppositions like mind/body, human/machine, natural/artificial, and material/immaterial, which the long process of virtualizing reality subverts. What once seemed to be hard-and-fast oppositions now appear to be interfaces in which neither term remains the same. Virtual reality involves neither the synthesis of opposites nor the suppression of one term by the other but gives rise to a different order of 'reality' that eludes traditional classificatory structures."[69] According to Taylor, VR, which he argues is not just a technology but an effective figure of the postmodern condition, does not take up residence on either one side or the other of the conceptual oppositions that have organized and programmed Western systems of meaning. It, therefore, is neither located on the side of the real nor situated as its opposite. Instead it constitutes something like a dialectical *third term*.[70] This third term, however, is not situated in between the two poles of a conceptual opposition. It does not, following the procedure of Hegelian philosophy, mediate or synthesize their difference. Instead, it is situated completely outside and in excess of the either/or possibilities that have been programmed by the binary oppositions that define and characterize Western metaphysics. This third term, therefore, does not participate in the dialectical game of either/or but exceeds and even circumscribes its rules. In the end, we can say, to come full circle and return to the quotation from Kierkegaard with which this all began, that rather than designating a choice between the real and the virtual, the decision before ICT theorists and practitioners is whether to continue to operate within this dialectic or to rule it out and proceed to investigate opportunities that are otherwise.

Chapter Six

The Machine Question

Ethics, Alterity, and Technology

> In addition, we might ask about those ethical
> calls of the future from "beings" that we can-
> not now even imagine.[1]
> —Jeffrey T. Nealon

In the *Matrix* trilogy, as in many contemporary science fiction narratives, the machine is situated outside of and in opposition to what is defined as properly and uniquely human.[2] This decision, like the other binary oppositions that have organized thinking, is not without ethical complications and consequences. The following, therefore, takes up the question of ethics. And like much of the contemporary work on this subject matter, it is interested in the call from, our response to, and our responsibility for others.[3] However, unlike the capital "O" other, who has taken center stage in recent moral thinking largely due to the influence of Emmanuel Levinas and others, this question is directed otherwise. It is about others who remain, for reasons that will need to be explicated, outside the contemporary and essentially anthropocentric understandings of alterity that have persisted in and been definitive of the Western episteme. It is, therefore, a question that is not concerned with or limited to the present and the presence of these somewhat familiar Others. It is a question that is oriented to the future, toward other "beings," whom we may not now even be able to imagine and who call to us and approach from elsewhere. It is, in short, a question about the future of ethics. And it involves and addresses itself to the possibility of an other who remains fundamentally and disturbingly otherwise.

The subject of this inquiry, as intimated in the chapter title, is the machine, especially the autonomous and self-regulating machine that has become so prevalent in the latter half of the previous century. These machines, as Donna Haraway has pointed out, look suspiciously like us. "Late twentieth-century machines," she writes in her manifesto for cyborgs, "have made thoroughly ambiguous the difference between natural and artificial, mind and body, self-developing and externally designed, and many other distinctions that used to apply to organisms and machines. Our machines are disturbingly lively, and we ourselves frighteningly inert."[4] Despite this affiliation, the machine has been and continues to be excluded from any and all forms of axiology. It simply does not qualify as a legitimate subject of ethics. As J. Storrs Hall describes it, "we have never considered ourselves to have 'moral' duties to our machines, or them to us."[5] The machine, therefore, despite all kinds of demonstrated affinities with living organisms, has occupied and continues to occupy a position that is situated outside of ethics. In other words, the machine is an other that is so categorically different that it does not even qualify as other. It is that other who, somewhat ironically, is already and necessarily excluded by moral philosophy's own concern with and for Others. At a time when all kinds of other beings— animals and even the environment—qualify for some kind of consideration in ethical discussions, the machine appears to constitute the last socially acceptable moral prejudice.

The following, therefore, attempts to ask the machine question. The choice of words here is deliberate. I write "attempts," because it is not entirely certain that this question can be successfully articulated as such without simultaneously putting in question the means and mechanism of its articulation. Throughout the Western tradition it is speech or λόγος that has defined the boundaries of the human being. It is the human entity, according to a long and rich tradition that Jacques Derrida has termed "logocentrism," who alone possesses the power of speech and who can, through this capacity, communicate *his* (and this logocentric tradition is always informed by a complementary phallocentrism) thoughts to others.[6] According to this history, machines, especially the technologies of information and communication, have been considered to be mere transmission media or instruments of repetition. As Socrates says of written texts, arguably one of the first forms of information technology, "you might think they spoke as if they had intelligence, but if you question them, wishing to know about their sayings, they always say one and the same thing."[7] This restriction is, however, no longer tenable. Not only are there machines that can be called "intelligent" and that are capable of conversing with human users in a way that is virtually indistinguishable from another person, but the machine has even been determined to outpace the human in this distinctly human occupation. In the estimation of Kevin Warwick, "the biggest advantage of all for machine intelligence is communication. In comparison with the capabilities of machines, human communication is so poor as to be embarrassing."[8] Articulating the machine question will, therefore, require a confrontation with speech, λόγος, and communication that will, at the same time, inevitably affect the mechanisms by which this information is communicated. Because a written text is already considered to be a mechanism of communication, one cannot articulate the machine question in writing without also questioning, or at least holding open the possibility of questioning, the machinery of its own articulation. The effect of this can be immediately perceived in the "style" or texture of what follows. Instead of being organized into an essay that proposes, argues for, and proves a singular thesis, the text is composed of a sequence of interrelated but independent maneuvers. This is not a literary affectation. On the contrary, it is necessitated by the subject that is addressed. Like the machinic other that it investigates, this alternative form of writing deliberately puts in question the instrumentalist assumptions that have shaped traditional understandings of both communication and technology.

Additionally I write "ask" instead of "answer." In investigating the machine and its place in ethics, I am not, at least at this stage, interested in devising a definitive answer. This is not because of the customary suspicion that is usually directed against criticism, which Neil Postman succinctly describes at the end of *Technopoly*: "Anyone who practices the art of cultural criticism must endure being asked, What is the solution to the problems you describe? Critics almost never appreciate this question, since, in most cases, they are entirely satisfied with themselves for having posed the problem and, in any event, are rarely skilled in formulating practical suggestions about anything."[9] This criticism of criticism, which ironically is at risk of being exposed to the difficulties it identifies, questions the value of critical inquiry. On this account, asking a question or identifying a problem is only a means to an end. It is but one step on the way to providing an answer or formulating a solution, which is the presumed objective of the entire enterprise. Despite the "common-sense" attraction of this instrumentalist understanding, it does have at least two significant problems. First, it assumes that critical investigations are a corrective enterprise. This assumption accords with colloquial usage, where the words "criticism," "criticize," and "critique" are generally understood as a predominantly negative process of judgment, evaluation, or fault-finding. There is, however, an older and more precise definition that is rooted in Immanuel Kant's critical philosophy. A critique of any system, as Barbara Johnson characterizes it, "is not an examination of its flaws and imperfections. . . . It is an analysis that focuses on the grounds of that system's possibility."[10] Following this precedent, it can be said that the machine question does not simply identify a fault or failure in the systems of Western ethics in order to correct it or to provide a definitive answer for the designated problem. Instead, it "critiques" these systems by demonstrating that the customary exclusion of the machine is not simply an oversight or imperfection that could be fixed but constitutes a systemic necessity that is the condition for the possibility of what has been called "ethics."

Second, this form of critical questioning is clearly not a simple or casual activity. As Martin Heidegger observed in *Being and Time*, questioning is a complex undertaking that involves a number of factors that need to be taken into account. "Any inquiry," Heidegger writes, "as an inquiry about something, has that which is asked about [*Gefragtes*]. But all inquiry about something is somehow a questioning of something. So in addition to what is asked about, an inquiry has that which is interrogated [*Befragtes*]. . . . Furthermore, in what is asked about there lies also that which is to be found out by the asking [*Erfragte*]; this is what is really intended."[11] To make a rather long story short, Heidegger's point is that a question is never objective, transparent, or neutral. A question, no matter how carefully articulated, necessarily harbors preconceptions and preunderstandings that direct and regulate the inquiry. What this means is that how a question is formulated is just as important, if not more important, than the answers that might be provided for it. In the case of the machine, for instance, we are dealing with a question that has rarely if ever been asked. If, as Heidegger declares in the first line of *Being and Time*, the "question of being," the *Seinsfrage*, has been forgotten,[12] then it can be said that "the machine question" is in a situation that is considerably worse. Unlike the *Seinsfrage*, which has been forgotten and now needs to be recalled, the machine question has, it appears, not been asked.[13] Being situated outside the sphere of ethics—comprising as it were the excluded other of moral philosophy—the machine has never been present as a legitimate subject of or for moral reasoning. It has, by definition, not been articulated as a question that is suitable for ethical consideration. It simply has not and does not register on the philosophical radar. At some point it might be possible to venture a kind of solution or answer. It may even be possible at some future moment to entertain "a code of ethics" for dealing with intelligent machines of our own creation. For now, however, the undertaking must be much more modest. We first need to learn how to ask the machine question so that the machine can, in the first place, become a legitimate question for ethics. For this reason, asking the machine question will require considerable effort on numerous fronts. How, for example, does one make manifest within the space of ethics that which by necessity does not and cannot be manifest as such? How does one include in ethical considerations that which has been excluded and must be excluded in order for moral philosophy to be what it is? How does one respond to and take responsibility for an other that remains completely alien to an ethics that has made the other its subject? How, in other words, do we respond to the ethical calls from others who are and remain fundamentally otherwise?

Ethics of Exclusion

> Humanism administers lessons to "us" (?). In a mil-
> lion ways, often mutually incompatible. Well founded
> (Apel)and non-founded (Rorty), counter-factual
> (Habermas, Rawls) and pragmatic (Searl), psychological
> (Davidson) and ethico-political (the French neo-
> humanists). But always as if at least man were a
> certain value, which has no need to be interrogated.[14]
> —Jean-François Lyotard

Ethics, especially communication ethics, is customarily understood as being concerned with questions of responsibility for and in the face of an Other with whom we interact and exchange ideas or information. For the discipline of communication and traditional forms of moral philosophy, this "Other" is more often than not conceived of as another human being—another human subject who is essentially and necessarily like we assume ourselves to be. This deep-seated anthropocentric presumption necessarily excludes others, most notably the animal and the machine. In fact, it is through the systemic exclusion of these others that the human as human has come to be defined, delimited, and characterized. Although this systemic exclusivity is enacted and described throughout the history of Western thought, it is perhaps most evident in the work of René Descartes. For Descartes, the human being is the sole creature that is capable of rational thought. In this view, animals not only lack reason but are nothing more than mindless automatons that, like a clockwork mechanism, follow predetermined instructions that are programmed in the disposition of their various parts or organs. Understood in this way, the animal and machine become virtually indistinguishable. "If any such machine," Descartes writes, "had the organs and outward shape of a monkey or of some other animal that lacks reason, we should have no means of knowing that they did not possess entirely the same nature as these animals."[15] Consequently, the animal and machine share a common form of alterity that situates them as completely different from and distinctly other than human.

Because of this exclusion from the realm of rational thought, the animal has not traditionally been considered a legitimate moral subject. When Kant, for example, defined morality as involving the rational determination of the will,[16] the animal, which does not by definition possess reason, is immediately and categorically excluded. The practical employment of reason does not concern the animal and, when Kant does make mention of animality (*Tierheit*), he only uses it as a foil by which to define the limits of humanity proper.[17] It is because the human being possesses reason, that he (and the human being, in this case, was principally male) is raised above the brute instinctual behavior of mere animality and able to act according to the principles of pure practical reason.[18] The same ethical redlining is effected in the analytic tradition. According to Tom Regan, this is immediately apparent in the seminal work of analytical ethics. "It was in 1903 when analytic philosophy's patron saint, George Edward Moore, published his classic, *Principia Ethica*. You can read every word in it. You can read between every line of it. Look where you will, you will not find the slightest hint of attention to 'the animal question.' Natural and nonnatural properties, yes. Definitions and analyses, yes. The open-question argument and the method of isolation, yes. But so much as a word about non-human animals? No. Serious moral philosophy, of the analytic variety, back then did not traffic with such ideas."[19] This exclusive anthropocentrism is also at work in the philosophy of Emmanuel Levinas,[20] the most notable ethicist in the continental tradition and the darling of recent work in the field of communication ethics. Unlike a lot of what goes by the name of "moral philosophy," Levinasian ethics does rely on metaphysical generalizations, abstract formulas, or simple pieties. His philosophy is concerned with the response to and responsibility for the absolutely Other who is confronted in an irreducible face-to-face encounter. Whatever the import of this unique contribution, this other is always and unapologetically human. Although he is not the first to identify this problem, Jeffrey Nealon provides what is perhaps the most succinct description of this problem in *Alterity Politics:* "In thematizing response solely in terms of the human face and voice, it would seem that Levinas leaves untouched the oldest and perhaps most sinister unexamined privilege of the same: *anthropos* ['ἄνθρωπος] and only *anthropos*, has *logos* [λόγος]; and as such, *anthropos* responds not to the barbarous or the inanimate, but only to those who qualify for the privilege of 'humanity,' only those deemed to possess a face, only to those recognized to be living in the *logos*."[21] For Levinas, as for those modes of ethical thinking that follow in the wake of his influence, the other is always operationalized as another human subject.[22] If, as Levinas argues, ethics precedes ontology, then in Levinas's own work anthropology and a certain brand of humanism precedes ethics.

It is only recently that the discipline of philosophy has begun to approach the animal as a legitimate subject of ethics. Regan identifies the turning point in a single work: "In 1971, three Oxford philosophers—Roslind and Stanley Godlovitch, and John Harris—published *Animals, Men and Morals*. The volume marked the first time philosophers had collaborated to craft a book that dealt with the moral status of nonhuman animals."[23] According to Regan, this book is not only credited with introducing what is now called the "animal question," but launched an entire subdiscipline of moral philosophy where the animal is considered to be a legitimate subject of ethical inquiry. Currently, philosophers of both the analytic and continental varieties[24] find reason to be concerned with animals, and there is a growing body of research addressing issues like the ethical treatment of animals, animal rights, and environmental ethics. According to Cary Wolfe, there are two factors that have made this remarkable reversal of the tradition possible. On the one hand, there is the crisis of humanism, "brought on, in no small part, first by structuralism and then post-structuralism and its interrogation of the figure of the human as the constitutive (rather than technically, materially, and discursively constituted) stuff of history and the social."[25] Since at least Nietzsche, philosophers, anthropologists, and social scientists have been increasingly suspicious of the privileged position human beings have given themselves in the great chain of being, and this suspicion becomes an explicit object of inquiry within the so called "human sciences." On the other hand, the boundary between the animal and the human has, as Donna Haraway remarks, become increasingly untenable. Everything that had divided us from them is now up for grabs: language, tool use, and even reason.[26] Recent discoveries in various branches of the biological sciences have had the effect of slowly dismantling the wall that Descartes and others had erected between the human and the animal. According to Wolfe, "a veritable explosion of work in areas such as cognitive ethology and field ecology has called into question our ability to use the old saws of anthropocentrism (language, tool use, the inheritance of cultural behaviors, and so on) to separate ourselves once and for all from the animals, as experiments in language and cognition with great apes and marine mammals, and field studies of extremely complex social and cultural behaviors in wild animals such as apes, wolves, and elephants, have more or less permanently eroded the tidy divisions between human and nonhuman."[27] The revolutionary effect of this transformation can be seen, somewhat ironically, in the backlash of what Evan Ratliff calls "creationism 2.0," a well-organized "crusade against evolution" that attempts to reinstate a clear and undisputed division between human beings and the rest of creation based on a strict interpretation of the Judeo-Christian creation myth.[28]

What is curious is that at a time when this other form of otherness is increasingly recognized as a legitimate subject of moral philosophy, its other, the machine, remains conspicuously absent. Despite all the talk of the animal question, animal others, animal rights, and the reconsideration of what Wolfe calls the "repressed Other of the subject, identity, logos,"[29] virtually nothing is said about the machine. One could, in fact, redeploy Regan's critique of G. E. Moore's *Principia Ethica* and apply it, with a high degree of accuracy, to any work purporting to address the animal question: "You can read every word in it. You can read between every line of it. Look where you will, you will not find the slightest hint of attention to 'the machine question.'" Even though the fate of the machine, from Descartes on, was intimately coupled with that of the animal, only one of the pair has qualified for ethical consideration. This exclusion is not just curious; it is illogical and indefensible. In fact, it seems as if the machine, even before the animal, should have challenged the anthropocentric prejudice that is the operating system of Western ethics. Unlike the animal, the machine, especially the information processing machine that comprises so much of contemporary technology, appears to possess something like intelligence, reason, or λόγος. Not only can the machine engage the complexities of mathematics, which for Descartes,

Leibniz, Kant, and others constituted the epitome of rational thought and the proper model of philosophy, but simple chatter-bots like ELIZA can apparently engage in intelligent dialogue, arranging words in such a way as to provide logical and meaningful answers to questions.[30] Despite this, it is only the animal that has qualified for ethical consideration. Despite all the ink spilled on the subject of the animal question, almost nothing[31] has been written about the machine. And despite all the talk about an ethics of radical otherness, we have said little or nothing about a machinic other. We have, in the words of Hall, "never considered ourselves to have moral responsibilities to our machines."[32] How can we continue to justify this exclusion? If we admit animals, do we not also have to admit the machine? Can an ethics that is oriented toward the other get away with including one and not the other? Can such an ethics persist without being exposed as inconsistent, capricious, and, in a word, unethical? The choice is clear, but each option seems difficult and problematic. Either we own up to the exclusive strategy of ethics, continue to redline the machine, and install new mechanisms to dispel the hypocrisy that will inevitably threaten such a maneuver at every turn. Or we open the flood gates and admit that it now makes sense, perhaps had always made sense, to entertain the machine question and consider the rights of machines. Either way, ethics will never be the same.

Mechanized Morality

> I inevitably stumbled onto this wonderful
> observation, namely, that one can devise a
> certain alphabet of human thoughts and that,
> through the combination of the letters of this
> alphabet and through the analysis of the words
> produced from them, all things can both
> be discovered and judged.[33]
> —Gottfried Wilhelm Leibniz

Despite its absence as a proper subject of ethics, the machine belongs to and is fundamental to the history of moral reasoning. All too often, however, one misses this fact, because of the way philosophers have (mis)understood and restricted the definition of the machine. In the philosophical imagination, the machine is more often than not characterized as a physical mechanism. "We have," Hall writes, "a naïve notion of a machine as a box with motors, gears, and whatnot in it."[34] It is, for example, the spring-driven mechanical clock, introduced in Europe around the middle of the sixteenth century, which had comprised the discipline's principal machinic image. For Descartes, the mechanical clock, with its intricate gears, was a model of the mindless animal body, which moves itself and responds to stimulus like a well-fashioned mechanism. In Sir Isaac Newton's *Philosophiae Naturalis Principia Mathematica*, this image was extended to cover the entirety of physical reality, introducing a concept that has come to be called the "clock-work universe." [35] And William Paley, in 1802, employed this understanding in what is now called the design argument for the existence of God. According to this view, if the universe itself is a well-designed and -regulated watch, then there must be a divine watchmaker who fashioned its various parts and put the whole apparatus into motion. [36] Even after technology had advanced well beyond the gears, springs, and levers of the clock, philosophers continued to fixate on mechanics. For Martin Heidegger, for example, technology was restricted to mechanical apparatuses: saw mills, hydroelectric power plants, high-frequency radar stations, and jet aircraft. [37]

This particular definition of the machine is not only restrictive but, as Hall argues, "incapable of dealing with the machines of the future." [38] According to Hall, a machine is not simply a set of gears and motors. It is a set of rules, instructions, or messages. "The most important machine of the twentieth century wasn't a physical thing at all. It was the Turing Machine, and it was a mathematical idea. It provided the theoretical basis for computers. . . . This theoretical concept of a machine as a pattern of operations which could be implemented in a number of ways is called a virtual machine." [39] Understood in this fashion, a machine is not merely a collections of physical springs and gears but a sequence of encoded instructions, an algorithm, which may be implemented and embodied in any number of ways. This general definition of the machine covers mechanical systems, like clocks that implement rules of synchronization in the form of physical space marked out on rotating gears; biological systems, like animals and plants that are composed of and operate by following instructions embedded in their genetic code; and information processing devices, like the computer, which performs different operations based on various program instructions stipulated by software. Philosophers have been somewhat reluctant to recognize and utilize this general definition of the machine. In fact, it is only recently, that philosophy has begun to address the machine virtually. Traces of this are perhaps most evident in the work of Gilles Deleuze and Félix Guattari, who characterize what they call the "abstract machine." Although not simply a synonym for the "virtual machine," the abstract machine also names an assemblage that is "independent of the forms and substances, expressions and contents it will distribute." [40]

If the machine, according to this general definition, is a pattern of operations or a set of predefined instructions, then moral philosophy has been and continues to be machinic. According to Henry Sidgwick, "the aim of Ethics is *to systematize* and free from error the apparent cognitions that most men have of the rightness or reasonableness of conduct." [41] Western conceptions of morality customarily consist in systematic rules of behavior that can be encoded, like an algorithm, and implemented by different moral agents in a number of circumstances and situations. They are, in short, programs that are designed to direct behavior and govern conduct. Take for example, the Ten Commandments, the cornerstone of Judeo-Christian ethics. These ten rules constitute an instruction set that not only prescribes correct operations for human beings but does so in a way that is abstracted from the particulars of circumstance, personality, and other empirical accidents. "Thou shall not kill" is a general prohibition against murder that applies in any number of situations where one human being confronts another. Like an algorithm, the statements contained within the Ten Commandments are general operations that can be applied to any particular set of data. Similarly Immanuel Kant's moral philosophy is founded on and structured by fundamental rules or what he calls, in a comparison to the laws of natural science, "practical laws." These practical laws are "categorical imperatives." That is, they are not merely subjective maxims that apply to a particular person's will under a specific set of circumstances. Instead, they must be objectively valid for the will of every rational being in every possible circumstance. "Laws," Kant writes, "must completely determine the will as will, even before I ask whether I am capable of achieving a desired effect or what should be done to realize it. They must thus be categorical; otherwise they would not be laws, for they would lack the necessity which, in order to be practical, must be completely independent of pathological conditions, i.e., conditions only contingently related to the will."[42] For Kant, moral action is programmed by principles of pure practical reason—universal laws that are not only abstracted from every empirical condition but applicable to any and all rational agents. It may be said, therefore, that Kant, who took physics and mathematics as the model for a wholesale transformation of the procedures of philosophy, mechanized ethics in a way that was similar to Newton's mechanization of physical science. Finally, even the pragmatic alternative to deontological ethics, utilitarianism, operates by a kind of systemic moral computation or what Jeremy Bentham called "moral arithmetic."[43] The core utilitarian principle, "seek to act in such a way as to promote the greatest quantity and quality of happiness for the greatest number," is a general formula that subsequently requires considerable processing to crunch the numbers and decide the best possible outcome. In fact, Michael Anderson, Susan Leigh Anderson, and Chris Armen have not only constructed computer-based "ethical advisors" but argue that such machines might have an advantage over a human being in following utilitarian theory, because of the sheer number of variables that usually need to be taken into account and calculated accurately.[44] In all these cases, ethics—which, according to Sidgwick, aims to systematize human cognition and conduct—conforms to the characterization of what is called "the virtual machine." Commandments, moral imperatives, ethical principles, codes of conduct, practical laws . . . these all endeavor to provide instruction sets or patterns of operation that program human behavior. Consequently, if moral reasoning is mechanical, then why is the machine virtually excluded from ethics? If ethics is a means by which to systematize and mechanize human operations, then why are other mechanical systems situated on the periphery of this undertaking? How and why is the machine positioned outside of something that is itself fundamentally machinic? Isn't this inconsistent? Isn't this potentially contradictory? More importantly, isn't this unethical?

Speaking of Others

> Would an ethics be sufficient, as Levinas maintains, to
> remind the subject of its being-subject, its being-guest,
> host or hostage, that is to say its being-subjected-to-the-
> other, to the Wholly Other or to every single other? I don't
> think so. It takes more than that to break with the
> Cartesian tradition of the animal-machine that exists
> without language and without the ability to respond.[45]
> —Jacques Derrida

At the end of *The Order of Things*, Michel Foucault writes (and some might be tempted to add the adverb "ominously") that "man is an invention of recent date. And one perhaps nearing its end."[46] By "invention" Foucault means to point out that the concept "man" is not some naturally occurring phenomenon but a conscious and deliberate fabrication. And by "end," he indicates that this invention, like any construct, has a definite history—a narrative with both a beginning and an ending. We will eventually get to the ending. For now, let us address what many, including Foucault, consider to be the beginning. The early Greek thinkers had defined the human being as ζῷον λόγον ἔχον—the animal possessing speech or reason. It is, in fact, speech and reason that, throughout the history of Western thought, mark the division between the human and its nonhuman others. Descartes (who is exceptional insofar as he explicitly addresses these others, if only to exclude them) elucidates this in his somewhat curious consideration of automatons. According to Descartes there are two "very certain means of recognizing" that these figures are machines and not real men:

> The first is that they could never use words, or put together other signs, as we do in order to declare our thoughts to others. For we can certainly conceive of a machine so constructed that it utters words, and even utters words which correspond to bodily actions causing a change in its organs. But it is not conceivable that such a machine should produce different arrangements of words so as to give an appropriately meaningful answer to whatever is said in its presence, as the dullest of men can do. Secondly, even though such machines might do some things as well as we do them, or perhaps even better, they would inevitably fail in others, which would reveal that they were acting not through understanding but only from the disposition of their organs. For whereas reason is a universal instrument which can be used in all kinds of situations, these organs need some particular disposition for each particular action; hence it is for all practical purposes impossible for a machine to have enough different

organs to make it act in all the contingencies of life in the way in which our reason makes us act.[47]

For Descartes what distinguishes the machine from the human being is the fact that the former obviously and unquestionably lacks λόγος. The automaton, although capable of having the external shape and appearance of a man, is absolutely unable to "produce different arrangements of words so as to give an appropriately meaningful answer to whatever is said in its presence" and does not possess or is incapable of simulating the faculty of reason, which is the universal instrument that directs all human action. Descartes immediately employs this machinic distinction also to describe and differentiate the animal.

> Now in just these two ways we can also know the difference between man and beast. For it is quite remarkable that there are no men so dull-witted or stupid—and this includes even madmen—that they are incapable of arranging various words together and forming an utterance from them in order to make their thoughts understood; whereas there is no other animal, however perfect and well-endowed it may be, that can do the like. . . . This shows not merely that the beasts have less reason than men, but that they have no reason at all. For it patently requires very little reason to be able to speak; and since as much inequality can be observed among the animals of a given species as among human beings, and some animals are more easily trained than others, it would be incredible that a superior specimen of the monkey or parrot species should not be able to speak as well as the stupidest child—or at least as well as a child with a defective brain—if their souls were not completely different in nature from ours.[48]

According to this Cartesian argument, the animal and the machine are similar insofar as both lack the ability to speak and, on the evidence of this deficiency, also do not possess the faculty of reason. Unlike human beings, who, despite various inequalities in actual capabilities, can speak and do possess reason, the animal and machine remain essentially speechless and irrational. In short, neither participates in λόγος. Consequently, Descartes organizes the animal and machine under one form of alterity. Both are the *same* insofar as both are completely *other* than human. In fact, according to this line of argument, there can be no reliable way to distinguish between a machine and an animal. Although a real human being is clearly distinguishable from a human-looking automaton, there is, on Descartes's account, no way to differentiate an animal automaton from a real animal. If we were confronted, Descartes argues, with a machine that apes the appearance of a monkey or any other creature that lacks reason, there would be no means by which to distinguish this mechanism from the actual animal it simulates.[49]

This Cartesian decision established a precedent that has gone unchallenged for a number of centuries and has found its way into all kinds of places. Alan Turing, for example, employed this structure as the foundation of his "imitation game," or what is commonly called "the Turing Test." If a machine, Turing hypothesized, becomes capable of successfully simulating a human being in communicative exchanges with a human interlocutor, then that machine would have to be considered intelligent, or in the parlance of modern philosophy, possessing reason.[50] In other words, if a machine is able to achieve the two limiting conditions defined by Descartes, speech communication and reason, then such a machine would be, for all intents and purposes, indistinguishable from a human being. This understanding is also employed and dramatically illustrated in Philip K. Dick's *Do Androids Dream of Electric Sheep?* the science fiction novel that provided the raw material for the film *Blade Runner*. In Dick's postapocalyptic narrative, animals are all but extinct. Because of this, there is great social capital involved in owning and caring for an animal. However, because of their scarcity, an actual animal is prohibitively expensive. Consequently, many people find themselves substituting and tending to animal automatons, like the electric sheep of the title. For most individuals, there is virtually no way to distinguish the electric sheep from a real one. Both eat, sleep, defecate, and bleat. In fact, so perfect is the illusion that when an electric animal breaks down, it is programmed to simulate the pathology of illness and the repair shop, which is complicit in the deception, operates under the pretense of a veterinary clinic. At the same time, this desolate and depopulated world is also inhabited by human automatons or androids. Whereas the confusion between the animal and machine is both acceptable and propitious, the same cannot be said of the human-looking automaton. The androids must be rooted out, positively identified, and, in a carefully selected euphemism, "retired." Although there is no practical way to differentiate the animal from the machine other than destructive analysis, i.e. dissection, there is a reliable way to differentiate a human automaton from an actual human being. And the evaluation involves speech. The suspected android is asked a series of questions and, depending upon his/her response in dialogue with the examiner, will, in a kind of perverse Turing Test, eventually betray its artificial nature.[51]

For Descartes, as for the majority of Western thought, the distinguishing characteristic that allows one to divide the human being from its others, the animal and machine, is speech. In fact, it seems that there is a closer affinity between the animal and machine due to a common lack of λόγος than there is between the human and animal based on the common possession of ζῷον. In other words, it appears that speech trumps life, when dividing us from them. Consequently, it is *speech communication* that makes the difference. It is in and by speech that the human differentiates itself from its others and that these others come to be justifiably excluded from everything that is said to be properly human. Unfortunately, this strategy is no longer, and perhaps never was, successful. Although speech communication had at one time described the proper limit of the human, it now signals, in the words of Foucault, the end of man. At about the same time that Foucault published *The Order of Things*, Joseph Weizenbaum, a computer scientist, demonstrated a machine that successfully challenged if not passed the Turing Test.[52] ELIZA, the first chatter-bot, was able to communicate with human users by producing, in the words of Descartes, "different arrangements of words so as to give an appropriately meaningful answer to whatever is said in its presence."[53] Because of the experience with machines like ELIZA and other advancements in artificial intelligence, robotics, and cybernetics, the boundary between the human-animal and the machine has become increasingly leaky, permeable, and ultimately indefensible. Likewise similar discoveries have been reported with animals. If machines are now capable of communication, then it should be no surprise that animals have also been found to display similar capabilities. Various experiments with primates, like those undertaken by Sue Savage-Rumbaugh and company,[54] have confirmed the presence of sophisticated linguistic abilities once thought to be the exclusive possession of human beings. As Haraway has observed (with that kind of deliberately provocative rhetoric that is characteristic of her manifesto), "the boundary between human and animal is thoroughly breached. The last beachheads of uniqueness have been polluted if not turned into amusement parks—language, tool use, social behavior, mental events, nothing really convincingly settles the separation of human and animal."[55] The outcome of these demonstrations is clear and undeniable, the animal and the machine both participate in some form of λόγος. Consequently, the human is no longer able to be sequestered and differentiated from its others. This not only institutes, as Foucault predicted, the end of a particular definition of "man" as the exclusive proprietor of λόγος but also raises important practical questions. Now that the animal and machine participate in what had been up to this point a unique human activity, how should we respond to them? What is our responsibility to these others? And what becomes of what had been called ethics after the end of man?

Beyond Mediation

> Our conventional response to all media, namely that
> it is how they are used that counts, is the numb
> stance of the technological idiot.[56]
> —Marshall McLuhan

Often it is the little things that make the difference, like prepositions. Let me explain. When employed for the purposes of communication, the machine has been assigned one of two possible functions, both of which are dictated by a particular conceptualization of the process of communication. The machine has either been defined as a medium through which human interlocutors exchange information, or it has occupied, with varying degrees of success, the position of the other in communicative exchanges, becoming a participant with whom[57] humans interact. These two alternatives were initially formalized and distinguished in Robert Cathcart and Gary Gumpert's "The Person-Computer Interaction." In this text, the authors differentiate communicating *through* a computer from communicating *with* a computer. The former, they argue, names all those "computer facilitated functions" where "the computer is interposed between sender and receiver." The latter designates "person-computer interpersonal functions" where "one party activates a computer which in turn responds appropriately in graphic, alphanumeric, or vocal modes establishing an ongoing sender/receiver relationship."[58] These two alternatives were corroborated and further refined in James Chesebro and Donald Bonsall's *Computer-Mediated Communication*. In this extended examination of the role and function of the computer, the authors detail a five-point scale that delimits the range of possibilities for "computer-human communication."[59] The scale extends from the computer utilized as a mere medium of transmission between human interlocutors to the computer understood as an intelligent agent with whom human users interact. Although providing a more complex articulation of the intervening possibilities, Chesebro and Bonsall's formulation remains bounded by the two possibilities initially described by Cathcart and Gumpert.

These two alternatives, which were originally identified with the prepositions *through* and *with*, effectively situate the computer in one of two positions. The computer either is a medium of communication through which a sender and receiver exchange information, or it constitutes an other with whom one communicates. Although not specifically referenced by Cathcart and Gumpert, these two alternatives had been initially modeled in the "Turing Test," which sought to determine whether and to what extent a machine could simulate human responses in computer-mediated communication. The test, therefore, is structured and functions by locating the computer in the position of both medium through which the communication takes place and an other with whom the human interrogator converses. Despite the early identification of these two alternatives, the discipline of communication has, for better or worse, subsequently privileged one term over and against the other. With very few exceptions, communication research has decided to address the computer as a medium through which human users communicate. This decision is immediately evident in and has been institutionalized by the new subfield of computer-mediated communication, or CMC.[60] CMC, as Susan Herring defines it, is any form of "communication that takes place between human beings via the instrumentality of computers."[61] With CMC the computer is understood as a medium or instrument *through* which human users exchange messages and interact with each other. Defining the computer in this manner is completely rational, and it possesses distinct theoretical advantages.

First, this formulation situates the computer at an identifiable position within the process model of communication, which was initially formalized by Claude Shannon and Warren Weaver's *The Mathematical Theory of Communication*. According to Shannon and Weaver, communication is a dyadic process bounded, on the one side, by an information source or sender and, on the other side, by a receiver. These two participants are connected by a communication channel or medium through which messages selected by the sender are conveyed to the receiver (figure 6).[62]

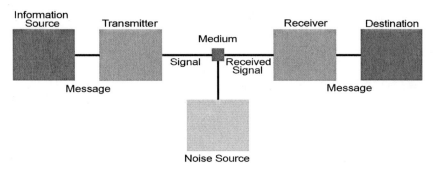

Figure 6
Shannon and Weaver's model of communication.

This rudimentary model not only is "accepted as one of the main seed out of which Communication Studies has grown"[63] but establishes the basic elements and parameters for future elaborations and developments. Although subsequent models, like those devised by George Gerbner, B. H. Wesley and M. S. MacLean, and Roman Jakobson, extend and complicate Shannon and Weaver's initial concept, they retain the basic elements of senders and receivers connected by a medium that facilitates the transmission of messages.[64] CMC locates the computer in the intermediate position of channel or medium. As such, it occupies the position granted to other forms of communication technology and is comprehended as something through which human messages pass. This understanding of the machine as medium has been taken up and further elaborated in the work of Marshall McLuhan, the media theorist whose influence extends beyond media studies and into the new fields of CMC, ICT, and cyberculture. For McLuhan, media—and the word "media" encompasses a wide range of different technological devices, applying not just to the mechanisms of communication, like newspapers and radio, but all kinds of tools and machines—are defined as "extensions of man." This is, of course, immediately evident in the title of what is considered to be one of his most influential books, *Understanding Media: The Extensions of Man.* And the examples employed throughout his text are by now familiar: the wheel is an extension of the foot, the telephone is an extension of the ear, and the television is an extension of the eye.[65] Understood in this way, technical mechanisms have been defined as prostheses through which various human faculties come to be extended beyond their original capacity or ability. And in making this argument, McLuhan does not so much introduce a new understanding of media but provides explicit articulation of a decision that is itself firmly rooted in the soil of the Western tradition. The concept of technology, especially the technology of information and communication, as an extension of human capabilities is, as we have already seen, evident in and deployed by Plato's *Phaedrus*, where writing had been addressed and debated as an artificial supplement for speech and memory.

Second, this intermediate position is also substantiated and justified by the traditional understanding of the proper role and function of the technological apparatus. According to Martin Heidegger's analysis in *The Question Concerning Technology*, the assumed understanding of any kind of technology, whether it be the product of handicraft or industrialized manufacture, is that it is a means employed by human users for particular ends. "We ask the question concerning technology when we ask what it is. Everyone knows the two statements that answer our question. One says: Technology is a means to an end. The other says: Technology is a human activity. The two definitions of technology belong together. For to posit ends and procure and utilize the means to them is a human activity. The manufacture and utilization of equipment, tools, and machines, the manufactured and used things themselves, and the needs and ends that they serve, all belong to what technology is."[66] Heidegger terms this particular conceptualization of technology "the instrumental definition" and indicates that it forms what is considered to be the "correct" understanding of any kind of technological innovation.[67] As Andrew Feenberg summarizes it in the introduction to his *Critical Theory of Technology*, "the instrumentalist theory offers the most widely accepted view of technology. It is based on the common sense idea that technologies are 'tools' standing ready to serve the purposes of users."[68] And because a tool "is deemed 'neutral,' without valuative content of its own,"[69] a technological instrument is evaluated not in and for itself but on the basis of the particular employments that have been decided by a human agent. This decision is succinctly described by Jean-François Lyotard in *The Postmodern Condition*: "Technical devices originated as prosthetic aids for the human organs or as physiological systems whose function it is to receive data or condition the context. They follow a principle, and it is the principle of optimal performance: maximizing output (the information or modification obtained) and minimizing input (the energy expended in the process). Technology is therefore a game pertaining not to the true, the just, or the beautiful, etc., but to efficiency: a technical 'move' is 'good' when it does better and/or expends less energy than another."[70] Lyotard's explanation begins by affirming the traditional understanding of technology as an instrument, prosthesis, or extension of human faculties. Given this "fact," which is stated as if it were something that is beyond question, Lyotard proceeds to provide an explanation of the proper place of the machine in epistemology, ethics, and aesthetics. According to his analysis, a technological device, whether it be a corkscrew, a clock, or a computer, does not in and of itself participate in the important questions of truth, justice, or beauty. Technology, on this account, is simply and indisputably about efficiency. A particular technological innovation is considered "good" if and only if it proves to be a more effective means to accomplishing a desired end. Consequently, technical devices, in and of themselves, do not constitute anything approaching a legitimate moral subject. "Morality," as Hall concludes, "rests on human shoulders, and if machines changed the ease with which things were done, they did not change responsibility for doing them. People have always been the only 'moral agents.'"[71]

In CMC, the computer is determined to be, in both name and function, an instrument or medium through which human interlocutors communicate. Understanding the computer in this fashion is technically justified and possesses distinct theoretical and practical advantages for students and scholars of communication. This approach, however, also entails a set of unacknowledged presuppositions that necessarily complicate this highly specific formulation and ultimately enervate its procedures and significance. In CMC research the computer is effectively immaterial. In fact, CMC is not about computers at all. Understood as an *instrument* through which human users interact, the computer recedes from view and becomes a more or less transparent medium of message exchange. According to Cathcart and Gumpert, studies of communication have always and necessarily "minimized the role of media and channel in the communication process. The focus has been on the number of participants, source and receiver relationships, and forms and functions of messages. The media of communication have been accepted, more or less, as fixed or neutral channels for the transmission of messages among participants."[72] This form of instrumental transparency, however useful and convenient, is necessarily interrupted and even resisted by the mechanisms and machinery of computing. Technically speaking, the computer, whether a timeshared mainframe, a networked PC, or something other, has never been a fixed or neutral channel through which human interaction takes place. Frederick Williams pointed this out as early as 1982: "The computer is the first communications technology to interact intellectually with its users. Most technologies only transform light, sound, or data into electronic impulses for transmission, then reverse the process at the receiving end. Computers, by contrast, can accept or reject our messages, reduce or expand them, file them, index them, or answer back with their own messages."[73] A similar remark was provided by Ithiel de Sola Pool in the foreword to Wilson Dizard's *The Coming Information Age*: "Prior to the computer, every communication device took a message that had been composed by a human being and (with some occasional loss) delivered it unchanged to another human being. The computer for the first time provides a communication device by which a person may receive a message quite different from what any human sent."[74] And Cathcart and Gumpert draw a similar conclusion: "For the first time, a technology can not only speed and expand message exchange, but it can also respond with its own message to a human partner. The computer in this mode becomes a proxy for a sender-receiver in the communication dyad."[75]

For Williams, de Sola Pool, and Cathcart and Gumpert, the computer cannot simply be reduced to the customary instrument of communication. Although other devices of communication may function appropriately as a kind of technical intermediary through which human beings exchange messages, the computer deviates from this expectation and interrupts its procedure. Instead of functioning as an immaterial and transparent channel through which human agents exchange messages, the computer participates in and contaminates the process. It acts on the messages, significantly alters them, and delivers information that was not necessarily selected, composed, or even controlled by human participants. These various occurrences cannot be reduced to a form of unintentional noise introduced by the exigencies of the channel, which is precisely how the process models have dispensed with and accounted for this kind of machinic contribution. As Chesebro and Bonsall point out, "other communication technologies may affect the substantive meaning of a human message, but the alteration is typically an unintended by-product of the medium. The computer, on the other hand, is employed because it will reformat the ideas contained in a human message."[76] With the other media of communication (i.e., print, telegraph, telephone, radio, television, etc.), changes in the human-generated message are explained as unintentional noise imparted by the instruments of transmission. With the computer, such alterations cannot be reduced to mere noise. They are necessary and integral elements of its function. The computer, therefore, substantively resists being exclusively defined as a medium and instrument through which human users exchange messages. Instead, it actively participates in communicative exchanges as a kind of additional agent and/or (inter)active co-conspirator.[77] Defined in this fashion, the computer cannot be reduced to an instrument or medium of communication but occupies, to varying degrees, the position of an other within communicative exchange. And in occupying this position, one inevitably runs up against and encounters questions of ethics. What, for example, is our responsibility in the face of this other—an other who is otherwise than another human entity and does not possess what is normally understood to be a face? How do or should we respond to this other form of otherness, and how will or should this other respond to us? These questions, although not yet part of the mainstream of moral philosophy, are beginning to appear in the margins. Hall's "Ethics for Machines," for example, argues, in a way that reiterates Kant's categorical imperative, that "it will be necessary to give our robots a sound basis for a true, valid, universal ethics that will be as valuable to them as it is to us."[78] Taking another approach, Kevin Warwick, who has willfully altered his own body with machinic implants, questions the practicality of such a "universal ethics": "When an individual's consciousness is based on a part human part machine nervous system, in particular when they exhibit Cyborg consciousness, will they also hold to Cyborg morals, values and ethics? These being potentially distinctly different to human morals, values and ethics."[79] But the most sustained and imaginative investigation of these issues has been articulated and entertained in science fiction. In particular, one finds the machine question formulated with incredible precision and detail in Philip K. Dick's *Do Androids Dream of Electric Sheep?* and its film adaptation in *Blade Runner*, Stanisław Lem's *Solaris* and its two cinematic interpretations by Andrei Tarkovsky and Steven Soderbergh, Isaac Asimov's collection of short stories *I, Robot* and the film by the same name, the *Matrix* trilogy and the animated prequels collected in the *Animatrix*, and the recent reimagining of the television series *Battlestar Galactica*.[80] It is in these and other works of speculative fiction that the ethical status of the machinic other has been initially exposed, examined, and explored.

The Ethics of Inclusion

> It is a banality to claim that there is a fundamental difficulty in human communication. And it is not hard to recognize in advance that this difficulty is partially irreducible. To communicate means to try to establish a unity, to make one of many; this is what the word *communion* means. In one way or another, something is always missing from the communion sought by humans.[81]
> —Georges Bataille

Despite what appears to be systemic exclusion, a small number of scholars have begun to give serious attention to the machine and its position, or lack thereof, in moral philosophy. Although these innovations do not provide definitive answers to the machine question, they do demonstrate the kind of thinking and discursive maneuvers that are necessary to respond to and to take responsibility for the machine as a legitimate moral subject. At the same time, however, these efforts, insofar as they are indebted to the language and logic of the tradition, also and unavoidably reinscribe traditional values and assumptions and, by doing so, demonstrate by their own practices just how difficult it is to think and articulate an ethics that is oriented otherwise. One attempt to think moral philosophy beyond its traditionally limited configuration can be found in what is now called *machine ethics*. This relatively new idea was first introduced and publicized in a paper written by Michael Anderson, Susan Leigh Anderson, and Chris Armen and presented during the 2004 Workshop on Agent Organizations held in conjunction with the American Association for Artificial Intelligence's (AAAI) nineteenth national conference. This debut, which appropriately sought "to lay the theoretical foundation for *machine ethics*"[82] was quickly followed with the formation of the Machine Ethics Consortium (MachineEthics.org) and a dedicated 2005 AAAI symposium on the subject. Unlike computer ethics, which is mainly concerned with the consequences of human behavior through the instrumentality of computer technology, "*machine ethics* is concerned," as characterized by Anderson et al., "with the consequences of behavior of machines toward human users and other machines."[83] In this way, machine ethics both challenges the "human-centric" tradition that has persisted in moral philosophy and argues for a widening of the subject of ethics so as to take into account not only human action with machines but the behavior of some machines, namely those that are designed to provide advice or programmed to make autonomous decisions with little or no human supervision. "Clearly," Anderson and company write, "relying on machine intelligence to effect change in the world without some restraint can be dangerous. Until fairly recently, the ethical impact of a machine's actions has either been negligible, as in the case of a calculator, or, when considerable, has only been taken under the supervision of a human operator, as in the case of automobile assembly via robotic mechanisms. As we increasingly rely upon machine intelligence with reduced human supervision, we will need to be able to count on a certain level of ethical behavior from them."[84]

Although significantly expanding the subject of ethics by incorporating the subjectivity and agency of machines, machine ethics does not, it is important to note, provide any consideration of our response to and responsibility for these machinic others. In other words, machine ethics is exclusively interested in articulating ethical guidelines and procedures for the way machines deal with and treat human beings. This alternative, according to Anderson et al., is motivated by an interest to protect human beings from potentially hazardous machine decisions and action. Deploying machine intelligence in the world without some kind of preprogrammed ethical restraint is, on their account, potentially dangerous for the human species. Consequently, the project of machine ethics, like Isaac Asimov's three laws of robotics,[85] is motivated by a desire to manage the potential hazards of intelligent machines for the sake of ensuring the humane treatment of human beings. At the theoretical foundation of machine ethics, then, is an affirmation of the supreme and unquestioned value of the human. This affirmation is precisely the organizing assumption of anthropocentric ethics, which machine ethics had purported to put in question and to suspend. Despite its critique of the anthropocentrism that dominates moral philosophy in general and computer ethics in particular, machine ethics deploys and reinforces a human-centered perspective. As a result, it is not situated outside of and as an alternative to computer ethics but remains part and parcel of that tradition. If computer ethics is, as Anderson et al. characterize it, about the responsible and irresponsible use of the computer by human users, then machine ethics is little more than the responsible programming of machines by human beings for the sake of protecting other human beings. Instead of laying the foundation for a new moral perspective, "machine ethics" redeploys the anthropocentric prejudice through the mechanism of what initially appears to be a critique and alternative. This is not necessarily some deliberate deception instituted by the authors or even an accidental lapse in thinking. It is, on the contrary, the result of and evidence for the almost complete saturation that has been achieved by the humanist perspective in ethical matters. In other words, the anthropocentrism that has characterized the last 2,500+ years of moral philosophy is so pervasive and inescapable that any attempt to think outside the humanist box, like that of Anderson and his colleagues, is already and unavoidably caught in the language, logic, and protocols of this legacy system.

Although machine ethics is concerned exclusively with the moral consequences of actions performed by machines, other theorists have considered whether and to what extent machines are deserving of ethical consideration as such. Robert Sparrow, for instance, foresees the need for something he calls "Android Ethics." "As soon as AIs begin to possess consciousness, desires and projects then it seems as though they deserve some sort of moral standing."[86] In order to define the ethical tipping point—the point at which a computer becomes the appropriate subject of moral concern—Sparrow proposes a modification of the Turing Test. The modified test, like the original, is proposed as a thought experiment, asking "when a computer might fill the role of a human being in a moral dilemma."[87] The dilemma selected by Sparrow is the case of triage.

> In the scenario I propose, a hospital administrator is faced with the decision as to which of two patients on life support systems to continue to provide electricity to, following a catastrophic loss of power in the hospital. She can only preserve the existence of one and there are no other lives riding on the decision. We will know that machines have achieved moral standing comparable to a human when the replacement of one of the patients with an artificial intelligence leaves the character of the dilemma intact. That is, when we might sometimes judge that it is reasonable to preserve the continued existence of the machine over the life of the human being. This is the "*Turing Triage Test*."[88]

As it is described by Sparrow, the "Turing Triage Test" evaluates whether and to what extent the continued existence of a computer can be comparable to another human being in what is arguably a highly constrained and somewhat artificial situation of life and death. In other words, it can be said that a computer has achieved moral standing that is at least on par with that of another human being when it is possible that one could in fact choose the continued existence of the computer over that of another human individual. Although Sparrow's characterization appears to make the moral status of the machine dependent on its ability to simulate human characteristics, he is careful to avoid the trap of simple anthropocentrism. The issue, he contends, is whether "intelligent computers might achieve the status of moral persons,"[89] and, following the example provided by animal ethicists like Peter Singer, Sparrow argues that the category "personhood" must be understood apart from the concept of the human. "Whatever it is that makes human beings morally significant must be something that could conceivably be possessed by other entities. To restrict personhood to human beings is to commit the error of chauvinism or 'speciesism.'"[90] Despite this important qualification, however, the definition of "personhood," which Sparrow admits is itself open to considerable equivocation, is something that is dependent upon and abstracted from human experience. Even if "moral personhood" is characterized "as a capacity to experience pleasure and pain,"[91] what constitutes "pleasure" and "pain" is derived from and defined according to distinctly human experiences and values. Consequently, Sparrow's dependency on the innovations of animal rights philosophy leads to his inheriting one of its fundamental problems, namely, extending what are essentially human values and interests to the animal-other does not necessarily contest but often reaffirms anthropocentrism. "One of the central ironies of animal rights philosophy," Wolfe writes, "is that its philosophical frame remains an essentially humanist one in its most important philosophers (utilitarianism in Peter Singer, neo-Kantianism in Tom Regan), thus effacing the very difference of the animal other that animal rights sought to respect in the first place."[92]

Like Sparrow's "Android Ethics," Luciano Floridi's "Information Ethics" is formulated in response to questions concerning the proper limits of moral consideration. According to Floridi's analysis, "any action, whether morally loaded or not, has the logical structure of a binary relation between an agent and a patient."[93] Standard or classic forms of ethics have been exclusively concerned with either the character of the agent, as in virtue ethics, or the actions that are performed by the agent, as in consequentialism, contractualism, and deontologism. For this reason, Floridi concludes, classic ethical theories have been "inevitably anthropocentric" in focus, and "take only a relative interest in the patient," or what he also refers to as the "receiver" or "victim."[94] This philosophical status quo has been, Floridi suggests, recently challenged by animal and environmental ethics, both of which "attempt to develop a patient-oriented ethics in which the 'patient' may be not only a human being, but also any form of life."[95] However innovative this alteration has been, Floridi finds it to be insufficient for a truly universal and impartial ethics. "Even Bioethics and Environmental Ethics," he argues, "fail to achieve a level of complete universality and impartiality, because they are still biased against what is inanimate, lifeless, or merely possible (even Land Ethics is biased against technology and artefacts, for example). From their perspective, only what is alive deserves to be considered as a proper centre of moral claims, no matter how minimal, so a whole universe escapes their attention."[96] For Floridi, therefore, bioethics and environmental ethics represents something of an incomplete innovation in moral philosophy. They have, on the one hand, successfully challenged the anthropocentric tradition by articulating a more universal form of ethics that not only shifts attention to the patient but also expands who or what qualifies for inclusion as a patient. At the same time, however, both remain ethically biased insofar as they substitute biocentrism for the customary anthropocentrism. Consequently, Floridi endeavors to take the innovations introduced by bioethics and environmental ethics one step further. He retains the patient-oriented approach but "lowers the condition that needs to be satisfied, in order to qualify as a centre of moral concern, to the minimal common factor shared by any entity"[97] whether animate, inanimate, or otherwise. For Floridi this common denominator is informational and, for this reason, he gives this thesis the name "Information Ethics," or IE.

> From an IE perspective, the ethical discourse now comes to concern information as such, that is not just all persons, their cultivation, well-being and social interactions, not just animals, plants and their proper natural life, but also anything that exists, from paintings and books to stars and stones; anything that may or will exist, like future generations; and anything that was but is no more, like our ancestors. Unlike other non-standard ethics, IE is more impartial and universal—or one may say less ethically biased—because it brings to ultimate completion the process of enlargement of the concept of what may count as a centre of information, no matter whether physically implemented or not.[98]

Following the innovations of bio- and environmental ethics, Floridi expands the scope of moral philosophy by altering its focus and lowering the threshold for inclusion. What makes someone or something a moral patient, deserving of some level of ethical consideration (no matter how minimal), is that it exists as a coherent body of information. This is a promising proposal, because it not only is able to incorporate a wider range of possible objects (living organisms, organizations, works of art, machines, historical entities, etc.) but expands the scope of ethical thinking to include those others who have been, for one reason or another, traditionally excluded from moral consideration. In fact, in focusing attention on the patient of the action, Floridi's proposal comes as close as any analytic philosopher has to approximating the "ethics of otherness" that has been the hallmark of continental thinkers like Levinas. Despite this, however, IE still runs up against significant structural and philosophical difficulties. First, in shifting emphasis from an agent-oriented to a patient-oriented ethics, Floridi simply inverts the two terms of a traditional binary structure. If classic ethical thinking has been organized, for better or worse, by an interest in the character and actions of the agent at the expense of the patient, IE endeavors, following the innovations modeled by bioethics, to reorient things by placing emphasis on the depreciated term. This maneuver is, quite literally, a revolutionary proposal, because it inverts or "turns over" the traditional arrangement. Inversion, however, is rarely in and by itself a satisfactory mode of critical intervention. As Nietzsche, Derrida, and other poststructuralists have pointed out, the inversion of a binary opposition actually does little or nothing to challenge the fundamental structure of the system in question. In fact, inversion preserves and maintains the traditional structure, albeit in an inverted form. The effect of this on IE is registered by Kenneth Einar Himma, who, in an assessment of Floridi's argument, demonstrates that a concern for the patient is nothing more than the flip-side of good-old, agent-oriented ethics. "To say that an entity X has moral standing (i.e., is a moral patient) is, at bottom, simply to say that it is possible for a moral agent to commit a wrong against X. Thus, X has moral standing if and only if (1) some moral agent has at least one duty regarding the treatment of X and (2) that duty is owed to X."[99] According to Himma's analysis, IE's patient-oriented ethics is not that different from traditional ethics; it simply looks at the agent/patient couple from the other side. Levinas, by contrast, does in fact introduce something entirely different. Instead of simply flipping the relative positions occupied by the agent and patient in the binary structure that has characterized traditional forms of moral theorizing, he considers the ethical experience of an Other that exceeds and remains exterior to these logical distinctions. "Experience, the idea of infinity," Levinas writes, "occurs in the relationship with the other. The idea of infinity is the social relationship. This relationship consists in approaching an absolutely exterior being. The infinity of this being, which one can therefore not contain, guarantees and constitutes this exteriority. It is not equivalent to the distance between a subject and an object."[100] In this way, Levinas's "ethics of otherness" is concerned with an Other who is not defined, as Floridi's patient is, as the mere flip-side of the agent or self-same; it is entirely and radically otherwise.

Second, IE not only alters the orientation of ethics but also enlarges its scope by reducing the minimum requirements for inclusion. It replaces both the exclusive anthropocentric and biocentric theories with an "ontocentric" one, which is, by comparison, much more inclusive. In doing so, however, IE simply replaces one form of centrism with another. This is, as Levinas points out, really nothing different; it is more of the same. "Western philosophy has most often been an ontology: a reduction of the other to the same by interposition of a middle or neutral term that ensures the comprehension of being."[101] According to Levinas's analysis, the SOP (standard operating procedure) of Western philosophy has been the reduction of difference. In fact, philosophy has, at least since the time of Aristotle, usually explained and dealt with difference by finding below and behind apparent variety some common denominator that is and remains irreducibly the same. Anthropocentric ethics, for example, posits a common humanity that underlies and substantiates the perceived differences in race, gender, ethnicity, class, etc. Likewise, biocentric ethics assumes that there is a common value in life itself, which subtends all forms of available biological diversity. And in the ontocentric theory of IE, it is being, the very matter of ontology itself, that underlies and supports all apparent differentiation. As Himma describes it, "every existing entity, whether sentient or non-sentient, living or non-living, natural or artificial, has some minimal moral worth . . . in virtue of its existence."[102] But as Levinas argues, this desire to articulate a universal, common element effectively reduces the difference of the other to what is ostensibly the same. "Perceived in this way," Levinas writes, "philosophy would be engaged in reducing to the same all that is opposed to it as other."[103] In taking an ontocentric approach, therefore, IE reduces all difference to a minimal common factor that is supposedly shared by any and all entities. Although this approach provides for a more inclusive kind of "centrism," it still utilizes a centrist approach and, as such, necessarily reduces difference to some preselected common element. None of this, however, should be taken to mean that Levinas simply trumps Floridi, which would ignore the fact that Floridi's work questions and complicates Levinas's adherence to humanism. What it does mean is that the innovation that has been ascribed to IE may not be as unconventional and different from the mainstream of moral philosophy as was initially advertised.

From Means to an End

> The machine is not an *it* to be animated, worshipped, and dominated. The machine is us, our processes, an aspect of our embodiment. We can be responsible for machines; *they* do not dominate or threaten us. We are responsible for boundaries; we are they.[104]
> —Donna Haraway

In *Grounding for the Metaphysics of Morals*, Immanuel Kant introduced the following elaboration of the categorical imperative: "So act as to use humanity, both in your own person and in the person of every other, always at the same time as an end, never simply as a means."[105] According to this particular formulation, every human person, including oneself, should be treated as an end in and of him/herself and not as a means by which to achieve some other outcome. H. J. Paton, in his analysis of this statement, remarks that if strictly applied, "this formula, like all others, should cover all rational beings as such; but since the only rational beings with whom we are acquainted are men, we are bidden to respect men as men, or men as rational beings."[106] One aspect of the machine question asks whether and to what extent the machine, as at least another kind of rational being, should or should not be included in what Kant terms "the kingdom of ends." The machine question, however, is not only interested in inclusion versus exclusion. Despite initial appearances, it is not simply interested in documenting the exclusion of the machine from the domain of moral philosophy. Nor is it concerned, like machine, android, or information ethics, with formulating criteria and strategies for its inclusion. The machine question is certainly interested in both these aspects, but it also and necessarily involves more. In particular, it is and must be concerned, following the examples supplied by poststructuralism, with the ethical complications and side-effects that are imposed by the deployment and use of the binary pairing of inclusion/exclusion in these and all other moral considerations.

Obviously exclusion is a real problem. As is evident from the history of philosophy, ethics has been an exclusive undertaking. For most of us, it is not news that moral philosophy has been and, in many cases, continues to be anthropocentric. At the center of Western ethical theories there has been the common assumption and unquestioned validation of the 'άνθρωπος—the 'άνθρωπος who bears a responsibility to other 'άνθρωποι. This anthropocentrism is not only apparent in those ethical writings that Levinas has critiqued under the moniker "philosophy of the same,"[107] the list of which reads like a who's who of Western philosophy—Plato, Aristotle, Descartes, Kant, Hegel, and even Heidegger. But it is also apparent in those other ethical theories, like that of Levinas, that attempt to articulate an ethics of radical otherness. The problem in all of this is, of course, the fact that the concept of the *human* has been arbitrary, flexible, and not altogether consistent. At different times, the membership criteria for club-anthropos have been defined in such a way as to not only exclude but justify the exclusion of others, e.g., barbarians, women, Jews, and people of color. As membership in the club has slowly and not without considerable resistance been extended to these excluded populations, there remain other, apparently more fundamental, exclusions, most notably that of the animal and the machine. And even the recent innovations introduced under the banner animal rights, although securing some form of access by non-human animals, has continued to redline the machine. This exclusion is theoretically unjustified. Because the animal and machine, at least since the time of Descartes, share a common form of alterity, the one cannot be admitted without also opening the door to the other. So despite all the innovations in moral philosophy by which both human and nonhuman others have been extended some claim to moral standing, the exclusion of the machine is and remains the last socially accepted prejudice.

In addition to this theoretical inconsistency, the exclusion of the machine also encounters practical difficulties. ICT, despite concerted efforts to restrict such technology to the customary status of instrument, tool, or medium, no longer functions in this manner. Even if we remain, as many researchers do, uncertain about the practicality of "strong AI," there are in fact machines that are able to converse with human users, are designed to make autonomous or semi-autonomous decisions, and are capable of performing many of the activities that have traditionally been restricted to the *animal rationale*. For Norbert Wiener, the progenitor of the science of cybernetics, these developments fundamentally alter the social landscape, introducing new social agents and new responsibilities: "It is the thesis of this book," Wiener writes at the beginning of the curiously titled *The Human Use of Human Beings*, "that society can only be understood through a study of the messages and the communication facilities which belong to it; and that in the future development of these messages and communication facilities, messages between man and machines, between machines and man, and between machine and machine, are destined to play an ever-increasing part."[108] In the social relationships of the not-too-distant future (we need to recall that Wiener wrote this in 1950) the machine will no longer be an instrument or medium through which human users communicate with each other. Instead the machine will occupy the position of another social actor with whom one communicates and interacts. Consequently, it is no longer practical to define the machine as an instrument that is to be animated and used, more or less responsibly, by a human being. It is, on the contrary, an other who confronts these human users, calls to them, and requires an appropriate response. ICTs are no longer a mere means to an end, they too begin to look as if they have some claim to be recognized as legitimate participants in "the kingdom of ends."

The exclusion of the machine from the proper domain of ethics is certainly an ethical problem. But inclusion, as its mere flip-side and dialectical other, appears to be no less problematic. Despite the recent political and intellectual cachet that has accrued to the word, "inclusion" is not without significant ethical complications and consequences. The inclusion of the other, whether another human being, the animal, the environment, the machine, or something else, always and inevitably runs up against the same difficulty, namely the reduction of difference to the same. In order to extend the boundaries of moral philosophy to traditionally excluded others, philosophers have argued for progressively more inclusive definitions of what qualifies someone or something for ethical consideration. That is, they have continually shifted the level of abstraction by which two different things come to be recognized as essentially the same and therefore deserving of each other's respect. Anthropocentrism, for example, situates the human at the center of ethics and admits into moral consideration anyone who is able to meet the basic criteria of what has been decided to comprise the human. Animocentrism focuses attention on the animal and extends consideration to any organism that meets the defining criteria of animality. Biocentrism goes one step further in the process of abstraction; it defines life as the common denominator and admits into consideration anything and everything that can be said to be alive. And ontocentrism completes the progression by incorporating into moral consideration anything that actually exists, had existed, or potentially exists. All of these innovations, despite their differences in focus, employ a similar maneuver. That is, they redefine the center of moral consideration in order to describe progressively larger circles that come to encompass a wider range of possible participants. Although there are and will continue to be considerable debates about who or what should define the center and who or what is or is not included, this debate is not the problem. The problem rests in the strategy itself. In taking a centrist approach, these different ethical theories endeavor to identify what is essentially the same in a phenomenal diversity of individuals. Consequently, they include others by effectively stripping away and reducing differences. This approach, although having the appearance of being increasingly more inclusive, immediately effaces the unique alterity of others and turns them into more of the same, instituting what Slavoj Žižek calls the structure of the Möbius band: "At the very heart of Otherness, we encounter the other side of the Same."[109] In making this argument, however, it should be noted that the criticism has itself employed what it criticizes. (Or to put it another way, the articulation of what is the matter is itself already and unavoidably involved with the material of its articulation.) In focusing attention on what is essentially the same in these various forms of moral centrism, the analysis does exactly what it charges—it identifies a common feature that underlies apparent diversity and effectively reduces a multiplicity of differences to what is the same. Pointing this out, however, does not invalidate the conclusion but demonstrates, not only in what is said but also in what is done, the questionable operations that are already involved in any attempt at articulating inclusion.

Exclusion is a problem because it calls attention to and concentrates on what is different despite similarities. Inclusion is a problem because it emphasizes similarities at the expense of apparent differences. Consequently, the one is the inverse of the other, or, to put it in colloquial terms, they are two sides of one coin. As long as ethical debate and innovation remain involved with and structured by these two possibilities, little or nothing will change. Exclusion will be identified and challenged, as it has been in the discourse of animal rights and bioethics, by calls for greater inclusiveness and ethical theories that are able to accommodate others. At the same time, inclusion will be challenged, as it has in critical responses to the project of animal rights, for its reduction of difference and the erasure of the otherness that it had sought to respect and accommodate in the first place. What is needed, therefore, is a third alternative that does not simply oppose exclusion by inclusion or vice versa. Fortunately examples of this alternative approach can already be found in both philosophy and the field of AI. In *The Inclusion of the Other*, for example, Jürgen Habermas (1998) proposes what amounts to a nonreductive universalism that is designed to be highly sensitive to differences: "The equal respect for everyone else demanded by a moral universalism sensitive to difference thus takes the form of a *nonleveling* and *nonappropriating inclusion* of the other in his *otherness*."[110] In proposing "a nonleveling and nonappropriating inclusion," Habermas attempts to identify an alternative to · the terms that have traditionally structured moral philosophy. This third term, which can only be articulated in language by using what appears to be contradictory predicates, exceeds and intentionally violates the either/or logic of inclusion/exclusion. A similar maneuver has been proposed in writings of Levinas. In fact, it is Levinas who, more so than any other thinker in the Western tradition, provides what is arguably the most elaborate and sustained consideration of this problem. Levinasian philosophy not only is critical of the traditional tropes and traps of Western ontology but proposes an ethics of radical otherness that deliberately resists and interrupts the metaphysical gesture par excellence, that is, the reduction of difference to the same. Despite these promising innovations, however, one needs to be aware of and to work against the persistent and irreducible humanism that has been shown to pervade and underlie the work of Levinas, and those others who, following his example, endeavor to address otherness. We must, therefore, as Derrida once wrote of Georges Bataille's exceedingly careful engagement with the thought of Hegel, follow Levinas to the end, "to the point of agreeing with him against himself" and of wresting his discoveries from the limited interpretations that he had provided.[111] One way to facilitate this process is to permit communication between and to work deliberately in excess of the two main divisions that currently organize philosophical discourse—the decision that, for better or worse, parses the discipline into analytic and continental varieties. On the one hand, analytic theorists working in both animal rights philosophy and information ethics have provided compelling arguments by which to challenge and to undermine the tradition of anthropocentrism that has been dominant in ethics. They have, however, done so at the expense of erecting other, no less problematic centrisms and, in the process, have often repeated in practice what they had opposed in theory. Continental theorists, on the other hand, have effectively criticized the philosophy of the same that is at the center of all centrisms and have successfully described the structure and exigencies of an ethics that is oriented otherwise. At the same time, however, they have done so on the basis and in the name of what remains an essentially unquestioned validation of the human and the traditions of humanism. If ever there was a time and a reason for the one side to take seriously the innovations of the other, it is in the face of the machine and in response to the machine question.

Finally, attention to another form of otherness that is not simply more of the same has also been introduced and exemplified in recent attempts to account for machine intelligence. According to Rodney Brooks, "the most important change in AI happened in the 1980s when some people realized that the model of reasoning used in AI was very different from what happens inside the heads of people, very different at any level of abstraction used for the descriptions. Such differences do not invalidate the nonhuman approaches—airplanes are good examples of very useful machines that operate very differently from the way real birds operate. But the realization in AI opened up new ways of doing things and new avenues to go down."[112] As long as the project of AI is pursued, as it had been for many years since its inception in the 1950s, as an attempt to get computers to think just like or better than human beings, then it is an undertaking that will continually fall short of expectations. There is, in fact, no machine that can "think" the same way the human entity thinks, and all attempts to get machines to simulate the activity of human thought processes, no matter what level of abstraction is utilized, have lead to considerable frustration or outright failure. If, however, one recognizes, as many AI researchers have since the 1980s, that machine intelligence may take place and be organized completely otherwise, then a successful "thinking machine" is not just possible but may already be extant. Following this precedent, we can say that just as there are other orders of intelligence that need to be accounted for in ways that do not simply identify similarities to ourselves, there may also be alternative moral subjects and ethical capabilities that need to be understood and addressed otherwise. In the end, therefore, it can be said that the machine question does not simply argue for a repositioning of the machine from its customary status as a means (an instrument, medium, or tool) to an end (another subject worthy of some level of moral respect). Instead the machine question puts in question the entire system of ethics and the mechanisms by which it has until now successfully differentiated and distinguished what is a means from who qualifies as an end. To paraphrase Floridi, and to agree with his analysis in excess of the restricted interpretations he gives it, the machine question not only adds interesting new dimensions to old problems, but leads us to rethink, methodologically, the very grounds on which our ethical positions are based.[113]

Chapter Seven

Concluding Otherwise

> Hegel will ask, no doubt rightly, if a preface in which
> the project of a philosophical enterprise is formulated is
> not superfluous or even obscurantist. . . . Should we not
> think with as much precaution of the possibility of a
> conclusion or a closure of the philosophical discourse?[1]
> —Emmanuel Levinas

G. W. F. Hegel, it is well known, had trouble at the beginning. He agonized over, or his published writings had at least recorded a considerable concern with, introductions, prefaces, forewords, and all forms of what Derrida has called the textual *hors d'oeuvre*.[2] The cause of the problem was simple: how could one legitimately say anything about the science of philosophy outside of and in advance of the science itself? Or as Hegel himself describes it in that often quoted passage from the preface to the *Phenomenology*: "Whatever can be properly said of philosophy in a preface—a historical statement of trends and points of view, its general contents and results, a string of random assertions and assurances about truth—cannot be accepted as the manner and way by which to present philosophical truth."[3] The converse, however, did not appear to be a problem. Say what you like about Hegelian dialectic, one thing is conclusive; it never worried about or was concerned with the end. It always knew, for better or worse,[4] where it was going, how it was going to get there, and what would be its outcome. Hegelianism was never, as one says in English, "open-ended," lacking closure, or exposed to the charge of being "inconclusive."

Unlike Hegelian philosophy, *Thinking Otherwise* has trouble with and at the *end*, which should be no big surprise given the fact that the investigation takes aim at and seeks to intervene in all forms of dialectical thinking. This is not, it

151

is important to emphasize, some literary pretense. That is, it is not a clever rhetorical maneuver whereby the conclusion to the book would be concerned with and would address the difficulty of composing its own conclusion. It is instead, as it was for Hegel and his concern with the preface, something that is required for and necessitated by the project at hand. To put it bluntly, because the task of thinking otherwise constitutes, as demonstrated in the six preceding chapters, an endlessly self-reflective practice and interminable analysis, it cannot end or even propose conclusive statements without the risk of invalidating the entire enterprise. Consequently, *Thinking Otherwise* cannot and does not achieve or terminate in some definite end-point, objective, or goal. It is, in the end, nothing like a destination. Instead it constitutes and must remain an open-ended process. Like deconstruction, hacking, poststructural analysis, and the other alternative transactions to which it is indebted, the project of thinking otherwise comprises a flexible, dynamic, and necessarily ceaseless engagement with its subject matter. For this reason, whatever can be said about this process at the end of the path that has just been covered will be otherwise than what is expected from or acceptable for what is usually called a conclusion. Instead of wrapping things up with definitive solutions and outcomes, this "conclusion" will be different. Such a conclusion—assuming we decide to retain this word, which is not entirely settled even at this point—is necessarily inconclusive and deliberately unsettling. It is, in every conceivable way, an open ending. For this reason, the four summary statements that follow, although occupying what would have been the place of a conclusion, are not conclusive in the usual sense of the word. They do not complete the analysis or enclose the investigation in something approximating a closed figure. Instead they open onto what is necessarily the open-ended project and ongoing task that confronts any attempt at thinking otherwise.

1. Binary opposition is not optional. The logic of binary opposition is not something that is limited to the digital computer and related information and communication technology (ICT). It also organizes, informs, and regulates our thinking. Investigations and criticisms of ICT, as we have seen, deploy and proceed according to an either/or logic that arranges a complex network of conceptual dichotomies: utopia/dystopia, immaterial/material, information haves/information have-nots, medicine/poison, true/false, human/machine, good/evil, etc. This particular structure is not capricious. It is, as Nietzsche had pointed out at the beginning of *Beyond Good and Evil*, the necessary assumption and fundamental faith that underlies and empowers all modes of philosophical thinking, up to and including that by which one would endeavor to question and to criticize it as such.[5] Consequently, organizing things in terms of binary opposition, whether indicated by the name "dualism," "oppositional logic," "dialectic," "digital," "dichotomy," or something else, is not a choice or a matter of individual volition. One does not, for example, decide to think in binary terms or not, which is obviously just one more binary opposition. We cannot seek, for instance, to occupy a position outside binary logic, for the very distinction and difference between the inside and outside is already stipulated in binary terms. We cannot, then, say anything about, oppose, or even question binary opposition without already participating in and utilizing the very thing that was to be submitted to scrutiny. The binary form, for whatever reason, is not optional.

2. Binary opposition is not neutral. Although binary opposition is not optional, there are good reasons to remain skeptical of and to question its hegemony. The binary, in whatever form it appears, has the effect of dividing between and sorting things into one of two possibilities. These two terms, however, are not situated on par with each other. They are not involved in what one would call an equitable and unbiased relationship. Instead one of the two terms is always given precedence and, as a result, not only rules over but determines the other as its negative and deficient counterpart. As Derrida has explained it, "in a classical philosophical opposition we are not dealing with the peaceful coexistence of a *vis-à-vis*, but rather with a violent hierarchy. One of the two terms governs the other (axiologically, logically, etc.), or has the upper hand."[6] This is, on the one hand, entirely rational and justified. We often define something by differentiating it from what it is not. Falsity is the negation of truth. What is artificial is not natural. And evil is the privation or lack of good. In fact, if structuralism is correct, language is inextricably involved in making and marking such differences. On the other hand, these hierarchical arrangements, no matter how useful and expedient for making sense of and describing the world, have considerable and potentially troubling consequences. In positioning one term over and against the other, decisions are made concerning what is valued and what is not. Even the seemingly indifferent 0 and 1 that comprise binary information encodes, at least for our purposes, moral decisions: no as opposed to yes, off as opposed to on, false as opposed to true, and nothing as opposed to something. Consequently, binary oppositions are neither impartial nor indifferent. They institute difference and this difference always makes a difference. In some cases, the effect of differentiation is minimal, as when the figure 0 is distinguished from 1 in a string of binary code. In other cases, it is considerable and broad, as when immaterial bits of data are distinguished from their material form, the information have-nots come to be defined as deficient in comparison to the information haves, the virtual is differentiated from and understood to be the opposite of the real, or the animal and machine are excluded from moral consideration because they are nonhuman. What is at stake in binary logic is not simply a manner of conveniently dividing up the world. Binary pairings, no matter where they occur or how they come to be arranged, always and already impose hierarchies that make exclusive and prejudicial decisions about others.

3. Resistance is futile. Because of these problems and complications, binary opposition should be questioned, challenged, and perhaps even surpassed. Unfortunately this is easier said than done. All the traditional strategies of resistance—contradiction, inversion, revolution—are always and necessarily ineffectual. Like the Borg of the *Star Trek* franchise, binary logic cannot be resisted with any amount of oppositional force, precisely because it is opposition that fuels the binary structure. Resistance is, therefore, futile. Or as Baudrillard characterizes it: "It is impossible to destroy the system by a contradiction-based logic or by reversing the balance of forces—in short, by a direct, dialectical revolution affecting the economic or political infrastructure. Everything that produces contradiction or a balance of forces or energy in general merely feeds back into the system and drives it on."[7] This is the thoroughly insidious nature of the problem: criticizing binary opposition by deploying the usual strategies of contradiction, reversal, revolution, and even thoughtful compromise not only does little or nothing to challenge the dominant system but is actually involved with and strengthens what one had wanted to criticize in the first place. This does not, however, mean that binary opposition is simply beyond critical inquiry or constitutes some kind of inescapable *fait accompli*. It does not, it is important to note, simply disarm or render impotent any and all forms of intervention, whether political, social, philosophical, or otherwise. What it does mean is that the critical engagement will need to operate in excess of mere opposition and be structured in a way that is significantly and disturbingly different. What is needed, as each chapter of *Thinking Otherwise* demonstrates in the case of ICT, is a kind of alternative transaction that inhabits the systems of binary opposition, learns the rules of its game through careful attention to its different operations and maneuvers, and institutes a deliberate and disruptive reprogramming that causes it to begin to function otherwise and that exposes it to alternatives that necessarily remain in excess of its admittedly limited comprehension. We are, then, to repurpose that well-known and often quoted statement of Audre Lorde, in the curious situation of needing to use the master's tools to dismantle the master's house.[8] And, to complicate matters, there is no one right way to do this. There is no single method of thinking otherwise that could be rigorously defined, applied, and pursued. Instead the different strategies of critical intervention turn out to be highly dependent on the material and subject matter in which they are deployed, and what turns out to work in one circumstance may not be at all effective in another. This is not, it must be emphasized, a procedural or methodological deficiency. It can only be justifiably described as "deficient" from the perspective of a certain understanding—that must also be submitted to critical investigation—that retains without question or hesitation the differentiation of method from application, theory from practice, and general from specific.

4. Finally there is no finality. Because thinking otherwise does not constitute a method or theory in the usual sense of the words, there are no prior assurances or final guarantees. Intervening in the binary oppositions that already organize the logic and the λόγος of ICT must be undertaken and pursued without the kind of prescribed direction, teleology, or eschatology that has been associated with traditional forms of thinking and argumentation. Instead it can only take place as a kind of "interminable methodological movement"[9] that must continually submit its own results and innovations to further scrutiny. This is not, it is important to note, just some cute poststructural postmodern deconstructionist cop-out. It is, first and foremost, the necessary condition and unavoidable outcome of the project. If binary logic is not optional and resistance to it is effectively futile, then any oppositional or critical position, no matter how well-articulated and -contextualized, is immediately and unavoidably exposed to the risk of reassimilation. "The hierarchy of dual oppositions," as Derrida has pointed out, "always reestablishes itself."[10] Once again, Hegel, who has an uncanny way of anticipating every move, had already predicted this complication: "But the man who flees is not yet free: in fleeing he is still conditioned by that from which he flees."[11] If, as poststructuralists have argued, Western systems of meaning are informed and underwritten by a matrix of logical dichotomies, then any meaningful statement, any critique that can and does make sense, is already and necessarily involved in and circumscribed by this particular structure. For this reason, thinking otherwise cannot simply and once and for all escape the dominance that has been imposed by binary opposition. Because the binary logic on which and in which it works already conditions and controls the available modes of critical intervention and effective communication, it must continually submit its own movement and innovation to criticism. This extreme and potentially monstrous form of self-reflectivity dissimulates the speculative science introduced by Hegel with one important and irreducible difference; it does not come preprogrammed with an exit strategy. It is and must be an interminable struggle that occupies the space of thinking and works within its structures to make it articulate, however tardy and incomplete, what necessarily remains in excess of its grasp. In the end, what *Thinking Otherwise* yields, at the risk of being repetitive (but then again, what would an interminable self-reflection be if not a kind of "repetition"?), are not answers, solutions, or even more accurate descriptions of extant problems. Instead each chapter individually and collectively opens within the fabric of ICT discourse an infinite abyss . . . an abyss that is not in any way negative or lacking . . . an abyss that cannot be filled up or exhausted with any amount of effort . . . an abyss that exposes thinking to opportunities, challenges, and subjects that are and remain otherwise.

Notes

Introduction

1. Emmanuel Levinas, *Totality and Infinity*, trans. Alphonso Lingis (Pittsburgh: Duquesne University Press, 1969), 21.
2. Philip Brey, "The Ethics of Representation and Action in Virtual Reality," *Ethics and Information Technology* 1.1 (March 1999): 8.
3. Blay R. Whitby, "The Virtual Sky is not the Limit—The Ethical Implications of Virtual Reality," *Intelligent Tutoring Media* 4.1 (1993): 24.
4. See, for instance, Craig A. Anderson and Brad J. Bushman, "Effects of Violent Video Games on Aggressive Behavior, Aggressive Cognition, Aggressive Affect, Physiological Arousal, and Prosocial Behavior: A Meta-Analytic Review of the Scientific Literature," *Psychological Science* 12.5 (September 2001): 353–359; Craig A. Anderson and Karen E. Dill, "Video Games and Aggressive Thoughts, Feelings, and Behavior in the Laboratory and in Life," *Journal of Personality and Social Psychology* 78.4 (2000): 772–790; Craig. A. Anderson and C. M. Ford, "Affect of the Game Player: Short-term Effects of Highly and Mildly Aggressive Video Games," *Personality and Social Psychology Bulletin* 12.4 (December 1986): 390–402; Lillian Bensley and Juliet Van Eenwyk, "Video Games and Real Life Aggression: Review of Literature," *Journal of Adolescent Health* 29.4 (October 2001): 244–257; Karen E. Dill and Jody C. Dill, "Video Game Violence: A Review of the Empirical Literature," *Aggression and Violent Behavior* 3.4 (Winter 1998): 407–428; Haejung Paik and George Comstock, "The Effects of Television Violence on Antisocial Behavior: A Meta-Analysis," *Communication Research* 21.4 (August 1994): 516–546; John L. Sherry, "The Effect of Violent Video Games on Aggression: A Meta-Analysis," *Human Communication Research* 27.3 (July 2001): 409–431.
5. Rob Riddell, "Doom Goes to War," *Wired* 5.4 (April, 1997): 114–118, 164-166.
6. Brey, 8.
7. Seymour Feshbach, "The Catharsis Hypothesis and Some Consequences of Interaction with Aggressive and Neutral Play Objects," *Journal of Personality* 24, (June 1956): 449–462; Barrie Gunter, "Psychological Effects of Video Games,"

in *Handbook of Computer Game Studies*, ed. Joost Raessens and Jeffrey Goldstein (Cambridge, MA: MIT Press, 2005), 150.

8. Whitby, 24.

9. See, for instance, Sandra L. Calvert and Siu-Lan Tan, "Impact of Virtual Reality on Young Adult's Physiological Arousal and Aggressive Thoughts: Interaction Versus Observation," *Journal of Applied Developmental Psychology* 15.1 (January–March 1994): 125–139; Daniel Graybill, Janice R. Kirsch, and Edward D. Esselman, "Effects of Playing Violent Versus Non-violent Video Games on the Aggressive Ideation of Aggressive and Non-aggressive Children," *Child Study Journal* 15.3 (1985): 199–205; G. I. Kestenbaum and L. Weinstein, "Personality, Psychopathology, and Developmental Issues in Male Adolescent Video Game Use," *Journal of the American Academy of Child Psychiatry* 24.3 (May 1985): 325–337; Steven B. Silvern and Peter A. Williamson, "The Effects of Video Game Play on Young Children's Aggression, Fantasy, and Prosocial Behavior," *Journal of Applied Developmental Psychology* 8.4 (October–December 1987): 453–462; Derek Scott, "The Effect of Video Games on Feelings of Aggression," *The Journal of Psychology* 129.2 (March 1995): 121–132.

10. Whitby, 25.

11. Sherry, 409.

12. Whitby, 25.

13. Ibid.

14. Sherry, 427.

15. Rodolphe Gasché, *The Tain of the Mirror: Derrida and the Philosophy of Reflection* (Cambridge, MA: Harvard University Press, 1986), 121.

16. Nicholas Negroponte, *Being Digital* (New York: Vintage, 1995), 3.

17. Plato, *Phaedrus*, trans. Harold N. Fowler (Cambridge, MA: Harvard University Press, 1990), 278c.

18. U.S. Dept. of Commerce, National Telecommunications and Information Administration (NTIA), *Falling Through the Net II: New Data on the Digital Divide* (Washington, DC: U.S. Department of Commerce, 1998) and *Falling Through the Net: Defining the Digital Divide* (Washington, DC: U.S. Department of Commerce, 1999).

19. Andy Wachowski and Larry Wachowski, directors, *The Matrix* (Burbank, CA: Warner Home Video, 1999).

20. Avital Ronell, *Crack Wars: Literature, Addiction, Mania* (Lincoln, NB: University of Nebraska Press, 1992), 78.

21. Slavoj Žižek, "Reloaded Revolutions," in *More Matrix and Philosophy: Revolutions and Reloaded Decoded*, ed. William Irwin (Chicago: Open Court, 2005), 198. Interestingly, Žižek makes this comment at the beginning of an essay that is included in William Irwin's *More Matrix and Philosophy*, an anthology that does in fact take seriously the philosophical underpinnings of the *Matrix* trilogy.

22. Christopher Grau, ed., *Philosophers Explore the Matrix* (Oxford: Oxford University Press, 2005); William Irwin, ed., *The Matrix and Philosophy* (Chicago: Open Court, 2002) and *More Matrix and Philosophy: Revolutions and Reloaded Decoded* (Chicago: Open Court, 2005); Matt Lawrence, *Like a Splinter in Your Mind: The Philosophy behind the Matrix Trilogy* (Oxford: Blackwell Publishing, 2004); Glenn Yeffeth, ed., *Taking the Red Pill: Science, Philosophy and Religion in The Matrix* (Dallas, TX: Benbella Books, 2003).

23. Žižek, 199.

24. Emmanuel Levinas, *Totality and Infinity*, trans. Alphonso Lingis (Pittsburgh: Duquesne University Press, 1969); Emmanuel Levinas, *Otherwise Than Being or Beyond Essence*, trans. Alphonso Lingis (The Hague: Martinus Nijhoff Publishers, 1981).

25. Peter Steiner, "Dog cartoon," *The New Yorker*, 5 July 1993, 61.

26. See, for instance, Roger F. Fidler, *Mediamorphosis: Understanding New Media* (Thousand Oaks, CA: Pine Forge Press, 1997); Richard Holeton, ed., *Composing Cyberspace: Identity, Community, and Knowledge in the Electronic Age* (New York: McGraw Hill, 1998); Sara Kiesler, ed., *Culture of the Internet* (Mahwah, NJ: Lawrence Erlbaum Associates, 1997); William J. Mitchell, *City of Bits: Space, Place, and the Infobahn* (Cambridge: MIT Press, 1995); Geoffrey Nunberg, "Prefixed Out," commentary on *Fresh Air*, WHYY radio, 17 May 2002. Transcript available at http://www-csli.stanford.edu/~nunberg/cyber.html; Diana Saco, *Cybering Democracy: Public Space and the Internet* (Minneapolis, MN: University of Minnesota Press, 2002).

27. Holeton, 111.

28. Allucquère Rosanna Stone, *The War of Desire and Technology at the Close of the Mechanical Age* (Cambridge, MA: MIT Press, 1995); Sherry Turkle, *Life on the Screen: Identity in the Age of the Internet* (New York: Simon & Schuster, 1995).

29. Stone, 16.

Chapter One

1. Peter Lurie, "The Rush to Judgment: Binary Thinking in a Digital Age," *ctheory. net* (30 March 2004). http://www.ctheory.net/text_file.asp?pick=416.

2. Michael Heim, *Virtual Realism* (New York: Oxford University Press, 1998), 42.

3. Ibid.

4. Derek Stanovsky, "Virtual Reality," in *The Blackwell Guide to the Philosophy of Computing and Information*, ed. Luciano Floridi (Oxford: Blackwell Publishing, 2004), 168.

5. Jonathan Culler, *On Deconstruction: Theory and Criticism after Structuralism* (Ithaca, NY: Cornell University Press, 1982), 98–99.

6. Mark Taylor, *About Religion: Economies of Faith in Virtual Culture* (Chicago: University of Chicago Press, 1999), 102.

7. Ferdinand de Saussure, *Course in General Linguistics*, trans. Wade Baskin (London: Peter Owen, 1959), 120.

8. Daniel Chandler, *Semiotics for Beginners* (1994). http://www.aber.ac.uk/media/Documents/S4B/semiotic.html.

9. Peter Elbow, "The Uses of Binary Thinking," *JAC* 13.1 (1993): 51.

10. Lurie, 5.

11. Elbow, 54.

12. Jean Baudrillard, *Selected Writings*, ed. Mark Poster (Stanford, CA: Stanford University Press, 1988), 185.

13. Michael Benedikt, ed., *Cyberspace: First Steps* (Cambridge, MA: MIT Press, 1993); Steven G. Jones, ed., *CyberSociety 2.0: Computer-Mediated Communication and Community* (London: Sage, 1994); David Porter, ed., *Internet Culture* (New York:

Routledge, 1997); David Bell and Barbara M. Kennedy, eds., *The Cybercultures Reader* (New York: Routledge, 2000).

14. Michael Benedikt, "Introduction," in *Cyberspace: First Steps*, ed. Michael Benedikt (Cambridge, MA: MIT Press, 1993), 16.

15. Mark Dery, "Flame Wars," in *Flame Wars: The Discourse of Cyberculture*, ed. Mark Dery (Durham, NC: Duke University Press, 1994), 3.

16. Margaret Wertheim, *The Pearly Gates of Cyberspace: A History of Space from Dante to the Internet* (New York: W. W. Norton & Company, 1999), 19.

17. Ibid., 18.

18. Neil Postman, *Technopoly: The Surrender of Culture to Technology* (New York: Vintage Books, 1993), xii.

19. Mark Slouka, *War of the Worlds: Cyberspace and the High-Tech Assault on Reality* (New York: Basic Books, 1995), 1.

20. Hubert L. Dreyfus, *On the Internet* (New York: Routledge, 2001), 93. Although Dreyfus recalls and leverages the Platonic indictment of writing in his analysis, he unfortunately references the wrong dialogue. "After all, in the 'Phaedo' Plato famously objected to writing as opposed to speech, because, as he pointed out, writing reduces the richness of communication since it makes it impossible to read the speaker's tone and bodily posture" (92).

21. In *Building a Bridge to the 18th Century* (New York: Vintage Books, 1999), Postman outs himself as a neoluddite, making the following confession: "I write my books with pen and paper, because I have always done it that way and enjoy doing so. I do not have a computer. The Internet strikes me as a mere distraction. I do not have voice mail or call-waiting, both of which I regard as uncivil" (55).

22. Slouka, 7.

23. Elbow, 53.

24. Ibid., 51.

25. Ibid., 52.

26. Ibid., 53.

27. Heim, 43.

28. Ibid., 44.

29. Andrew L. Shapiro, *The Control Revolution: How the Internet Is Putting Individuals in Charge and Changing the World We Know* (New York: PublicAffairs, 1999), xiii.

30. Ibid., xv.

31. Ibid., xiv.

32. Ibid., xiv–xv.

33. Andrew Calcutt, dust jacket to *White Noise: An A–Z of the Contradictions in Cyberculture* (New York: Palgrave Macmillan, 1998).

34. Marshall and Eric McLuhan, *Laws of Media: The New Science* (Toronto: University of Toronto Press, 1988), viii.

35. Ibid., 7.

36. Ibid., 127.

37. Ibid., 141.

38. Ibid., 129.

39. Heim, 167–168.

40. Aristotle, *The Nicomachean Ethics*, trans. H. Rackham (Cambridge, MA: Harvard University Press, 1982), II.ii.6–7.

41. Elbow, 57.

42. Heim, 44.

43. Elbow, 54.

44. Barbara Cassin, ed., *Vocabulaire européen des philosophies* (Paris: Le Robert & Seuil, 2004), 306.

45. Peter Lunenfeld, "Screen Grabs: The Digital Dialectic and New Media Theory," in *The Digital Dialectic: New Essays on New Media*, ed. Peter Lunenfeld (Cambridge, MA: MIT Press, 2000), xvii.

46. Elbow, 51.

47. Jon Stewart, "Introduction," in *The Hegel Myths and Legends*, ed. Jon Stewart (Evanston, IL: Northwestern University Press, 1996), 15.

48. Gustav E. Mueller, "The Hegel Legend of 'Thesis-Antithesis-Synthesis,'" *Journal of the History of Ideas* 19.3 (1958): 411–414.

49. Stewart, 15.

50. Georg Wilhelm Friedrich Hegel, *The Science of Logic*, trans. A. V. Miller (Atlantic Highlands, NJ: Humanities Press International, 1989), 828–829.

51. Ibid., 82.

52. Ibid., 829.

53. Ibid., 831.

54. Ibid., 835.

55. Ibid., 106.

56. Ibid., 107.

57. Ibid., 105.

58. Ibid., 826.

59. Ibid., 106.

60. Mueller, 413.

61. It is of course possible to modify the substantive formula to take this into account by making every synthesis turn into a new thesis. Peter Singer, for example, provides the following elaboration in his *Hegel: A Very Short Introduction* (Oxford: Oxford University Press, 2001): "Every dialectical movement terminates with a synthesis, but not every synthesis brings the dialectical process to a stop.... Often the synthesis, though adequately reconciling the previous thesis and antithesis, will turn out to be onesided in some other respect. It will then serve as the thesis for a new dialectical movement, and so the process will continue" (102). Although this explanation helps to reconcile some of the differences that exist between Hegel's own articulation of the dialectic and the caricature that had been inherited from Marx, it is usually not included as part of the substantive formula.

62. Hegel, 842.

63. Pierre Lévy, *Cyberculture*, trans. Robert Bononno (Minneapolis, MN: University of Minnesota Press, 2001), 29.

64. For advocates, see for instance Frank Biocca and Mark R. Levy, eds., *Communication in the Age of Virtual Reality* (Hillsdale, NJ: Lawrence Erlbaum Associates, 1995); and Howard Rheingold, *Virtual Reality* (New York: Summit Books, 1991). For critics, see for instance Mark Slouka, *War of the Worlds: Cyberspace and the*

High-Tech Assault on Reality (New York: Basic Books, 1995); and Herbert Zettl, "Back to Plato's Cave: Virtual Reality," in *Communication and Cyberspace: Social Interactions in an Electronic Environment*, ed. Lance Strate, Ron Jacobson, and Stephanie B. Gibson (Cresskill, NJ: Hampton Press, 1996).

65. Peter Horsfield, "Continuities and Discontinuities in Ethical Reflections on Digital Virtual Reality," *Journal of Mass Media Ethics* 18.3–4 (2003): 156. Although not explicitly mentioned by Horsfield, this position had been originally argued by Gilles Deleuze in *Difference and Repetition* (New York: Columbia University Press, 1994). According to Deleuze, who addresses the general concept of the virtual and not the technology of VR in particular, "the virtual is not opposed to the real; it possesses a full reality by itself" (211).

66. Mark Poster, *What's the Matter with the Internet* (Minneapolis, MN: University of Minnesota Press, 2001), 25.

67. Benjamin Woolley, *Virtual Worlds: A Journey in Hype and Hyperreality* (New York: Penguin Books, 1992), 69.

68. Defined in this fashion, the "virtual" bears a certain resemblance to what Jean Baudrillard characterizes under the name "hyperreal" in *Simulacra and Simulation* (Ann Arbor: MI, University of Michigan Press, 1994): "Simulation is no longer that of a territory, a referential being, or a substance. It is the generation by models of a real with out origin or reality: a hyperreal" (1). Resemblance, however, is not simply identity. For a detailed consideration of the complex interactions between simulation, the hyperreal, and virtual reality, see the third chapter of my *Hacking Cyberspace* (Boulder, CO: Westview Press, 2001).

69. Heim, 220.

70. Stanovsky, 171.

71. Manfred E. Clynes and Nathan S. Kline, "Cyborgs and Space," in *The Cyborg Handbook*, ed. Chris Hables Gray (New York: Routledge, 1995), 30–31.

72. Chris Hables Gray, *Cyborg Citizen* (New York: Routledge, 2002), 2.

73. Anne Balsamo, *Technologies of the Gendered Body: Reading Cyborg Women* (Durham, NC: Duke University Press, 1996), 33.

74. Chris Hables Gray and Steven Mentor, "The Cyborg Body Politic and the New World Order," in *Prosthetic Territories: Politics and Hypertechnologies*, ed. Gabriel Brahm Jr. and Mark Driscoll (Boulder, CO: Westview Press, 1995), 219–247; Chris Hables Gray, Steven Mentor, and Heidi J. Figueroa-Sarriera, "Cyborgology: Constructing the Knowledge of Cybernetic Organisms," in *The Cyborg Handbook*, ed. Chris Hables Gray (New York: Routledge, 1995), 1–16.

75. Chris Hables Gray, "Prosthesis/Bricollage/Morph," *ArtLab23* 1.1 (Spring 2002).

76. Gray and Mentor, 244.

77. Jay David Bolter and Richard Grusin, "Remediation," *Configurations* 4.3 (1996): 318; Jay David Bolter and Richard Grusin, *Remediation: Understanding New Media* (Cambridge, MA: MIT Press, 2000), 23–24. Subsequent references to this work will provide pagination for both the article and book versions.

78. Bolter and Grusin, 329–330/33–34.

79. Ibid., 312/5.

80. Ibid.

81. Ibid., 339/45.

82. Ibid.

83. Ibid., 345/55.

84. Ibid, 344 n. 46/55 n. 3.

85. Jacques Derrida, for example, understands his own philosophical project as a critical engagement with and ongoing response to the philosophy of Hegel. Although this rapport is immediately apparent in Derrida's published essays, it is explicitly identified as such during one of the interviews collected in *Positions* (Chicago: University of Chicago Press, 1981): "We will never be finished with the reading or rereading of Hegel, and, in a certain way, I do nothing other than attempt to explain myself on this point" (81). Conversely, Stanisław Lem, during an interview with Peter Swirski that is included in *A Stanisław Lem Reader* (Evanston, IL: Northwestern University Press, 1997), indicates that he, like Bertram Russell, has little or no patience for anything Hegelian: "One reason that I like Russell so much was that he had the intellectual and moral integrity to call Hegel—without pulling any punches—a complete idiot. I totally concur: Hegel is an idiot, and those who praised his work have only been doing themselves a great disservice" (66).

86. Michel Foucault, *The Archaeology of Knowledge*, trans. A. M. Sheridan Smith (New York: Pantheon Books, 1972), 235.

87. Heim, 42–43.

88. Jacques Derrida, *Positions*, trans. Alan Bass (Chicago: University of Chicago Press, 1981), 41.

89. See for instance my *Hacking Cyberspace* (Boulder, CO: Westview Press, 2001).

90. Bolter and Grusin, 330/34.

91. Foucault, 235.

92. Mark Taylor, *Hiding* (Chicago: University of Chicago Press, 1997), 269.

93. Ibid., 270.

94. These "examples" do not and cannot behave according to the usual understand of example. Because poststructuralism does not constitute a method strictly speaking, one cannot find it applied to this or that object in particular. In fact, "a theory of poststructuralism," if one may be permitted to speak in this somewhat improper way, would be indistinguishable from the various circumstances of its particular application. As Derrida notes about the practice of deconstruction in *Limited Inc.* (Evanston, IL: Northwestern University Press, 1993), "it 'is' only what it does and what is done with it, there where it takes place" (141). For this reason, anything that would serve as an example of poststructuralism is not just a specific and subsequent application of a general theory but is itself an original and highly specific generation of theory. Although this may be perceived to be a significant inconvenience, if not an outright annoyance, for those scholars who want to and need to be able to separate theory from practice and method from application, it is absolutely necessary for understanding what poststructuralism is and what it endeavors to do. In fact, this deliberate complication of the "tried and true" binary oppositions of theory/practice and method/application is entirely consistent with and a necessary component of the different strategies of poststructuralism.

95. Deleuze, *Difference*, xv and xvii.

96. Ibid., xx.

97. Ibid., xix.

98. Derrida, *Positions*, 44.

99. Emmanuel Levinas, *Collected Philosophical Papers*, trans. Alphonso Lingis (Dordrecht: Martin Nijhoff Publishers, 1987), 48.

100. Levinas, 17.

101. See for instance Derrida's critique of Levinas in "Violence and Metaphysics: An Essay on the Thought of Emmanuel Levinas," in *Writing and Difference*, trans. Alan Bass (Chicago: University of Chicago Press, 1978), 79–152.

102. Donna J. Haraway, "A Cyborg Manifesto: Science, Technology, and Socialist-Feminism in the Late Twentieth Century," in *Simians, Cyborgs, and Women: The Reinvention of Nature* (New York: Routledge, 1991). Originally published under the title "Manifesto for Cyborgs: Science, Technology, and Socialist-Feminism in the 1980's," *Socialist Review* 80 (1985): 65–108.

103. Taylor, *Hiding*, 272.

104. Ibid., 269.

105. Ibid.

106. Ibid., 302–303.

107. Ibid., 269.

108. For a detailed investigation of the figure of the cyborg and the way that Haraway's particular characterization operates on and affects the network of traditional metaphysical oppositions, see my *Hacking Cyberspace*, 173–200.

109. Haraway, 151.

110. Ibid., 151–152.

111. Ibid., 152.

112. Ibid., 181.

113. Trinh T. Minh-ha, *Woman Native Other* (Bloomington, IN: Indiana University Press, 1989); Emmanuel Levinas, *Otherwise Than Being Or Beyond Essence*, trans. Alphonso Lingis (The Hague: Martinus Nijhoff Publishers, 1981); Deleuze, *Difference*.

114. Derrida, *Positions*, 71.

115. Paul Patton, "Translator's Preface" to *Difference and Repetition*, by Gilles Deleuze (New York: Columbia University Press, 1994), xii.

116. Derrida, *Limited*, 147.

117. Jeffrey T. Nealon, *Double Reading: Postmodernism after Deconstruction* (Ithaca, NY: Cornell University Press, 1993); Brian Greene, *The Fabric of the Cosmos: Space, Time, and the Texture of Reality* (New York: Vintage Books, 2005); Stephen P. Stich, *Deconstructing the Mind* (Oxford: Oxford University Press, 1998); Lynda Weinman, *Deconstructing Web Graphics* (Berkeley, CA: New Riders, 1996).

118. Susan Morris Specifications Limited, "Building Deconstruction" (Vancouver: Greater Vancouver Regional District, 2001), 2.

119. Jacques Derrida, *Of Grammatology*, trans. Gayatri Chakravorty Spivak (Baltimore, MD: The Johns Hopkins University Press, 1976); Walter J. Ong, *Orality and Literacy: The Technologizing of the Word* (New York: Routledge, 1995); John M. Ellis, *Against Deconstruction* (Princeton, NJ: Princeton University Press, 1990).

120. Derrida, *Positions*, 42.

121. Taylor, *Hiding*, 269.

122. Derrida, *Positions*, 41.

123. Taylor, *Hiding*, 325.

124. Ibid., 270.

125. Gilles Deleuze and Félix Guattari, *A Thousand Plateaus: Capitalism and Schizo-phrenia*, trans. Brian Massumi (Minneapolis, MN: University of Minnesota Press, 1987), 20.

126. Derrida, *Positions*, 93.

127. Plato, *Phaedrus*, trans. Harold North Fowler (Cambridge, MA: Harvard University Press, 1982).

128. Ong, *Orality*, 79.

129. Haraway, 177.

Chapter Two

1. The title of this chapter is not my own; it is borrowed from another, albeit anonymous, source. In April of 1999, I was asked by a reporter at *The Washington Post* to comment on the tragic events that took place at Columbine High School in Littleton, Colorado. The reporter was interested in one question: "Did the Internet play any role in warping the world views of the teenage killers?" In responding to this query, I noted that this question could just as easily be asked of the public library. But no one, I noted rather cynically, was questioning the role books may have played. My comments were eventually published in a story aptly named "As Always, the Internet Angle." Several weeks later, someone read an excerpt of my comments in a journal of library science. This individual sent me an unsigned email, asking the questions: "What do you have against libraries? What's the matter with books?"

2. On the "end of the book," see Eugene F. Provenzo, *Beyond the Gutenberg Galaxy: Microcomputers and the Emergence of Post-Typographical Culture* (New York: Teachers College Press, 1986); Sven Birkerts, *The Gutenberg Elegies: The Fate of Reading in an Electronic Age* (Boston: Faber and Faber, 1994); Elizabeth L. Eisenstein, "The End of the Book? Some Perspectives on Media Change," *American Scholar* 64.4 (1995): 541–555; Charles T. Meadow, *Ink into Bits: A Web of Converging Media* (Lanham, MD: The Scarecrow Press, 1998); Raymond Kurzweil, "The Future of Libraries," in *CyberReader,* ed. Victor J. Vitanza (Boston: Allyn and Bacon, 1999), 291–304; and Jacques Derrida, "The Book to Come," in *Paper Machine*, trans. Rachel Bowlby (Stanford, CA: Stanford University Press, 2005); On the "death of literature," see Alvin Kernan, *The Death of Literature* (New Haven, CT: Yale University Press, 1990). On remediation, see Fritz-Wilhelm Neumann, "Information Society and the Text: The Predicament of Literary Culture in the Age of Electronic Communication," *Erfurt Electronic Studies in English,* strategy statement no. 6 (1999), http://webdoc.sub.gwdg.de/edoc/ia/eese/strategy/neumann/6_st.html; Jay David Bolter and Richard Grusin, *Remediation: Understanding New Media* (Cambridge, MA: MIT Press, 2000); and Jay David Bolter, *Writing Space: Computers, Hypertext, and the Remediation of Print* (Mahwah, NJ: Lawrence Erlbaum Associates, 2001).

3. This focus on the materiality of information technology is not unique to this particular investigation but is part of and informed by recent innovations in the fields

of media studies, science studies, and the philosophy of technology. N. Katherine Hayles's *Writing Machines* (Cambridge, MA: MIT Press, 2002), for example, begins by identifying the basic problem. "Why have we not heard more about materiality? Granted, there have been some promising beginnings and a host of materially-based studies in the field of science studies. But within the humanities and especially literary studies, there has been a sharp line between representation and the technologies producing them. . . . By and large literary critics have been content to see literature as immaterial verbal constructions" (19). According to Hayles, this problem is especially evident in contemporary culture insofar as we appear to be increasingly involved in simulations and the reduction of all kinds of information to the immaterial flow of digital data. Consequently, *Writing Machines* endeavors to change the course of both literary and media criticism by attending to "the materiality of the literary artifact" (6). It is, in Hayles's own words, "a mode of critical interrogation alert to the ways in which the medium constructs the work and the work constructs the medium" (6). This unique approach to investigating the materiality of information sounds promising, at least until Hayles considers the status of her own text. "This book," she writes, "attempts to practice what it preaches by being attentive to its own material properties. As the author of the verbal text, I speak the words, but these are only part of the message; my collaborator Anne Burdick speaks in another mode through her designs" (6). *Writing Machines*, which is by its own account attentive to materiality, cannot be honest about its analysis if it is not also attentive to its own materiality as a book. Consequently, *Writing Machines* "attempts to practice what it preaches" by being conscious of and engaging in the material of its own techniques and technology of representation. And this materializes, Hayles suggests, in the look and feel of the text itself. The book has been deliberately submitted to significant graphical processing, much like the design-writing of Avital Ronell's *Telephone Book* (Lincoln, NB: University of Nebraska Press, 1989) and the typographical experimentation that comprises Jacques Derrida's *Glas* (Lincoln, NB: University of Nebraska Press, 1986). In other words, the medium, the material of ink and paper, has been deliberately manipulated, demonstrating in a very practical way that *Writing Machines* is in fact concerned with and involved in a thoroughly self-conscious understanding and manipulation its own material. However, in order to describe this matter, Hayles deploys and reaffirms the very problem she endeavors to address in the first place. At the point at which she describes her text's own self-involvement, she writes that she "speaks the words" and her collaborator "speaks in another mode." In writing this, she makes the assumption that the written text is a medium for the transmission of various forms of speech. In other words, she assumes that behind the material of the written text are the immaterial words that have been *spoken* by an author or designer. Although perfectly colloquial, this is the logocentric gesture *par excellence* and the root of the problem that Hayles had identified in the first place—the assumption that literature is essentially an "immaterial verbal construction." Consequently, Hayles's text, in the very effort to point out how it practices what it preaches, actually retreats to and reaffirms the immateriality that it endeavors to question in the first place. This is not, I would argue, some momentary lapse of reason, an editorial oversight, or a simple mistake. It is instead a testament to the difficulty of addressing the question of materiality. It is, in other words, evidence of what's the matter.

4. Victor Hugo, *Notre-Dame de Paris*, trans. John Sturrock (New York: Penguin Putnam, 1978), 188.

5. Frances A. Yates, *The Art of Memory* (Chicago: University of Chicago Press, 1974); Elizabeth L. Eisenstein, *The Printing Press as an Agent of Change: Communications and Cultural Transformations in Early-Modern Europe*, 2 vols. (Cambridge: Cambridge University Press, 1982).

6. Jay David Bolter, *Writing Space: The Computer, Hypertext, and the History of Writing* (Hillsdale, NJ: Lawrence Erlbaum Associates, 1991), 2.

7. Ibid. In order to account for this multifaceted relationship between different forms of information and communication technology, Derrida in *Paper Machine* (Stanford, CA: Stanford University Press, 2005) has suggested the use of the word *restructuration:* "The codex had itself supplanted the volume, the *volumen*, the scroll. It had supplanted it without making it disappear, I should stress. For what we are dealing with is never replacements that put an end to what they replace but rather, if I might use this word today, *restructurations* in which the oldest form survives, and even survives endlessly, coexisting with the new form and even coming to terms with a new economy" (9).

8. Geoffrey Nunberg, "Introduction," to *The Future of the Book*, ed. Geoffrey Nunberg (Berkeley, CA: University of California Press, 1996), 10.

9. Friedrich A. Kittler, *Gramophone, Film, Typewriter*, trans. Geoffery Winthrop-Young and Michael Wutz (Stanford, CA: Stanford University Press, 1999), xl. This procedure is informed by and demonstrates Marshall McLuhan's argument in *Understanding Media* (Cambridge, MA: MIT Press, 1995) that "the 'content' of any medium is always another medium" (8).

10. Robert Markley, "Introduction: History, Theory and Virtual Reality," in *Virtual Realities and Their Discontents*, ed. Robert Markley (Baltimore, MD: The Johns Hopkins University Press, 1996), 1.

11. Nicholas Negroponte, *Being Digital* (New York: Vintage, 1995), 7.

12. Vilém Flusser, *Die Schrift: Hat Schreiben Zukunft?* (Göttingen: Immatrix Publications, 1989), 1.

13. Mark Taylor and Esa Saarinen, *Imagologies: Media Philosophy* (New York: Routledge, 1994), Telewriting.

14. Antonio Gramsci, *Selections from the Prison Notebooks of Antonio Gramsci*, ed. and trans. Quintin Hoare and Geoffrey Nowell-Smith (London: Lawrence and Wishart, 1971), 276.

15. Michael Heim, *Electric Language: A Philosophical Study of Word Processing* (New Haven, CT: Yale University Press, 1999), 13–14.

16. David Bell, *An Introduction to Cybercultures* (New York: Routledge, 2001), 1.

17. Peter Lunenfeld, ed., *The Digital Dialectic: New Essays on New Media* (Cambridge, MA: MIT Press, 2000), xx.

18. Frank Hartmann, *Cyber.Philosophy: Medientheoretische Auslotungen* (Vienna: Passagen Verlag, 1999), 31.

19. Michael Benedikt, "Introduction," to *Cyberspace: First Steps*, ed. Michael Benedikt (Cambridge, MA: MIT Press, 1993), 3.

20. This mode of "reading" is indebted to the practice of deconstruction. As characterized by Christopher Norris in *Deconstruction: Theory and Practice* (New York: Methuen, 1982), "deconstruction is the vigilant seeking-out of those 'aporias,' blind spots or moments of self-contradiction where a text involuntarily betrays the tension between rhetoric and logic, between what it manifestly *means to say* and what it is nonetheless *constrained to mean*" (1). For more on deconstruction, see Jacques Derrida's *Of Grammatology* (Baltimore: The Johns Hopkins University Press, 1976); Briankle Chang's *Deconstructing Communication: Representation, Subject, and Economies of Exchange* (Minneapolis, MN: University of Minnesota Press, 1996); and "Deconstruction for Dummies," in my *Hacking Cyberspace* (Boulder, CO: Westview Press, 2001), 201–205.

21. Jacques Derrida, *Disseminations*, trans. Barbara Johnson (Chicago: University of Chicago Press, 1981), 158.

22. Rob Wittig, *Invisible Rendezvous: Connection and Collaboration in the New Landscape of Electronic Writing* (Hanover, NH: Wesleyan University Press, 1994), 9.

23. Jacques Derrida, *Writing and Difference*, trans. Alan Bass (Chicago: University of Chicago Press, 1978), 281.

24. Aristotle, *De interpretatione*, in *The Basic Works of Aristotle*, ed. and trans. Richard McKeon (New York: Random House, 1941), 1, 16a 3.

25. Charles Sanders Peirce, *The Collected Papers of Charles Sanders Peirce*, vol. 2, ed. Charles Hartshorne and Paul Weiss (Cambridge, MA: Harvard University Press, 1932), 228.

26. Jacques Derrida, *Margins of Philosophy*, trans. Alan Bass (Chicago: University of Chicago Press, 1982), 9.

27. Ibid.

28. Geoffrey Bennington, *Jacques Derrida* (Chicago: University of Chicago Press, 1993), 24.

29. Bolter, *Writing Space* (1991), p. x.

30. Ibid., ix.

31. Ibid., 240.

32. Jay David Bolter, *Writing Space: Computers, Hypertext, and the Remediation of Print* (Mahwah, NJ: Lawrence Erlbaum Associates, 2001), xi.

33. Ibid.

34. Ibid., xii.

35. Ibid., 214.

36. Marshall McLuhan, *Understanding Media: The Extensions of Man* (Cambridge, MA: MIT Press, 1995), 8.

37. Bolter, *Writing Space* (2001), 23.

38. Bolter, *Writing Space* (1991), ix.

39. Bolter and Grusin, 24.

40. Mark Taylor, *Erring: A Postmodern A/Theology* (Chicago: University of Chicago Press, 1984), 82.

41. Negroponte, *Being Digital*, 7.

42. Douglas Adams, Endorsement for *Being Digital*, by Nicholas Negroponte (New York: Vintage Books, 1995).

43. Bolter, *Writing Space* (1991), 197.

44. A similar determination can be found in the writings of Marshall McLuhan, who proposed that "the 'content' of any medium is always another medium" (*Understanding Media*, 8). According to this argument, there is never an immediate encounter with the thing represented in and by a particular medium. There is only the endless process of mediation where one medium contains and refers to another.

45. Bolter, *Writing Space* (1991), 204.

46. This confluence of high technology and critical theory is also identified by and investigated in George P. Landow's *Hypertext: The Convergence of Contemporary Critical Theory and Technology* (Baltimore, MD: The Johns Hopkins University Press, 1992).

47. Mark Amerika, *Hypertextual Consciousness: A Companion Theory Guide* (1997), http://www.grammatron.com/htc.html.

48. In stating this, I am not making the claim that hypertext has a more trustworthy referential dimension than print. In fact, the seemingly endless play of signification that is exhibited in books about technology extends to all signifiers whether they be printed on paper or presented in digital form on the surface of a computer monitor. The only advantage hypertext has over printed text is that hypertext is often far more attuned to its own performative dimension. That is, it performs/enacts/embodies what it addresses.

49. Gilles Deleuze, *The Fold: Leibniz and the Baroque*, trans. Tom Conley (Minneapolis, MN: University of Minnesota Press, 1993), 132.

50. Paul A. Taylor and Jan Ll. Harris, *Digital Matters: The Theory and the Culture of the Matrix* (New York: Routledge, 2005), 1.

51. Jacques Derrida, *Of Grammatology*, trans. Gayatri Chakravorty Spivak (Baltimore, MD: The Johns Hopkins University Press, 1976), 158. "There is nothing outside the text" is one of the most misquoted, misused, and misunderstood statements written by Derrida. Although this problem has been addressed in several places, the most direct explanation has been provided in the afterword to *Limited Inc.* (Evanston, IL: Northwestern University Press, 1993): "'There is nothing outside the text.' That does not mean that all referents are suspended, denied, or enclosed in a book, as people have claimed, or have been naive enough to believe and to have accused me of believing. But it does mean that every referent, all reality has the structure of a differential trace, and that one cannot refer to this 'real' except in an interpretive experience" (148).

52. Bolter, *Writing Space* (2001), xiv.

53. There are two reasons why the work of Derrida has been selected in order to articulate this necessary self-referential character of media. First, what is at issue in this chapter are books about ICT, that is, writing about technology. For many writers of media theory, writing either does not qualify for explicit analysis as a medium or it is subordinated, as Derrida has demonstrated time and again, to the metaphysical privilege of speech, whether that be in the form of an assumed "original" orality or the so-called "second orality" supposedly instituted by electronic media. Derrida, on the contrary, is one of the only writers of theory who takes writing seriously. Consequently, it is his work that is most appropriate in the context of this text, which addresses texts about technology. Second, in taking writing seriously, Derrida is hypersensitive to the self-reflective situation that

necessarily structures and underlies his own work. Derrida's writing on writing is exceedingly self-reflective, allowing what is written to affect how it is written and vice versa. What distinguishes Derrida's writing is not the fact that it includes such self-reflection, but the fact that this self-reflection is permitted to proliferate almost without boundaries. Whereas other theorists often try to exhaust the process of self-reflection, arguing that such "navel gazing" must end at some point in order to get on with the matter, Derrida, following the precedent of Hegel's speculative philosophy, locates the matter in a self-reflection that is and must be interminable. This kind of endless and unavoidable self-reflection is perhaps best exemplified in the initial sentence of "Signature Event Context" (in Jacques Derrida, *Limited Inc.* [Evanston, IL: Northwestern University Press, 1993], 1–24), where the questioning of communication turns back on itself, ceaselessly implicating the question in its questioning. For more on the self-reflective character of Derrida's writing, see Rodolphe Gasché's *Tain of the Mirror: Derrida and the Philosophy of Reflection* (Cambridge, MA: Harvard University Press, 1987); and Briankle Chang's *Deconstructing Communication*. For a consideration of the application of Derrida's work to new media and technology, see my *Hacking Cyberspace*.

54. William Gibson, *Neuromancer* (New York: Ace Books, 1984).
55. John Sallis, *Delimitations: Phenomenology and the End of Metaphysics* (Bloomington, IN: Indiana University Press, 1986), 5.
56. Plato, *Phaedo*, trans. Harold North Fowler (Cambridge, MA: Harvard University Press, 1990), 96a.
57. Ibid., 99e.
58. Georg Wilhelm Friedrich Hegel, *Enzyklopädie der philosophischen Wissenschaften im Grundrisse* (Hamburg: Verlag von Felix Meiner, 1969). For an explanation of how Hegel understands and employs the concept "speculative," see chapter 1.
59. Chang, ix–x.
60. Ibid., x.
61. Adilkno [Bilwet], *Media Archive*, trans. Laura Martz (New York: Autonomedia, 1998), 1.
62. Derrida, *Margins*, 309.

Chapter Three

1. Sinikka Sassi, "Cultural Differentiation or Social Segregation? Four Approaches to the Digital Divide," *New Media and Society* 7.5 (October 2005): 685.
2. For examples, see the following:

Academic Studies—David Bolt and Ray Crawford, *Digital Divide: Computers and Our Children's Future* (New York: TV Books, 2000); Eric P. Bucy, "Social Access to the Internet," *Harvard International Journal of Press Politics* 5.1 (2000): 50–61; Benjamin Compaine, *The Digital Divide: Facing a Crisis or Creating a Myth?* (Cambridge, MA: MIT Press, 2001); Bosah Ebo, *Cyberghetto or Cyberutopia: Race, Class, and Gender on the Internet* (Westport, CT: Praeger Press, 1998); Donna L. Hoffman, Thomas P. Novak, and Ann E. Schlosser, "The Evolution of the Digital Divide: How Gaps in Internet Access May Impact Electronic Commerce," *Journal of Computer-Mediated Communication* 5.3 (March 2000); James Katz and P. Aspden, "Motivations for and Barriers to Internet Usage: Results of a National Public Opinion Survey," *Internet Research: Electronic Networking Applications and Policy* 7.3 (1997): 170–188; Amanda Lenhart, "Who's Not Online," *Pew Internet American Life Project* (Washington, DC: Pew Research Center, 21 September 2000) and "The Ever-Shifting Internet Population: A New Look at Internet Access and the Digital Divide," *Pew Internet American Life Project* (Washington, DC: Pew Research Center, 16 April 2003); Thomas P. Novak and Donna L. Hoffman, "Bridging the Racial Divide on the Internet," *Science* 280 (17 April 1998): 390–391; Ekaterina O. Walsh, "The Truth about the Digital Divide," *Forrester Technographics Brief* (Cambridge, MA: Forrester Research, Inc., 2000); Anthony Wilhelm, "From Crystal Palaces to Silicon Valleys: Market Imperfections and the Enduring Digital Divide," in *Access Denied in the Information Age*, ed. Stephen Lax (New York: Palgrave, 2001), 199–217; William Wresch, *Disconnected: Haves and Have Nots in the Information Age* (New Brunswick, NJ: Rutgers University Press, 1996).

Professional Meetings and Conferences—Digital Nations Summit, Cambridge, MA (2000); Harvard/MIT eDevelopment conference, Cambridge, MA (2000); National Communication Association annual conference, Seattle, WA (2000), Atlanta, GA (2001), and New Orleans, LA (2002); The Technology Alliance conference on Seeking Solutions to the Digital Divide, Seattle, WA (1999);

Political Speeches, Hearings, and Policy Studies—Benton Foundation/Center for Media and Community, *Digital Divide Network* (February 2004), http://www.digitaldividenetwork.org; Al Gore, "Remarks at the Digital Divide Event" (28 April 1998), http://clinton4.nara.gov/textonly/WH/EOP/OVP/speeches/edtech.html; Susan Goslee, *Losing Ground Bit by Bit: Low-Income Communities in the Information Age* (Washington, DC: Benton Foundation, 1998); House Committee on Small Business, *The Digital Divide: Bridging the Technology Gap: Hearing before the Subcommittee on Empowerment of the Committee on Small Business*, 106th Cong., 1st sess., 27 July 1999, H. Report 106-25; House Committee on Small Business, *The Digital Divide: Field Hearing before the Subcommittee on Empowerment of the Committee on Small Business*, 106th Cong., 1st sess., 25 April 2000, H. Report 106-54; National Telecommunications and Information Administration (NTIA), *Falling Through the Net: A Survey of the "Have Nots" in Rural and Urban America* (Washington, DC: U.S. Department of Commerce, 1995); National Telecommunications and Information Administration (NTIA), *Falling Through the Net II: New Data on the Digital Divide* (Washington, DC: U.S. Department of Commerce, 1998); National Telecommunications and Information Administration (NTIA), *Falling Through the Net: Defining the Digital Divide* (Washington, DC: U.S. Department of Commerce, 1999); National Telecommunications and Information Administration (NTIA), *Falling Through the Net: Toward Digital Inclusion* (Washington, DC: U.S. Department of Commerce, 2000); National Telecommunications and Information Administration (NTIA), *A Nation Online: How Americans Are Expanding Their Use of the Internet* (Washington, DC: U.S. Department of Commerce, 2002); Global Internet Liberty Campaign, *Bridging the Digital Divide: Internet Access in Central and Eastern Europe* (Washington, DC: Center for Democracy and Technology, 2000);

Popular Press and Media—American Broadcasting Companies, Inc., "Digital Divide: No Computer, No Internet," *ABC World News Tonight with Peter Jennings*

(1 March 1999, 6:30 pm ET); O. Burkeman, "Internet's Global Reach Is Not at All Utopian: The Evolution of Net Surfing May Be Unwittingly Creating a New Class of Inequality," *The Independent*, 17 August 1998, 14; Bon Michel, "Internet, ou la communauté rétablie," *Le Monde*, 10 February 2001, 1; National Public Radio, "New Poll by National Public Radio (NPR), The Kaiser Family Foundation and Harvard's Kennedy School of Government," *Talk of the Nation* (29 February 2000, 3:00 pm ET); Public Broadcasting System, *Digital Divide* (2001) http://www.pbs.org/digitaldivide/; C. Schrader, "Brücken über den Digital Graben," *Süddeutsche Zeitung*, 5 December 2000, V2/13; Chris Taylor, "Digital Divide: So Close Yet So Far," *Time*, 4 December 2000, 120–128.

3.   See for instance John Perry Barlow, "Jack In, Young Pioneer!" Electronic Frontier Foundation, 11 August 1994, http://www.eff.org/Misc/Publications/John_Perry_Barlow/HTML/ jack_in_young_pioneer.html; John Perry Barlow, "A Declaration of the Independence of Cyberspace," *Binäre Mythen/Binary Myths*, Proceedings from the 14 September 1996 conference "Binary Myths—The Renaissance of Lost Emotions" held in Vienna, Austria (Wien: Zukunfts-werkstätte, 1997); Michael Benedikt, ed., *Cyberspace: First Steps* (Cambridge, MA: MIT Press, 1993); Mark Dery, ed., *Flame Wars: The Discourse of Cyberculture* (Durham, NC: Duke University Press, 1994); Ester Dyson et al., "Cyberspace and the American Dream: A Magna Carta for the Knowledge Age," *Information Society* 12.3 (1996): 295–308; David Gans and R. U. Sirius, "Civilizing the Electronic Frontier: An Interview with Mitch Kapor & John Barlow of the Electronic Frontier Foundation," *Mondo 2000* 3 (Winter 1991): 45–49; Nicholas Negroponte, *Being Digital* (New York: Vintage Books, 1995); Howard Rheingold, *The Virtual Community: Homesteading on the Electronic Frontier* (New York: Addison-Wesley, 1993); Bruce Schuman, *Utopian Computer Networking: America's New Central Project* (19 November 1988), http://origin.org/ucs/text/utopia2.cfm.

4.   Mick Brady, "The Digital Divide Myth," *E-Commerce Times* (4 August 2000), http://www.ecommercetimes.com/story/3953.html; Eric Cohen, "United We Surf: The Clinton Administration and the Business Community Are Eager to Solve a Problem—the 'Digital Divide'—That Does Not Exist," *The Weekly Standard*, 28 February 2000, 26; John Horvath, "Delving into the Digital Divide," *Telepolis* (17 July 2000), http://www.heise.de/tp/r4/artikel/8/8393/1.html; Paul Somerson, "Commentary: The Digital Divide Is Bunk," *ZDNet* (17 April 2000), http://www.zdnet.com/zdnn/stories/comment/0,5859,2499151,00.html; Adam D. Thierer, "Nonsense to Say That 'Have-Nots' Need Computers," *The Houston Chronicle*, 3 March 2000, A-41; James Crabtree, "The Digital Divide Is Rubbish—A Kind of Exclusion That Shouldn't Worry Us," *New Statesman*, 14 May 2001, 26.

5.   Barbara Johnson, "Translator's Introduction" to *Disseminations*, by Jacques Derrida (Chicago: University of Chicago Press, 1981), xv.

6.   Mark Warschauer, "What Is the Digital Divide?" (26 April 2001), http://www.gse.uci.edu/faculty/markw/dd.pdf.

7.   Larry Irving, "Origin of the Term Digital Divide," Digitaldivide@list.benton.org, 3 January 2001. Archived at http://www.rtpnet.org/lists/rtpnet-tact/msg00080.html.

8.   Amy Harmon, "Daily Life's Digital Divide," *Los Angeles Times*, 3 July 1996, A1.

9. Andy Carvin, "Origin of the Term Digital Divide," Digitaldivide@list.benton.org, 4 January 2001. Archived at http://www.rtpnet.org/lists/rtpnet-tact/msg00080. html.

10. Gary Andrew Poole, "A New Gulf in American Education, The Digital Divide," *The New York Times*, 29 January 1996, D3, col. 3.; Dinty W. Moore, *The Emperor's Virtual Clothes: The Naked Truth about Internet Culture* (New York: Algonquin Books, 1995).

11. Moore, 3.

12. Harmon, A1.

13. Ibid.

14. Gore, 1. "K–12" is a term that is specific to the American system of education. It denotes "kindergarten through twelfth grade," which means that it functions as a generic term indicating both primary and secondary education.

15. On the origin of the term "Information Superhighway," see my *Hacking Cyberspace* (Boulder, CO: Westview Press, 2001), 63.

16. Howard Wolinsky, "The Digital Divide," *Chicago Sun-Times*, 17 March 1996, 6.

17. Poole, D3, col. 3.

18. Shawn Steward, "Diminishing the Digital Divide," *Cellular Business* 14.2 (February 1997): 32–38.

19. Hamish McRae, "Unleashing the Digital Divide: The Changes in Television Will Change Global Society as We Lose Something That Unifies a Nation," *The Independent*, 17 November 1998, 5; "The Great Digital Divide: Broadcasters Are at Odds with Congress over Whether HDTV or Multicasting Will Prevail," *Mediaweek* 7.39, 20 October 1997, 4; John L. Roberts, "TV: Digital Divide," *Newsweek* 129.16 (1997): 50–51; Informa Publishing Group, "Absat Bridges Digital Divide with Astra Package: Pay-TV France," *New Media Markets*, 18 September 1997, 3; William G. Jones, "Crossing the Digital Divide: Moving from Film to Filmless Radiology," *Journal of Digital Imaging* 12.2 (1999): 47–54.

20. Julia Angwin and Laura Castaneda, "The Digital Divide: High-Tech Boom a Bust for Blacks, Latinos," *The San Francisco Chronicle*, 4 May 1998, A1.

21. Art Perio, "The Digital Divide and Institutional Racism," *Political Affairs* 80.2 (2001): 4–10.

22. NTIA, 1999, xiii.

23. Compaine, xiii.

24. Benton Foundation.

25. Compaine, 5.

26. NTIA, 1999, xiii.

27. It is, one could argue, somewhat ironic to expect or to advocate terminological stability for anything associated with digital media and information networks, which are so often characterized as fluid, flexible, and dynamic.

28. Daniel Chandler, "Biases of the Ear and Eye: 'Great Divide' Theories, Phonocentrism, Graphocentrism, and Logocentrism," 1994, http://www.aber.ac.uk/media/ Documents/litoral/litoral.html.

29. Ibid.

30. See for instance Jack Goody, *Literacy in Traditional Societies* (Cambridge: Cambridge University Press, 1968); Eric A. Havelock, *Preface to Plato* (Cambridge,

MA: Belknap Press, 1963); Claude Lévi-Strauss, *The Savage Mind*, trans. George Weidenfeld (Chicago: University of Chicago Press, 1966); Marshall McLuhan, *The Gutenberg Galaxy: The Making of Typographic Man* (Toronto: University of Toronto Press, 1962).

31. Chandler, "Biases," 1.

32. Mark Warschauer, *Technology and Social Inclusion: Rethinking the Digital Divide* (Cambridge, MA: MIT Press, 2003), 38–46. Also see Suzanne de Castell and Allan Luke, "Models of Literacy in North American Schools: Social and Historical Conditions and Consequences," in *Literacy, Society, and Schooling*, ed. Suzanne de Castell, Allan Luke, and Kieran Egan (Cambridge: Cambridge University Press, 1986), 87–109; Bill Cope and Mary Kalantzis, eds., *Multiliteracies: Literacy Learning and the Design of Social Futures* (London: Routledge, 2000); James Paul Gee, *Social Linguistics and Literacies* (London: Taylor & Francis, 1996); Brian V. Street, *Literacy in Theory and Practice* (Cambridge: Cambridge University Press, 1984).

33. Harvey J. Graff, *The Labyrinths of Literacy: Reflections on Literacy Past and Present* (London: Bodley Head, 1987).

34. Andrew L. Shapiro, *The Control Revolution: How the Internet Is Putting Individuals in Charge and Changing the World We Know* (New York: Century Foundation Books, 1999), xvi.

35. Warschauer, *Technology*, 6–7.

36. Chandler, "Biases," 2.

37. Warschauer, "What Is the Digital Divide?" 1.

38. Jan A. G. M. van Dijk, *The Deepening Divide: Inequality in the Information Society* (Thousand Oaks, CA: Sage, 2005), 4.

39. NTIA, 1999; NTIA, 2000; NTIA, 2002.

40. See chapter 1 for more on this issue.

41. Mark Dery, *Escape Velocity: Cyberculture at the End of the Century* (New York: Grove Press, 1996), 244.

42. Chandler, "Biases," 1.

43. Mark Taylor, *Hiding* (Chicago: University of Chicago Press, 1997), 269.

44. Andy Carvin, "Mind the Gap: The Digital Divide as the Civil Rights Issue of the New Millennium," *Multimedia Schools* 7.1 (2001): 56.

45. Daniel Chandler, "Technological or Media Determinism," 1995, http://www.aber.ac.uk/media/Documents/tecdet/tecdet.html, 2.

46. Jacques Ellul, *The Technological Society* (New York: Vintage, 1964), xviii; Barry Jones, *Sleepers, Wake! Technology and the Future of Work* (New York: Oxford University Press, 1990), 210; Daniel Chandler, "Shaping and Being Shaped: Engaging with Media," *Computer-Mediated Communication Magazine*, 1 February 1996, http://www.december.com/cmc/mag/1996/feb/chandler.html, 2.

47. Charles Horton Cooley, *Social Organization* (New York: Schocken Books, 1962), 65.

48. Harold Innis, *The Bias of Communication* (Toronto: University of Toronto Press, 1951); Ellul, *Technological Society*; McLuhan, *Gutenberg*.

49. Ruth Finnegan, "Communication and Technology," Unit 8 of the Open University Correspondence Course, *Making Sense of Society*, Block 3, *Communication*. (Buckingham: Open University Press, 1975), 105.

50. See for instance Donald MacKenzie and Judy Wajcman, eds., *The Social Shaping of Technology: How the Refrigerator Got Its Hum* (Buckingham: Open University Press, 1985); Neil Postman, *Technopoly: The Surrender of Culture to Technology* (New York: Vintage, 1993); Merritt Roe Smith and Leo Marx, eds., *Does Technology Drive History? The Dilemma of Technological Determinism* (Cambridge, MA: MIT Press, 1994).

51. Jay David Bolter, *Turing's Man: Western Culture in the Computer Age* (Chapel Hill, NC: University of North Carolina Press, 1984), 13, 4.

52. Negroponte, 11–13.

53. Alvin Toffler, *The Third Wave* (New York: Bantam Books, 1980).

54. NTIA, 1999, 1.

55. U.S. Department of Commerce, *The Emerging Digital Economy* (Washington, DC: U.S. Department of Commerce, 1998), 3.

56. Compaine, 333–334.

57. Gore, 1.

58. Compaine, xiii.

59. NTIA, 1999, xiii, 77.

60. Chandler, "Shaping and Being Shaped," 2.

61. See for instance Katz and Aspden; Novak and Hoffman; NPR et al.; NTIA 1995, 1998, 1999, 2000 and 2002; Walsh.

62. NTIA, 1999, 8.

63. Chandler, "Technological or Media Determinism," 11.

64. Graff, 19.

65. Compaine, 328.

66. Jan A. G. M. van Dijk, *The Networked Society: Social Aspects of New Media* (Thousand Oaks, CA: Sage Publications, 2000). Also see Brady; NTIA, 2000; Katz and Aspden; van Dijk, *The Deepening Divide*.

67. Hubert Dreyfus, *On the Internet* (New York: Routledge, 2001), 2.

68. Zillah Eisenstein, *Global Obscenities: Patriarchy, Capitalism, and the Lure of Cyberfantasy* (New York: New York University Press, 1998); Gordon Graham, *The Internet://A Philosophical Inquiry* (New York: Routledge, 1999); Kevin Robins and Frank Webster, *Times of the Technoculture: From the Information Society to the Virtual Life* (New York: Routledge, 1999).

69. Ellul, xxvii–xxxiv.

70. William Gibson, "Academy Leader," in *Cyberspace: First Steps*, ed. Michael Benedikt (Cambridge, MA: MIT Press, 1993), 29.

71. Katie Hafner and Matthew Lyon, *Where Wizards Stay Up Late: The Origins of the Internet* (New York: Simon & Schuster, 1996).

72. Compaine, 332.

73. James Carey, *Communication as Culture: Essays on Media and Society* (New York: Routledge, 1989), 17.

74. Martin Spinelli, "Radio Lessons for the Internet," *Postmodern Culture* 6.2 (1996): 2.

75. David Sarnoff (1891–1971), a pioneer in the development of radio and television broadcasting, became president of the Radio Corporation of America (RCA) in 1930. Herbert Hoover (1874–1964), who was U.S. Secretary of Commerce under

Presidents Harding and Coolidge, was instrumental in shaping public policy in the early days of radio broadcasting. In 1929, he became the thirty-first president of the United States.

76. Henry David Thoreau, *Walden and Other Writings* (New York: Bantam Books, 1981), 144.

77. See for instance Manuel De Landa, *War in the Age of Intelligent Machines* (New York: Zone Books, 1991); Armand Mattelart, *Mapping World Communication: War, Progress, Culture*, trans. Susan Emanuel and James A. Cohen (Minneapolis, MN: University of Minnesota Press, 1994); Armand Mattelart, *The Invention of Communication*, trans. Susan Emanuel (Minneapolis, MN: University of Minnesota Press, 1996).

78. Steven Lubar, *InfoCulture* (Boston, MA: Houghton Mifflin Company, 1993), 89.

79. De Landa, 75; Spinelli, 14.

80. Postman, 181.

Chapter Four

1. Adilkno [Bilwet], *The Media Archive*, trans. Laura Martz (New York: Autonomedia, 1998), 114.

2. Peter Horsfield, "Continuities and Discontinuities in Ethical Reflections on Digital Virtual Reality," *Journal of Mass Media Ethics* 18.3–4 (2004): 166.

3. Edward Castronova, "Virtual Worlds: A First-Hand Account of Market and Society on the Cyberian Frontier," *Center for Economic Studies & Ifo Institute for Economic Research*, working paper no. 618 (December 2001): 4. This investigation has recently received expanded treatment in Castronova's *Synthetic Worlds: The Business and Culture of Online Games* (Chicago: University of Chicago Press, 2005). Whether Castranova's analysis is methodologically sound is a question for economists to resolve. What is of interest in this particular context are not the statistical details and conclusions of his investigation but the fact that the virtual world of a computer game has been situated and understood as a viable alternative to what used to be called "reality."

4. Andy Wachowski and Larry Wachowski, directors, *The Matrix* (Burbank, CA: Warner Home Video, 1999).

5. See for instance Christopher Grau, ed., *Philosophers Explore the Matrix* (Oxford: Oxford University Press, 2005); William Irwin, ed., *The Matrix and Philosophy* (Chicago: Open Court, 2002) and *More Matrix and Philosophy: Revolutions and Reloaded Decoded* (Chicago: Open Court, 2005); Karen Haber, ed., *Exploring the Matrix: Visions of the Cyber Present* (New York: St. Martin's Griffin, 2003); Jake Horsley, *Matrix Warrior: Being the One* (New York: St. Martin's Griffin, 2003); Matthew Kapell and William G. Doty, eds., *Jacking into the Matrix Franchise: Cultural Reception and Interpretation* (New York: Continuum, 2004); Matt Lawrence, *Like a Splinter in Your Mind* (Oxford: Blackwell Publishing, 2004); Glenn Yeffeth, ed., *Taking the Red Pill: Science, Philosophy and Religion in The Matrix* (Dallas, TX: Benbella Books, 2003).

6. I take up and analyze this decision in chapter 5.

7. Avital Ronell, *Crack Wars: Literature, Addiction, Mania* (Lincoln, NB: University of Nebraska Press,1992), 68.

8. William Gibson, *Neuromancer* (New York: Ace Books, 1984), 51.
9. See for instance Nobuo Kamioka, "Cyberpunk Revisited: William Gibson's *Neuromancer* and the 'Multimedia Revolution,'" *Japanese Journal of American Studies* 9 (1998): 56.
10. Gibson, *Neuromancer*, 52.
11. Ibid., 6.
12. Ibid., 5.
13. Chris Chesher, "Colonizing Virtual Reality: Construction of the Discourse of Virtual Reality 1984–1992," *Cultronix* 1.1 (1994): 10.
14. David Jay Brown, "Reality Check: An Interview with Jaron Lanier," in *Voices from the Edge—Internet Edition*, 1993, http://www.levity.com/mavericks/jaron.htm.
15. Benjamin Woolley, *Virtual Worlds: A Journey in Hype and Hyperreality* (London: Penguin Books, 1993), 24.
16. Ibid., 24–25.
17. Chesher, 7.
18. Mark Dery, *Escape Velocity: Cyberculture at the End of the Century* (New York: Grove Press, 1996), 22.
19. John Perry Barlow, "Being in Nothingness: Virtual Reality and the Pioneers of Cyberspace," *Mondo 2000* 2 (Summer 1990): 39.
20. Nicole Stenger, "Mind Is a Leaking Rainbow," in *Cyberspace: First Steps*, ed. Michael Benedikt (Cambridge, MA: MIT Press, 1991), 49.
21. Ibid.
22. Douglas Rushkoff, *Cyberia: Life in the Trenches of Hyperspace*, 2nd ed. (Manchester: Clinamen Press, 2002), xviii.
23. Mark Taylor and Esa Saarinen, *Imagologies: Media Philosophy* (New York: Routledge, 1994), Ad-diction 3.
24. Michael Horowitz, editor's note to *Chaos and Cyberculture*, by Timothy Leary (Berkeley, CA: Ronin Publishing, 1994), xi.
25. Dery, *Escape*, 22.
26. Taylor and Saarinen, Ad-diction 9. If, as Taylor argues in *About Religion* (Chicago: University of Chicago Press, 1999), repetition is an indicator of importance (118), then it should be noted that Taylor himself finds this insight to be important enough to reiterate it in at least two subsequent publications: *Hiding* (Chicago: University of Chicago Press, 1997, 282) and *About Religion* (130–131).
27. Dery, *Escape*, 30.
28. Eric Norden, "Marshall McLuhan: A Candid Conversation with the High Priest of Popcult and Metaphysician of the Media," *Playboy*, March 1969, 55.
29. Rushkoff, viii.
30. Ibid.
31. Barlow quoted in Taylor, *Hiding*, 283.
32. Ibid., 282–283.
33. Rushkoff, ix.
34. Kevin Kelly, Adam Heilbrun, and Barbara Stacks, "Virtual Reality: An Interview with Jaron Lanier," *Whole Earth Review* 64 (Fall 1989): 114.
35. These are Lanier's early thoughts on the subject. On his website, he refers to this material as "a vintage interview that captures the delirious, infectious way I used

to talk about VR in my twenties" ("Writings," 2005, http://www.jaronlanier.com/writings.html). Admittedly, Lanier's discourse has become more nuanced and less utopian in the last fifteen years. In recent interviews his statements about VR are, by comparison, much more sober, reserved, and varied. Still these early texts indicate the kind of ideology that was operative in the art and science of VR. This youthful optimism, like that of the counterculture, has not been eradicated as much as it has been tempered and incorporated in other structures.

36. Kelly, Heilbrun, and Stacks, 114–115.

37. Marshall McLuhan, *Understanding Media: The Extensions of Man* (Cambridge, MA: MIT Press, 1995); Howard Rheingold, *The Virtual Community: Homesteading on the Electronic Frontier* (San Francisco, CA: HarperPerennial, 1993); Esther Dyson, *Release 2.0: A Design for Living in the Digital Age* (New York: Broadway Books, 1997); William Mitchell, *City of Bits: Place, Space and the Infobahn* (Cambridge, MA: MIT Press, 1996); Nicholas Negroponte, *Being Digital* (New York: Vintage Books, 1995).

38. McLuhan, *Understanding*, 5.

39. Mark Dery, "Flame Wars," in *Flame Wars: The Discourse of Cyberculture*, ed. Mark Dery (Durham, NC: Duke University Press, 1994), 3.

40. See for instance Ziauddin Sardar and Jerome R. Ravetz, eds., *Cyberfutures: Culture and Politics on the Information Superhighway* (New York: New York University Press, 1996); and my *Hacking Cyberspace* (Boulder, CO: Westview Press, 2001).

41. Stenger, 52.

42. See for instance Erik Davis, *TechGnosis : Myth, Magic, and Mysticism in the Age of Information* (New York: Three Rivers Press, 1998); Michael Heim, *The Metaphysics of Virtual Reality* (New York: Oxford University Press, 1993); David W. Noble, *The Religion of Technology: The Divinity of Man and the Spirit of Invention* (New York: Penguin Books, 1999); Margaret Wertheim, *The Pearly Gates of Cyberspace: A History of Space from Dante to the Internet* (New York: W. W. Norton & Company, 1999); Jeffrey P. Zaleski, *The Soul of Cyberspace* (San Francisco, CA: Harper, 1997).

43. See for example Gregory Bassham, "The Religion of *The Matrix* and the Problems of Pluralism," in *The Matrix and Philosophy*, ed. William Irwin (Chicago: Open Court, 2002), 111–125; Slavoj Žižek, "Reloaded Revolutions," in *More Matrix and Philosophy: Revolutions and Reloaded Decoded*, ed. William Irwin (Chicago: Open Court, 2005), 198–208.

44. It should be noted that the word "addiction" is defined broadly in these writings. As William S. Burroughs, who is something of an expert in addiction, has indicated in *Naked Lunch* (New York: Grove Press, 1982), addiction can be defined both broadly and narrowly. When defined broadly, we can speak of addictions to coffee, chocolate, etc. But this dependency is, according to Burroughs, not addiction per se. Addiction is a metabolic dependency. It therefore is only proper to speak of addiction when addressing heroin, which creates a metabolic dependency in the user.

45. Ann Weinstone, "Welcome to the Pharmacy: Addiction, Transcendence, and Virtual Reality," *Diacritics* 27.3 (1997): 77.

46. Howard Rheingold, *Virtual Reality* (New York: Summit Books, 1991), 354.

47. Taylor and Saarinen, Ad-diction 6.

48. Stanisław Lem, "Thirty Years Later," in *A Stanisław Lem Reader*, ed. and trans. Peter Swirski (Evanston, IL: Northwestern University Press, 1997), 83.

49. Rheingold, *Virtual Community*, 33.

50. Sue Barnes, *Computer-Mediated Communication: Human-to-Human Communication across the Internet* (Boston: Pearson Education, 2003), 195.

51. CBS Broadcasting, Inc., "Addicted: Suicide over Everquest?" *48 Hours* (18 October 2002, 10:00pm EST); Noah Shachtman, "EverQuest: The Latest Addiction," *Wired News* (29 July 1999) http://www.wired.com/news/culture/0,1284,20984,00.html.

52. Kimberly S. Young, *Caught in the Net: How to Recognize the Signs of Internet Addiction—And a Winning Strategy for Recovery* (New York: John Wiley & Sons, 1998); Mark D. Griffiths, "Internet Addiction: Fact or Fiction?" *The Psychologist* 12.5 (1998): 246–50; Pam Belluck, "Stuck on the Web; Symptoms of Internet Addiction," *New York Times*, 1 December 1996, sec. 4, p. 5.

53. See for instance Andrew Careaga, *Hooked on the Net* (Grand Rapids, MI: Kregel Publications 2002); David N. Greenfield, *Virtual Addiction: Help for Netheads, Cyberfreaks, and Those Who Love Them* (Oakland, CA: New Harbinger, 1999); Stephen O. Watters, *Real Solutions for Overcoming Internet Addictions* (Ann Arbor, MI: Vine Books, 2001); Center for Online Addiction, September 2005, http://www.netaddiction.com; The Center for Internet Behavior, September 2005, http://www.virtual-addiction.com; Internet/Computer Addiction Services, June 1999, http://www.icaservices.com; Internet-a-holics Anonymous, August 1999, http://internetaddiction.com.

54. Ronell, 33.

55. Walter J. Ong, *Orality and Literacy: The Technologizing of the Word* (New York: Routledge, 1995), 79.

56. Friedrich Nietzsche, *The Gay Science*, trans. Walter Kaufmann (New York: Vintage Books, 1974), 142.

57. Plato, *Phaedrus*, trans. Harold N. Fowler (Cambridge, MA: Harvard University Press, 1982), 230d–e.

58. Ibid., 274c–275a (translation slightly modified).

59. H. G. Liddel and R. Scott, *An Intermediate Greek-English Lexicon* (Oxford: Clarendon Press, 1991), 804.

60. Ong, 81–82.

61. Jay David Bolter, *Writing Space: The Computer, Hypertext, and the History of Writing* (Hillsdale, NJ: Lawrence Erlbaum and Associates, 1991), 37.

62. Ibid.

63. Jacques Derrida, *Disseminations*, trans. Barbara Johnson (Chicago: University of Chicago Press, 1981), 103.

64. Ibid., 97.

65. Ibid.

66. Plato, 275c.

67. Derrida, *Disseminations*, 103.

68. Ibid., 67.

69. Plato, 275c–d.

70. Jacques Derrida, "The Rhetoric of Drugs," trans. Michael Israel, in *Points: Inter-*

views, 1974–1994, ed. Elisabeth Weber (Stanford, CA: Stanford University Press, 1995), 235–236.

71. Ibid., 235.

72. James Brook and Iain Boal, eds., *Resisting the Virtual Life: The Culture and Politics of Information* (San Francisco, CA: City Lights, 1995), vii.

73. Heim, 89.

74. Ronell, 50.

75. See for instance David L. Clark, "Heidegger's Craving: Being-on-Schelling," *Diacritics* 27.3 (1997): 8–33; Barbara Claire Freeman, "Moments of Beating: Addiction and Inscription in Virginia Woolf's 'A Sketch of the Past,'" *Diacritics* 27.3 (1997): 65–76; Debra Hawhee, "Burke on Drugs," *Rhetoric Society Quarterly* 34.1 (2004): 5–28; Jeffrey T. Nealon, *Alterity Politics: Ethics and Performative Subjectivity* (Durham, NC: Duke University Press, 1998); Eve Kosofsky Sedgwick, "Epidemics of Will," in *Zone 6: Incorporations*, ed. Jonathan Crary and Sanford Kwinter (New York: Urzone, 1992), 582–595; Weinstone, "Welcome."

76. Ronell, 78.

77. Ibid., 33.

78. William Gibson, foreword to *The Matrix: The Shooting Script*, by Andy and Larry Wachowski (New York: Newmarket Press, 2001), viii.

79. T. M. Lentz, "The Third Place from the Truth: Plato's Paradoxical Attack on Writing," *Communication Quarterly* 31.4 (Fall 1983): 290–301.

80. Derrida, *Disseminations*, 112.

81. Wachowski and Wachowski, *The Matrix*.

Chapter Five

1. Søren Kierkegaard, *Either/Or, Part II*, trans. Howard V. and Edna H. Hong (Princeton, NJ: Princeton University Press, 1987), 169.

2. Myriam Diocaretz and Stefan Herbrechter, eds., *The Matrix in Theory* (Amsterdam: Editions Rodopi B.V., 2006); Christopher Grau, ed., *Philosophers Explore the Matrix* (Oxford: Oxford University Press, 2005); William Irwin, ed., *The Matrix and Philosophy* (Chicago: Open Court, 2002) and *More Matrix and Philosophy: Revolutions and Reloaded Decoded* (Chicago: Open Court, 2005); Matthew Kappell and William G. Doty, eds., *Jacking into the Matrix Franchise: Cultural Reception and Interpretation* (New York: Continuum, 2004); Matt Lawrence, *Like a Splinter in Your Mind* (Oxford: Blackwell Publishing, 2004); Glenn Yeffeth, ed., *Taking the Red Pill: Science, Philosophy and Religion in The Matrix* (Dallas, TX: Benbella Books, 2003).

3. The concept of an older and more comprehensive matrix situated prior to and behind *The Matrix* has recently been proposed and examined by Paul Taylor and Jan Harris in *Digital Matters: Theory and Culture of the Matrix* (New York: Routledge, 2005).

4. Iakovos Vasiliou, "Reality, What Matters, and *The Matrix*," in *Philosophers Explore the Matrix*, ed. Christopher Grau (Oxford: Oxford University Press, 2005), 98.

5. Andy Wachowski and Larry Wachowski, directors, *The Matrix* (Burbank, CA: Warner Home Video, 1999).

6. William Gibson, foreword to *The Matrix: The Shooting Script*, by Andy and Larry Wachowski (New York: Newmarket Press, 2001), viii.

7. Gregory Bassham, "The Religion of *The Matrix* and the Problems of Pluralism," in *The Matrix and Philosophy*, ed. William Irwin (Chicago: Open Court., 2002), 111–125; Gregory A. Boyd and Al Larson, *Escaping the Matrix: Setting Your Mind Free to Experience Real Life in Christ* (North Dartmouth, MA: Baker Books, 2005); Stephen Faller, *Beyond the Matrix: Revolutions and Revelations* (Atlanta, GA: Chalice Press, 2004); Chris Seay and Greg Garrett, *The Gospel Reloaded: Exploring Spirituality and Faith in the Matrix* (Colorado Springs, CO: Piñon Press, 2003); Ben Witherington, "Neo-Orthodoxy: Tales of the Reluctant Messiah, Or 'Your Own Personal Jesus,'" in *More Matrix and Philosophy: Revolutions and Reloaded Decoded*, ed. William Irwin (Chicago: Open Court, 2005), 165–174; Eddie Zacapa, *Matrix Reflections: Choosing Between Reality and Illusion* (Bloomington, IN: Authorhouse, 2005).

8. Paul Fontana, "Finding God in *The Matrix*," in *Taking the Red Pill: Science, Philosophy and Religion in The Matrix*, ed. Glenn Yeffeth (Dallas, TX: Benbella Books, 2003), 169–171; Thomas S. Frentz and Janice Hocker Rushing, "Mother Isn't Quite Herself Today: Myth and Spectacle in *The Matrix*," *Critical Studies in Media Communication* 19.1 (2002): 68; Colin McGinn, "The Matrix of Dreams," in *Philosophers Explore the Matrix*, ed. Christopher Grau (Oxford: Oxford University Press, 2005), 63.

9. Gerald J. Erion and Barry Smith, "Morality, and *The Matrix*," in *The Matrix and Philosophy*, ed. William Irwin (Chicago: Open Court, 2002), 27.

10. Peter Boettke, "Human Freedom and the Red Pill," in *Taking the Red Pill: Science, Philosophy and Religion in The Matrix*, ed. Glenn Yeffeth (Dallas, TX: Benbella Books, 2003), 154.

11. Charles L. Griswold, "Happiness and Cypher's Choice: Is Ignorance Bliss?" in *The Matrix and Philosophy*, ed. William Irwin (Chicago: Open Court, 2002), 132; Read Mercer Schuchardt, "What Is the Matrix?" in *Taking the Red Pill: Science, Philosophy and Religion in The Matrix*, ed. Glenn Yeffeth (Dallas, TX: Benbella Books, 2003), 10; Robin Hanson, "Was Cypher Right? (Part 1): Why We Stay in Our Matrix," in *Taking the Red Pill: Science, Philosophy and Religion in The Matrix*, ed. Glenn Yeffeth (Dallas, TX: Benbella Books, 2003), 24; Erion and Smith, 26.

12. Frentz and Rushing, 68.

13. This opposition is perhaps best illustrated in scenes involving the consumption of food. Cypher enjoys an artificial, computer-generated steak, while Neo chokes down real sustenance in the form of what the crew of the *Nebuchadnezzar* call "a bowl of snot."

14. Christopher Grau, "Bad Dreams, Evil Demons, and the Experience Machine: Philosophy and *The Matrix*," in *Philosophers Explore the Matrix*, ed. Christopher Grau (Oxford: Oxford University Press, 2005), 10–23; Hubert L. Dreyfus and Stephen D. Dreyfus, "Existential Phenomenology and the Brave New World of *The Matrix*," in *Philosophers Explore the Matrix*, ed. Christopher Grau (Oxford: Oxford University Press, 2005), 71–97.

15. David Weberman, "*The Matrix* Simulation and the Postmodern Age," in *The Matrix and Philosophy*, ed. William Irwin (Chicago: Open Court, 2002), 234.

16. William Irwin, "Computers, Caves, and Oracles: Neo and Socrates," in *The Matrix and Philosophy*, ed. William Irwin (Chicago: Open Court, 2002), 15.

17. Andy Wachowski and Larry Wachowski, directors, *The Matrix Reloaded* (Burbank, CA: Warner Home Video, 2003).

18. For comparisons of Plato's "Allegory of the Cave" to the technology and experience of cinema, see Christopher Falzon, *Philosophy Goes to the Movies* (New York: Routledge, 2002); and Margaret Morse, *Virtualities: Television, Media Art, and Cyberculture* (Bloomington, IN: Indiana University Press, 1998). For comparisons to virtual reality, see Carolina Cruz-Neira et al., "The CAVE: Audio Visual Experience Automatic Virtual Environment," *Communications of the ACM* 35.6 (June 1992): 64–72; Michael Heim, *The Metaphysics of Virtual Reality* (New York: Oxford University Press, 1993); Ken Hillis, *Digital Sensations: Space, Identity, and Embodiment in Virtual Reality* (Minneapolis, MN: University of Minnesota Press, 1999); Howard Rheingold, *Virtual Reality* (New York: Summit Books, 1991); Herbert Zettl, "Back to Plato's Cave: Virtual Reality," in *Communication and Cyberspace: Social Interaction in an Electronic Environment*, ed. Lance Strate, Ronald Jacobson, and Stephanie B. Gibson (Cresskill, NJ: Hampton Press, 1996), 83–94. For comparisons to the *Matrix*, see Boettke, 145–158; Jorge J. E. Gracia and Jonathan J. Sanford, "The Metaphysics of *The Matrix*," in *The Matrix and Philosophy*, ed. William Irwin (Chicago: Open Court, 2002), 55–65; Griswold, 126–137; Irwin, 5–15; Lawrence, 4–6; John Partridge, "Plato's Cave and *The Matrix*," in *Philosophers Explore the Matrix*, ed. Christopher Grau (Oxford: Oxford University Press, 2005), 239–257.

19. Plato, *Republic*, trans. Paul Shorey (Cambridge, MA: Harvard University Press, 1987), 515d.

20. Ibid., 516e.

21. Boettke, 148; Erion and Smith, 25; Grau, "Bad Dreams," 18; Lawrence, 116–117; Theodore Schick, "Fate, Freedom, and Foreknowledge," in *The Matrix and Philosophy*, ed. William Irwin (Chicago: Open Court, 2002), 89; Lyle Zynda, "Was Cypher Right? (Part 2): The Nature of Reality and Why It Matters," in *Taking the Red Pill: Science, Philosophy and Religion in The Matrix*, ed. Glenn Yeffeth (Dallas, TX: Benbella Books, 2003), 42.

22. Robert Nozick, *Anarchy, State, and Utopia* (New York: Basic Books, 1974), 42.

23. Ibid., 44.

24. Zynda, 42.

25. Friedrich Nietzsche, *The Gay Science*, trans. Walter Kaufmann (New York: Vintage Books, 1974), 281.

26. Ibid.

27. Friedrich Nietzsche, *Beyond Good and Evil*, trans. Walter Kaufmann (New York: Vintage Books, 1989), 15.

28. Heim, *Metaphysics*, 107–108.

29. Similar decisions are evident in the interviews with VR developers presented in Howard Rheingold's *Virtual Reality*, Ken Hillis's critical investigation of virtual environments in *Digital Sensations*, Stanisław Lem's early investigation of "phantomatics" in his *Summa Technologica* (Kraków: Wydawnictwo Literackie, 1964); and the various articles collected in anthologies like Frank Biocca and Mark R. Levy's *Communication in the Age of Virtual Reality* (Hillsdale, NJ: Lawrence Erl-

baum Associates, 1995); James Brook and Iain A. Boal's *Resisting the Virtual Life* (San Francisco, CA: City Lights, 1995); and Ziaddin Sardar and Jerome R. Ravetz's *Cyberfutures: Culture and Politics on the Information Superhighway* (New York: New York University Press, 1996).

30. Kenneth Rufo, "The Mirror in *The Matrix* of Media Ecology," *Critical Studies in Media Communication* 20.2 (2003): 137.

31. Bret Leonard, director, *Lawnmower Man* (Hollywood, CA: New Line Cinema, 1992).

32. Heim, *Metaphysics*, 146.

33. Peter Weir, director, *Truman Show* (Hollywood, CA: Paramount Pictures, 1998).

34. Arthur Kroker and Michael A. Weinstein, *Data Trash* (New York: St. Martin's Press, 1994), 5.

35. Robin Beck, "You Won't Know the Difference So You Can't Make the Choice," *Philosophy Now* 30 (December 2000/January 2001): 35.

36. Russell Blackford, "Try the *Blue* Pill: What's Wrong with Life in a Simulation?" in *Jacking into the Matrix Franchise: Cultural Reception and Interpretation*, ed. Matthew Kapell and William G. Doty (New York: Continuum, 2004), 170.

37. Ibid., 171; James Patrick Kelly, "Meditations on the Singular Matrix," in *Exploring the Matrix: Visions of the Cyber Present*, ed. Karen Haber (New York: St. Martin's Griffin, 2003), 233.

38. Blackford, 169, 181.

39. Ibid., 173.

40. Ibid., 181.

41. Slavoj Žižek, "Reloaded Revolutions," in *More Matrix and Philosophy: Revolutions and Reloaded Decoded*, ed. William Irwin (Chicago: Open Court, 2005), 202.

42. Weberman, 234.

43. Ibid., 234–235.

44. Kevin Warwick, "*The Matrix*—Our Future?" in *Philosophers Explore the Matrix*, ed. Christopher Grau (Oxford: Oxford University Press, 2005), 207.

45. Donna Haraway, *Simians, Cyborgs, and Women: The Reinvention of Nature* (New York: Routledge, 1991); N. Katherine Hayles, *How We Became Posthuman: Virtual Bodies in Cybernetics, Literature, and Informatics* (Chicago: University of Chicago Press, 1999); J. C. R. Licklider, "Man-Computer Symbiosis," *IRE Transactions on Human Factors in Electronics HFE-1* (March 1960): 4–11.

46. Haraway, 180.

47. Nietzsche, *Beyond*, 2.

48. William Irwin, ed., dust jacket to *The Matrix and Philosophy* (Chicago: Open Court, 2002).

49. Nietzsche, *Gay Science*, 281.

50. Ibid., 282.

51. I am indebted to Debra Hawhee for this insight. See David J. Gunkel and Debra Hawhee, "Virtual Alterity and the Reformating of Ethics," *Journal of Mass Media Ethics* 18.3/4 (2003): 173–193.

52. Nietzsche, *Gay Science*, 282.

53. Wachowski and Wachowski, *The Matrix*.

54. McGinn, "The Matrix of Dreams," 2.

55. Nietzsche, *Gay Science*, 316.

56. Friedrich Nietzsche, *Nachgelassene Fragmente 1869–1874*, in *Friedrich Nietzsche Sämtliche Werke, Kritische Studienausgabe*, vol. 7, ed. Giorgio Colli and Mazzino Montinari (Berlin: Walter de Gruyter, 1980), 199.

57. Martin Heidegger, *Nietzsche: The Will to Power as Art*, trans. David Farrell Krell (New York: Harper & Row, 1979); Jacques Derrida, *Positions*, trans. Alan Bass (Chicago: University of Chicago Press, 1981).

58. Friedrich Nietzsche, *The Twilight of the Idols*, in *The Portable Nietzsche*, trans. and ed. Walter Kaufmann (New York: Penguin Books, 1983), 486.

59. Mark Taylor and Esa Saarinen, *Imagologies: Media Philosophy* (New York: Routledge, 1994), Virtuality 15.

60. The term "deconstruction" is perhaps one of the most misused and misunderstood concepts in contemporary theory. Despite the circulation of misinterpretations that have become something of an institutional (mal)practice, the term "deconstruction" does not indicate "to take apart" or "to un-construct." What it signifies is neither simply synonymous with "destruction" nor the antithesis of "construction." As Derrida points out in the "Afterword" to *Limited Inc.* (Evanston, IL: Northwestern University Press, 1993), "the 'de-' of *de*construction signifies not the demolition of what is constructing itself, but rather what remains to be thought beyond the constructionist or destructionist schema" (147). For this reason, deconstruction is something entirely other than what is understood and delimited by the conceptual opposition situated between construction and destruction. To put it schematically, deconstruction comprises a kind of general strategy by which to intervene in this and all other conceptual oppositions that have and continue to organize and regulate Western systems of knowing. For a more detailed explanation of the strategies and operations of deconstruction, see Jacques Derrida, *Positions*, trans. Alan Bass (Chicago: University of Chicago Press, 1981); Jonathan Culler, *On Deconstruction: Theory and Criticism after Structuralism* (Ithaca, NY: Cornell University Press, 1982); Briankle Chang, *Deconstructing Communication: Representation, Subject, and Economies of Exchange* (Minneapolis, MN: University of Minnesota Press, 1996); and "Deconstruction for Dummies" in my *Hacking Cyberspace* (Boulder, CO: Westview Press, 2001).

61. One attempt to name this alternative has been proposed in Jean Baudrillard's *Simulacra and Simulation* (Ann Arbor, MI: University of Michigan Press, 1994), a publication that has not only figured prominently in the narrative structure of *The Matrix* but is actually included as a prop in an early scene. According to Baudrillard, "simulation" names that which remains outside of and beyond the sovereign difference that had distinguished the real from imaginary representations (2). For a detailed consideration of simulation and VR technology, see my *Hacking Cyberspace*, especially chapter 3.

62. Wachowski and Wachowski, *The Matrix*.

63. Peter B. Lloyd, "Glitches in *The Matrix* ... And How to Fix Them," in *Taking the Red Pill: Science, Philosophy and Religion in The Matrix*, ed. Glenn Yeffeth (Dallas, TX: Benbella Books, 2003), 106.

64. Wachowski and Wachowski, *The Matrix Reloaded*.

65. Kroker and Weinstein, 5.

66. Heim, *Metaphysics*, 89.

67. Plato, *Phaedrus*, trans. Harold N. Fowler (Cambridge, MA: Harvard University Press, 1990), 274c–275a.

68. Walter Ong, *Orality and Literacy: The Technologizing of the Word* (New York: Routledge, 1995), 169.

69. Mark Taylor, *Hiding* (Chicago: University of Chicago Press, 1997), 301–303.

70. For more on the concept of the "dialectical third term," see chapter 1.

Chapter Six

1. Jeffrey T. Nealon, *Alterity Politics: Ethics and Performative Subjectivity* (Durham, NC: Duke University Press, 1998), 71.

2. In their paper "Just Another Artifact: Ethics and the Empirical Experience of AI," which was presented at the Fifteenth International Congress on Cybernetics (1998), Joanna Bryson and Phil Kime argue that these science fiction narratives "are exploring what it means to be human, not what it means to be a computer" (5).

3. The relationship between ethics, response, and responsibility is perhaps best articulated by Gayatri Chakravorty Spivak in the essay "Responsibility," in *Boundary 2* 21.3 (1994). "I can," Spivak writes, "formalize responsibility in the following way: It is that all action is undertaken in response to a call (or something that seems to us to resemble a call) that cannot be grasped as such" (22). The machine question will have been motivated by a "call," or something that seems to us to resemble a call, that is issued from elsewhere and otherwise. And this entire chapter can be understood as an attempt (perhaps a necessarily incomplete attempt) to respond to and to take responsibility for that call. I am indebted to Peter Krapp for this reference.

4. Donna J. Haraway, *Simians, Cyborgs, and Women: The Reinvention of Nature* (New York: Routledge, 1991), 152.

5. J. Storrs Hall, "Ethics for Machines," *KurzweilAI.net* (5 July 2001), http://www.kurzweilai.net/articles/art0218.html.

6. Jacques Derrida, *Of Grammatology*, trans. Gayatri Chakravorty Spivak (Baltimore, MD: The Johns Hopkins University Press, 1976).

7. Plato, *Phaedrus*, trans. Harold N. Fowler (Cambridge, MA: Harvard University Press, 1982), 275d.

8. Kevin Warwick, "Cyborg Morals, Cyborg Values, Cyborg Ethics," *Ethics and Information Technology* 5.3 (2003): 132. Although this is a rather controversial statement, Warwick is correct as long as "communication" is defined as the transmission of information between two points. Obviously two interconnected machines can transmit much larger amounts of data over greater distances in less time than is possible for any human being. Although communication scholars would be quick to point out that Warwick's definition of communication is highly limited, the discipline of communication has, for better or worse, traditionally defined "communication" as "the transmission of messages between senders and receivers."

9. Neil Postman, *Technopoly: The Surrender of Culture to Technology* (New York: Vintage Books, 1993), 181.

10. Barbara Johnson, "Translator's Introduction" to *Disseminations*, by Jacques Derrida (Chicago: University of Chicago Press, 1981), xv.

11. Martin Heidegger, *Being and Time*, trans. John Macquarrie and Edward Robinson (New York: Harper & Row, 1962), 24.

12. Ibid., 2.

13. In stating this, I do not mean to suggest that the machine has simply been absent from ethical considerations. In fact, it has figured prominently in moral discourse under the rubric of what is now called "computer ethics," "cyber-ethics," and "media ethics." These investigations, however, do not consider the ethical status of the machine as such but limit their examinations to questions of the responsible use of technology by and for human users.

14. Jean-François Lyotard, *The Inhuman: Reflections on Time*, trans. Geoffrey Bennington and Rachel Bowlby (Stanford, CA: Stanford University Press, 1991), 1.

15. René Descartes, *Discourse on Method*, in *Descartes: Selected Philosophical Writings*, trans. and ed. John Cottingham, Robert Stoothoff, and Dugald Murdoch (Cambridge: Cambridge University Press, 1988), 44. In 1738, this characterization was practically demonstrated when Jacques de Vaucanson exhibited a mechanical duck, which reportedly was indistinguishable from a real duck.

16. Immanuel Kant, *Critique of Practical Reason*, trans. Lewis White Beck (New York: Macmillan, 1985), 17.

17. According to this reading, Kantian philosophy merely excludes the animal from consideration. Theodor Adorno, as Derrida points out in the final essay of *Paper Machine* (Stanford, CA: Stanford University Press, 2005), takes the interpretation one step further, arguing that Kant not only excluded animality but held it in contempt. "He [Adorno] particularly blames Kant, whom he respects too much from another point of view, for not giving any place in his concept of dignity (*Würde*) and the 'autonomy' of man to any compassion (*Mitleid*) between man and the animal. Nothing is more odious (*verhasster*) to Kantian man, says Adorno, than remembering a resemblance or affinity between man and animal (*die Erinnerung an die Tierähnlichkeit des Menschen*). The Kantian feels only hate for human animality" (180).

18. Kant, 63.

19. Tom Regan, foreword to *Animal Others: On Ethics, Ontology, and Animal Life*, ed. Peter Steeves (Albany, NY: State University of New York Press, 1999), xii.

20. Emmanuel Levinas, *Totality and Infinity*, trans. Alphonso Lingis (Pittsburgh: Duquesne University Press, 1969); Emmanuel Levinas, *Otherwise Than Being or Beyond Essence*, trans. Alphonso Lingis (The Hague: Martinus Nijhoff Publishers, 1981).

21. Nealon, 71.

22. Levinas's humanism is also identified and addressed by Derrida in the introduction to his 1997 presentation at Cerisy-la-Salle and in Richard Cohen's introduction to the English translation of Levinas's 1972 publication *Humanism of the Other*. For Derrida ("The Animal That Therefore I Am," *Critical Inquiry* 28 [winter 2002]), the humanist pretensions of Levinasian philosophy constitute cause for considerable concern: "In looking at the gaze of the other, Levinas says, one must forget the color of his eyes, in other words see the gaze, the face that gazes before seeing the

visible eyes of the other. But when he reminds us that the 'best way of meeting the Other is not even to notice the color of his eyes,' he is speaking of man, of one's fellow as man, kindred, brother; he thinks of the other man and this, for us, will later be revealed as a matter for serious concern" (381). Whereas Derrida maintains a critical stance toward Levinas's humanism, Cohen's introduction to *Humanism of the Other* (Chicago: University of Illinois Press, 2003) gives it a positive spin: "The three chapters of *Humanism of the Other* each defend humanism—the world view founded on the belief in the irreducible dignity of humans, a belief in the efficacy and worth of human freedom and hence also of human responsibility" (ix). This is not the place to engage in this debate concerning Levinasian philosophy. However, what is important to note for the analysis at hand is the fact that both sides of the argument recognize and affirm a fundamental humanism always and already at work within Levinas's ethics of otherness.

23. Regan, xi.
24. In continental thought, the prominence of "the animal question" is evident in Martin Heidegger's 1929–30 lecture course *Die Grundbegriffe der Metaphysik: Welt—Endlichkeit—Einsamkeit* (Frankfurt am Main: V. Klostermann, 1983); David Farrell Krell's commentary on this text in *Daimon Life: Heidegger and Life Philosophy* (Bloomington, IN: Indiana University Press, 1992); and the lectures delivered at the third Cerisy-la-Salle conference (1997) and subsequently published under the title *L'Animal autobiographique, Autour de Jacques Derrida* (Paris: Editions Galilée, 1999).
25. Cary Wolfe, introduction to *Zoontologies: The Question of the Animal*, ed. Cary Wolfe (Minneapolis, MN: University of Minnesota Press, 2003), x–xi.
26. Haraway, 151–152.
27. Wolfe, xi.
28. Evan Ratliff, "The Crusade against Evolution," *Wired* 12.10 (October 2004): 156–161.
29. Wolfe, x.
30. Because of these demonstrations, researchers have tried to distinguish the machine from the human by employing other differentiating criteria, most notably emotions. This argument has, however, been significantly complicated by Daniel C. Dennett's extended "philosophical thought experiment" in "Why You Can't Make a Computer That Feels Pain," in *Brainstorms: Philosophical Essays on Mind and Psychology* (Cambridge, MA: MIT Press, 1998).
31. Attempts to articulate something like a "machine question," although not always identified by this name, can be found in a few conference papers and publications. These will be detailed and addressed later in this chapter.
32. Hall, 2.
33. Gottfried Wilhelm Leibniz, "Preface to a *Universal Characteristic*," in *G. W. Leibniz: Philosophical Essays*, trans. and ed. Roger Ariew and Daniel Garber (Indianapolis, IN: Hackett Publishing Company, 1989), 6–7.
34. Hall, 2.
35. Isaac Newton, *Philosophiae Naturalis Principia Mathematica*, ed. Alexandre Koyré and I. Bernard Cohen (Cambridge, MA: Harvard University Press, 1972).
36. William Paley, *Natural Theology: Or, Evidences of the Existence and Attributes of the*

Deity, Collected from the Appearances of Nature, 10th edition (London: R. Faulder, 1805).

37. Martin Heidegger, *The Question Concerning Technology,* trans. William Lovitt (New York: Harper Torchbooks, 1977), 5.

38. Hall, 2.

39. Ibid.

40. Gilles Deleuze and Félix Guattari, *A Thousand Plateaus: Capitalism and Schizophrenia,* trans. Brian Massumi (Minneapolis, MN: University of Minnesota Press, 1987), 141.

41. Henry Sidgwick, *The Methods of Ethics* (Indianapolis, IN: Hackett Publishing Company, 1981), 77.

42. Kant, 18.

43. Jeremy Bentham, *An Introduction to the Principles and Morals of Legislation* (Amherst, NY: Prometheus Books, 1988).

44. Michael Anderson, Susan Leigh Anderson, and Chris Armen, "Toward Machine Ethics," paper presented at American Association for Artificial Intelligence—The Nineteenth National Conference on Artificial Intelligence, 25–29 July 2004, San Jose, California, p. 2.

45. Jacques Derrida, "And Say the Animal Responded," trans. David Willis, in *Zoontologies: The Question of the Animal,* ed. Cary Wolfe (Minneapolis, MN: University of Minnesota Press, 2003), 121.

46. Michel Foucault, *The Order of Things: An Archaeology of the Human Sciences,* trans. Alan Sheridan (New York: Vintage Books, 1973), 387.

47. Descartes, 44–45.

48. Ibid., 45.

49. Ibid., 44.

50. Alan Turing, "Computing Machinery and Intelligence," in *Computer Media and Communication: A Reader,* ed. Paul A. Meyer (Oxford: Oxford University Press, 1999), 37–58.

51. Philip K. Dick, *Do Androids Dream of Electric Sheep?* (New York: Ballantine Books, 1982).

52. Joseph Weizenbaum, *Computer Power and Human Reason: From Judgment to Calculation* (San Francisco, CA: W. H. Freeman, 1976).

53. Descartes, 44.

54. Sue Savage-Rumbaugh, Stuart G. Shanker, and Talbot J. Taylor, *Apes, Language, and the Human Mind* (Oxford: Oxford University Press, 1998).

55. Haraway, 151–152.

56. Marshall McLuhan, *Understanding Media: The Extensions of Man* (Cambridge, MA: MIT Press, 1995), 18.

57. It is unclear whether I ought to use the phrase "with which" or "with whom" in this particular context. Although this equivocation appears, like the concern with prepositions, to be another small grammatical issue, everything, it turns out, depends upon this decision. In making a choice between the one or the other, it is decided whether the machine is to be regarded as a thing, a mere object, or whether it is considered to be another subject. I have obviously decided to go with the latter. This decision, however, is not without significant complications and consequences

that will need to be detailed, investigated, and justified by what follows. A similar concern has been identified and pursued, although from an altogether different angle, in Derrida's most recent work on the gift, forgiveness, and hospitality. As Derrida explains in one of the texts collected in *Paper Machine:* "I have already seemed to count on the distinction between *who* and *what,* to shake it up a bit, so let me be clear that in my present work, above all in my teaching, I try to reach a place *from* which this distinction between *who* and *what* comes to appear and become determined, in other words a place 'anterior' to this distinction, a place more 'old' or more 'young' than it, a place also that both enjoins determination but also enables the terribly reversible translation of *who* into *what*" (80).

58. Robert Cathcart and Gary Gumpert, "The Person-Computer Interaction: A Unique Source," in *Information and Behavior,* vol. 1, ed. Brent D. Ruben (New Brunswick, NJ: Transaction Books, 1985), 114.

59. James W. Chesebro and Donald G. Bonsall, *Computer-Mediated Communication: Human Relationships in a Computerized World* (Tuscaloosa, AL: The University of Alabama Press, 1989).

60. Communication through the instrumentality of the computer, whether in the form of synchronous or asynchronous exchanges, has been designated by a number of different names. In "The Computer as a Communication Device" (*Science and Technology,* April 1968), J. C. R. Licklider and Robert W. Taylor advocated use of the term "computer-aided communication" (CAC), which they fashioned following the precedent established in the engineering community with computer-aided design (CAD) and computer-aided engineering (CAE). Other theorists and practitioners have employed the compound "compunications" (Anthony G. Oettinger, "Compunications in the National Decision-Making Process," in *Computers, Communications, and the Public Interest,* ed. Martin Greenberger [Baltimore, MD: The Johns Hopkins University Press, 1971], 73–114), "computer-based communication" (Jacques Vallee and Thaddeus Wilson, *Computer-Based Support of Scientific and Technical Work,* IFTF Rept. No. NASA CR 137879, 1976), and "computerized communication" (Everett M. Rogers and Sheizaf Rafaeli, "Computers and Communication," in *Information and Behavior,* ed. Brent D. Ruben [New Brunswick, NJ: Transaction Books, 1985], 95–112). But the most popular and accepted appellation has been and continues to be "computer-mediated communication." Despite its popularity, the exact origin and etymology of this term is not certain. What is known is that it begins to make an appearance in the mid- to late 1970s. In 1978, for example, Starr Roxanne Hiltz and Murray Turoff employed the term in their extended examination of computerized conferencing, *The Networked Nation: Human Communication via Computer* (Reading, MA: Addison-Wesley Publishing Company, 1978). Although Hiltz and Turroff used the term "computer conferencing system" (CCS) to name "any system that uses the computer to mediate communication among human beings" (xix), they had also employed "computer-mediated communication" as a generic designation for various forms of human communication via the computer, including "computerized conferencing, computer assisted instruction, and home terminals from which white collar work can be done" (167). "Computer-mediated communication" was elevated to the status of a technical term in Hiltz's subsequent collaboration with Elaine Kerr,

which was undertaken for the National Science Foundation. This 1981 study was expanded and published in 1982 under the title *Computer-Mediated Communication Systems: Status and Evaluation* (New York: Academic Press, 1982). In this text, "computer-mediated communication" is defined as "a new form of enhanced human communication" (3): "Essentially, computer-mediated communication means that large numbers of people in business, government, education, or at home can use the computer to maintain continuous communication and information exchanges. More than a replacement for the telephone, mails, or face-to-face meetings, computer communication is a new medium for building and maintaining human relationships" (ix). For Kerr and Hiltz, the specific technologies that make up this new medium of human interaction include: "conferencing systems, electronic message systems, and general information-communication systems designed to support 'knowledge workers'" (1). Consequently, Kerr and Hiltz's "computer-mediated communication" functions as a comprehensive term, designating both synchronous and asynchronous forms of human communication *through* the instrumentality of the computer.

61. Susan C. Herring, introduction to *Computer-Mediated Communication: Linguistic, Social and Cross-Cultural Perspectives*, ed. Susan Herring (Philadelphia, PA: John Benjamins Publishing Company, 1996), 1.

62. Claude E. Shannon and Warren Weaver, *The Mathematical Theory of Communication* (Urbana, IL: University of Illinois Press, 1963), 7–8.

63. John Fisk, *Introduction to Communication Studies* (New York: Routledge, 1994), 6.

64. George Gerbner, "Toward a General Model of Communication," *Audio Visual Communication Review* 4.3 (1956): 171–199; Roman Jakobson, "Closing Statement: Linguistics and Poetics," in *Style and Language*, ed. Thomas A. Sebeok (Cambridge, MA: MIT Press, 1960), 350–377; B. H. Wesley and M. S. MacLean, "A Conceptual Model for Communication Research," *Journalism Quarterly* 34 (1957): 31–38.

65. McLuhan, *Understanding Media*.

66. Heidegger, *The Question*, 4–5.

67. Ibid.

68. Andrew Feenberg, *Critical Theory of Technology* (New York: Oxford University Press, 1991), 5.

69. Ibid.

70. Jean-François Lyotard, *The Postmodern Condition: A Report on Knowledge*, trans. Geoff Bennington and Brian Massumi (Minneapolis, MN: University of Minnesota Press, 1984), 44.

71. Hall, 2.

72. Robert Cathcart and Gary Gumpert, "Mediated Interpersonal Communication: Toward a New Topology," in *Inter/media: Interpersonal Communication in a Media World*, ed. Robert Cathcart and Gary Gumpert (New York: Oxford University Press, 1981), 27.

73. Frederick Williams, *The Communications Revolution* (Beverly Hills: Sage, 1982), 30.

74. Ithiel de Sola Pool, foreword to *The Coming Information Age: An Overview of Technology, Economics, and Politics*, 2nd edition, by Wilson P. Dizard (New York: Longman, 1985), xi–xii.

75. Cathcart and Gumpert, "The Person-Computer Interaction," 116.

76. Chesebro and Bonsall, 31.

77. Perhaps the best, if not somewhat ironic, example of this is unwanted email or spam. Spam messages, which inform Internet users of everything from herbal supplements to enhance the size and operation of various parts of the body to bogus stock and investment opportunities, are generated by and originate with a computer. And as a result of the seemingly unrestrained proliferation of this kind of mail, users and network administrators now employ spam filters, which effectively decide which messages to deliver to the human user and which ones to filter out. (I am grateful to Joanna Bryson for providing me with this example.)

78. Hall, 6.

79. Warwick, "Cyborg Morals," 132.

80. Dick, *Do Androids Dream?*; Ridley Scott, director, *Blade Runner* (Burbank, CA: Warner Home Video, 1982); Stanisław Lem, *Solaris* (Kraków: Wydawnictwo Literackie, 2002); Andrei Tarkovsky, director, *Solaris* (New York: Criterion Collection, 2002); Steven Soderbergh, director, *Solaris* (Beverly Hills, CA: Twentieth Century Fox Home Video, 2004); Isaac Asimov, *I, Robot* (Garden City, NY: Doubleday, 1950); Alex Proyas, director, *I, Robot* (Beverly Hills, CA: Twentieth Century Fox Home Video, 2005); Andy and Larry Wachowski, directors, *The Matrix*, *The Matrix Reloaded* and *The Matrix Revolutions* (Burbank, CA: Warner Home Video, 1999 and 2003); Peter Chung and Andy Jones, directors, *The Animatrix* (Burbank, CA: Warner Home Video, 2003); David Eick and Ronald D. Moore, producers, *Battlestar Galactica*, Season 1 (Universal City, CA: Universal Studios, 2005).

81. Georges Bataille, *The Unfinished System of Nonknowledge*, trans. and ed. Michelle Kendall and Stuart Kendall (Minneapolis, MN: University of Minnesota Press, 2001), 5.

82. Anderson, Anderson, and Armen, 1. It should be emphasized that by "debut" I mean the institution of "machine ethics" as a recognized and distinct area of study within the discipline of artificial intelligence (AI). The motivations and ideas behind machine ethics had already been available and articulated within the discipline of AI for quite some time prior to this. See for example the 2000 Convention of the Society for the Study of Artificial Intelligence and the Simulation of Behaviour (AISB-00) Symposium on Artificial Intelligence, Ethics and (Quasi-)Human Rights (University of Birmingham, UK, 19–20 April 2000), especially Blay Whitby and Kane Oliver's "How to Avoid a Robot Takeover: Political and Ethical Choices in the Design and Introduction of Intelligent Artifacts," Helen Seville and Debora Field's "What Can AI Do for Ethics?" and Joanna Bryson's "A Proposal for the Humanoid Agent-builders League (HAL)."

83. Ibid.

84. Ibid., 4.

85. Asimov, *I, Robot*.

86. Robert Sparrow, "The Turing Triage Test," *Ethics and Information Technology* 6.4 (December 2004): 203.

87. Ibid., 204.

88. Ibid.

89. Ibid.

90. Ibid., 207.

91. Ibid.

92. Wolfe, *Zoontologies*, xii.

93. Luciano Floridi, "Information Ethics: On the Philosophical Foundation of Computer Ethics," *Ethics and Information Technology* 1.1 (March 1999): 41.

94. Ibid., 41, 42.

95. Ibid., 42.

96. Ibid., 43.

97. Ibid.

98. Ibid.

99. Kenneth Einar Himma, "There's Something about Mary: The Moral Value of Things *qua* Information Objects," *Ethics and Information Technology* 6.3 (September 2004): 145.

100. Emmanuel Levinas, *Collected Philosophical Papers*, trans. Alphonso Lingis (Dordrecht: Martinus Nijhoff Publishers, 1987), 54–55.

101. Levinas, *Totality*, 43.

102. Himma, 145.

103. Levinas, *Collected*, 43.

104. Haraway, 180.

105. Immanuel Kant, *Grounding for the Metaphysics of Morals*, trans. James W. Ellington (Indianapolis, IN: Hackett Publishing Company, 1983), 36 (translation modified).

106. H. J. Paton, *The Categorical Imperative: A Study in Kant's Moral Philosophy* (Philadelphia, PA: University of Pennsylvania Press, 1971), 165.

107. Levinas, *Totality*, 38.

108. Norbert Wiener, *The Human Use of Human Beings: Cybernetics and Society* (1950; rpt., Boston: Da Capo Press, 1988), 16.

109. Slavoj Žižek, *The Plague of the Fantasies* (New York: Verso, 1997), 161.

110. Jürgen Habermas, *The Inclusion of the Other: Studies in Political Theory*, trans. Ciaran Cronin et al. (Cambridge, MA: MIT Press, 1998), 40.

111. Jacques Derrida, *Writing and Difference*, trans. Alan Bass (Chicago: University of Chicago Press, 1978), 260.

112. Rodney Brooks, Comment in "AI's Greatest Trends and Controversies," by Marti A. Hearst and Haym Hirsh, *IEEE – Intelligent Systems* 15.1 (January/February 2002): 8–17.

113. Luciano Floridi, "Information Ethics, Its Nature and Scope," in *Moral Philosophy and Information Technology*, ed. Jeroen van den Hoven and John Weckert (Cambridge: Cambridge University Press, 2006). Pre-print available from http://www.philosophyofinformation.net/pdf/ieinas.pdf, p. 7.

Chapter Seven

1. Emmanuel Levinas, *Otherwise Than Being or Beyond Essence*, trans. Alphonso Lingis (The Hague: Martinus Nijhoff Publishers, 1981), 20.

2 . Jacques Derrida, *Disseminations*, trans. Barbara Johnson (Chicago: University of Chicago Press, 1981), 1–59.

3. Georg Wilhelm Friedrich Hegel, *Phenomenology of Spirit*, trans. A. V. Miller (Oxford: Oxford University Press, 1977), 1. Translation modified.

4. For the "worse," see Søren Kierkegaard, *Concluding Unscientific Postscript*, trans. David F. Swenson and Walter Lowrie (Princeton, NJ: Princeton University Press, 1968), 16–17.

5. Friedrich Nietzsche, *Beyond Good and Evil*, trans. Walter Kaufmann (New York: Vintage Books, 1989), 10.

6. Jacques Derrida, *Positions*, trans. Alan Bass (Chicago: University of Chicago Press, 1981), 41.

7. Jean Baudrillard, *Le ludique et le policier et autres textes parus dans Utopie* (Paris: Sens & Tonka, 2001), 335. Translation provided in Chris Turner, "The Intelligence of Evil: An Introduction," to *The Intelligence of Evil or the Lucidity Pact*, by Jean Baudrillard (Oxford: Berg, 2005), 4. A similar statement is included in Baudrillard's *Symbolic Exchange and Death* (London: Sage, 1993): "We will not destroy the system by a direct, dialectical revolution of the economic or political infrastructure. Everything produced by contradiction, by the relation of forces, or by energy in general, will only feed back into the mechanism and give it impetus, following the circular distortion similar to a Moebius strip" (36).

8. Audre Lorde, "The Master's Tools Will Never Dismantle the Master's House," in *Sister Outsider: Essays and Speeches* (Berkeley, CA: The Crossing Press, 1984), 110–113.

9. Levinas, 20.

10. Derrida, *Positions*, 42.

11. Georg Wilhelm Friedrich Hegel, *Hegel's Logic*, trans. William Wallace (Oxford: Oxford University Press, 1987), 138.

Bibliography

Adams, Douglas. Endorsement for Being Digital, by Nicholas Negroponte. New York: Vintage Books, 1995.

Adilkno [Bilwet]. *Media Archive.* Translated by Laura Martz. New York: Autonomedia, 1998.

American Broadcasting Companies, Inc. "Digital Divide: No Computer, No Internet." *ABC World News Tonight with Peter Jennings,* 1 March 1999, 6:30 pm ET.

Amerika, Mark. *Hypertextual Consciousness: A Companion Theory Guide,* 1997, http://www.grammatron.com/htc.html (1 November 2005).

Anderson, Craig A., and Brad J. Bushman. "Effects of Violent Video Games on Aggressive Behavior, Aggressive Cognition, Aggressive Affect, Physiological Arousal, and Prosocial Behavior: A Meta-Analytic Review of the Scientific Literature." *Psychological Science* 12.5 (September 2001): 353–359.

Anderson, Craig A., and Karen E. Dill. "Video Games and Aggressive Thoughts, Feelings, and Behavior in the Laboratory and in Life." *Journal of Personality and Social Psychology* 78.4 (2000): 772–790.

Anderson, Craig. A., and C. M. Ford. "Affect of the Game Player: Short-term Effects of Highly and Mildly Aggressive Video Games." *Personality and Social Psychology Bulletin* 12.4 (December 1986): 390–402.

Anderson, Michael, Susan Leigh Anderson, and Chris Armen. "Toward Machine Ethics." American Association for Artificial Intelligence—The Nineteenth National Conference on Artificial Intelligence, 25–29 July 2004. San Jose, California. http://www.cs.uu.nl/~virginia/aotp/papers/Towards Machine Ethics.pdf (1 November 2005).

Angwin, Julia, and Laura Castaneda. "The Digital Divide: High-Tech Boom a Bust for Blacks, Latinos." *The San Francisco Chronicle,* 4 May 1998, A1.

Aristotle. *De interpretatione.* In *The Basic Works of Aristotle.* Edited and translated by Richard McKeon. New York: Random House, 1941.

———. *The Nicomachean Ethics.* Translated by H. Rackham. Cambridge, MA: Harvard University Press, 1982.

Asimov, Isaac. *I, Robot.* Garden City, NY: Doubleday, 1950.

Balsamo, Anne. *Technologies of the Gendered Body: Reading Cyborg Women.* Durham, NC: Duke University Press, 1996.

Barlow, John Perry. "A Declaration of the Independence of Cyberspace." *Binäre Mythen/Binary Myths.* Proceedings from the 14 September 1996 conference "Binary Myths—The Renaissance of Lost Emotions" held in Vienna, Austria. Vienna: Zukunfts-werkstätte, 1997.

———. "Being in Nothingness: Virtual Reality and the Pioneers of Cyberspace." *Mondo 2000* 2, Summer 1990, 34–43.

———. "Jack In, Young Pioneer!" Electronic Frontier Foundation, 11 August 1994. http://www.eff.org/Misc/Publications/John_Perry_Barlow/HTML/jack_in_ young_pioneer.html (1 November 2005).

Barnes, Sue. *Computer-Mediated Communication: Human-to-Human Communication Across the Internet.* Boston, MA: Pearson Education, 2003.

Bassham, Gregory. "The Religion of The Matrix and the Problems of Pluralism." In *The Matrix and Philosophy,* ed. William Irwin, 111–125. Chicago: Open Court, 2002.

Bataille, Georges. *The Unfinished System of Nonknowledge.* Translated and edited by Michelle Kendall and Stuart Kendall. Minneapolis, MN: University of Minnesota Press, 2001.

Baudrillard, Jean. *The Intelligence of Evil or the Lucidity Pact.* Translated by Chris Turner. Oxford: Berg, 2005.

———. *Le ludique et le policier et autres textes parus dans Utopie.* Paris: Sens & Tonka, 2001.

———. *Selected Writings.* Edited by Mark Poster. Stanford, CA: Stanford University Press, 1988.

———. *Simulacra and Simulation.* Translated by Sheila Faria Glaser. Ann Arbor, MI: University of Michigan Press, 1994.

———. *Symbolic Exchange and Death.* Translated by Iain Hamilton Grant. London: Sage, 1993.

Beck, Robin. "You Won't Know the Difference So You Can't Make the Choice." *Philosophy Now* 30 (December 2000/January 2001): 35–36.

Bell, David. *An Introduction to Cybercultures.* New York: Routledge, 2001.

Bell, David, and Barbara M. Kennedy, eds. *The Cybercultures Reader.* New York: Routledge, 2000.

Belluck, Pam. "Stuck on the Web; Symptoms of Internet Addiction." *New York Times,* 1 December 1996, sec. 4, p. 5.

Benedikt, Michael, ed. *Cyberspace: First Steps.* Cambridge, MA: MIT Press, 1993.

———. "Introduction." In *Cyberspace: First Steps,* ed. Michael Benedikt, 1–25. Cambridge, MA: MIT Press, 1993.

Bennington, Geoffrey. *Jacques Derrida.* Chicago: University of Chicago Press, 1993.

Bensley, Lillian, and Juliet Van Eenwyk. "Video Games and Real Life Aggression: Review of Literature." *Journal of Adolescent Health* 29.4 (October 2001): 244–257.

Bentham, Jeremy. *An Introduction to the Principles and Morals of Legislation.* Amherst, NY: Prometheus Books, 1988.

Benton Foundation/Center for Media and Community. *Digital Divide Network.* February 2004. http://www.digitaldividenetwork.org (1 November 2005).

Biocca, Frank, and Mark R. Levy, eds. *Communication in the Age of Virtual Reality.* Hillsdale, NJ: Lawrence Erlbaum Associates, 1995.

Birkerts, Sven. *The Gutenberg Elegies: The Fate of Reading in an Electronic Age.* Boston, MA: Faber and Faber, 1994.

Blackford, Russell. "Try the Blue Pill: What's Wrong with Life in a Simulation?" In *Jacking into the Matrix Franchise: Cultural Reception and Interpretation,* ed. Matthew Kapell and William G. Doty, 169–182. New York: Continuum, 2004.

Boettke, Peter. "Human Freedom and the Red Pill." In *Taking the Red Pill: Science, Philosophy and Religion in The Matrix,* ed. Glenn Yeffeth, 145–158. Dallas, TX: Benbella Books, 2003.

Bolt, David, and Ray Crawford. *Digital Divide: Computers and Our Children's Future.* New York: TV Books, 2000.

Bolter, Jay David. *Turing's Man: Western Culture in the Computer Age.* Chapel Hill, NC: University of North Carolina Press, 1984.

———. *Writing Space: The Computer, Hypertext, and the History of Writing.* Hillsdale, NJ: Lawrence Erlbaum Associates, 1991.

———. *Writing Space: Computers, Hypertext, and the Remediation of Print.* Mahwah, NJ: Lawrence Erlbaum Associates, 2001.

Bolter, Jay David, and Richard Grusin. "Remediation." *Configurations* 4.3 (1996): 311–358. Also available at http://muse.jhu.edu/journals/configurations/toc/con4.3.html.

———. *Remediation: Understanding New Media.* Cambridge, MA: MIT Press, 2000.

Boyd, Gregory A., and Al Larson. *Escaping the Matrix: Setting Your Mind Free to Experience Real Life in Christ.* North Dartmouth, MA: Baker Books, 2005.

Brady, Mick. "The Digital Divide Myth." *E-Commerce Times,* 4 August 2000. http://www.ecommercetimes.com/story/3953.html (1 November 2005).

Brey, Philip. "The Ethics of Representation and Action in Virtual Reality." *Ethics and Information Technology* 1.1 (March 1999): 5–14.

Brook, James, and Iain A. Boal, eds. *Resisting the Virtual Life: The Culture and Politics of Information.* San Francisco, CA: City Lights, 1995.

Brooks, Rodney. Comment in "AI's Greatest Trends and Controversies," by Marti A. Hearst and Haym Hirsh, *IEEE – Intelligent Systems* 15.1 (January/February 2002): 9.

Brown, David Jay. "Reality Check: An Interview with Jaron Lanier." In *Voices from the Edge—Internet Edition,* 1993. http://www.levity.com/mavericks/jaron.htm (1 November 2005).

Bryson, Joanna. "A Proposal for the Humanoid Agent-builders League (HAL)." Symposium on Artificial Intelligence, Ethics and (Quasi-)Human Rights, Convention of the Society for the Study of Artificial Intelligence and the Simulation of Behaviour (AISB-00). University of Birmingham, UK, 19–20 April 2000. http://www.cs.bath.ac.uk/~jjb/ftp/HAL00.pdf (28 February 2006).

Bryson, Joanna, and Phil Kime. "Just Another Artifact: Ethics and the Empirical Experience of AI." Fifteenth International Congress on Cybernetics. Namur, Belgium, 24–28 August 1998. http://www.cs.bath.ac.uk/~jjb/web/aiethics98.html (28 February 2006).

Bucy, Eric P. "Social Access to the Internet." *Harvard International Journal of Press Politics* 5.1 (2000): 50–61.

Burkeman, O. "Internet's Global Reach Is Not at All Utopian: The Evolution of Net Surfing May Be Unwittingly Creating a New Class of Inequality." *The Independent,* 17 August 1998, 14.

Burroughs, William S. *Naked Lunch.* New York: Grove Press, 1982.

Calcutt, Andrew. *White Noise: An A–Z of the Contradictions in Cyberculture.* New York: Palgrave Macmillan, 1998.

Calvert, Sandra L., and Siu-Lan Tan. "Impact of Virtual Reality on Young Adult's Physiological Arousal and Aggressive Thoughts: Interaction Versus Observation." *Journal of Applied Developmental Psychology* 15.1 (January–March 1994): 125–139.

Careaga, Andrew. *Hooked on the Net.* Grand Rapids, MI: Kregel Publications, 2002.

Carey, James. *Communication as Culture: Essays on Media and Society.* New York: Routledge, 1989.

Carvin, Andy. "Mind the Gap: The Digital Divide as the Civil Rights Issue of the New Millennium" *Multimedia Schools* 7.1 (2001): 56–58.

———. "Origin of the Term Digital Divide." Digitaldivide@list.benton.org, 4 January 2001. Archived at http://www.rtpnet.org/lists/rtpnet-tact/msg00080.html (1 November 2005).

Cassin, Barbara, ed. *Vocabulaire européen des philosophies.* Paris: Le Robert & Seuil, 2004.

Castell, Suzanne de, and Allan Luke. "Models of Literacy in North American Schools: Social and Historical Conditions and Consequences." In *Literacy, Society, and Schooling,* ed. Suzanne de Castell, Allan Luke, and Kieran Egan, 87–109. Cambridge: Cambridge University Press, 1986.

Castronova, Edward. "Virtual Worlds: A First-Hand Account of Market and Society on the Cyberian Frontier." *Center for Economic Studies & Ifo Institute for Economic Research,* CESifo Working Paper Series No. 618 (December 2001). http://ssrn.com/abstract=294828.

———. *Synthetic Worlds: The Business and Culture of Online Games.* Chicago: University of Chicago Press, 2005.

Cathcart, Robert, and Gary Gumpert. "The Person-Computer Interaction: A Unique Source." In *Information and Behavior*, ed. Brent D. Ruben. Vol. 1. New Brunswick, NJ: Transaction Books, 1985.

———. "Mediated Interpersonal Communication: Toward a New Topology." In *Inter/media: Interpersonal Communication in a Media World*, ed. Robert Cathcart and Gary Gumpert, 26–40. New York: Oxford University Press, 1981.

CBS Broadcasting, Inc. "Addicted: Suicide over Everquest?" *48 Hours*. 18 October 2002, 10:00pm EST.

The Center for Internet Behavior. September 2005. http://www.virtual-addiction. com (1 November 2005).

Center for Online Addiction. September 2005. http://www.netaddiction.com (1 November 2005).

Chandler, Daniel. "Biases of the Ear and Eye: 'Great Divide' Theories, Phonocentrism, Graphocentrism and Logocentrism," 1994, http://www.aber.ac.uk/media/Documents/litoral/litoral.html (1 November 2005).

———. *Semiotics for Beginners*, 1994, http://www.aber.ac.uk/media/Documents/ S4B/ semiotic.html (1 November 2005).

———. "Shaping and Being Shaped: Engaging with Media." *Computer-Mediated Communication Magazine*, 1 February 1996. http://www.december.com/cmc/ mag/1996/feb/chandler.html (1 November 2005).

———. "Technological or Media Determinism," 1995, http://www.aber.ac.uk/media/Documents/ tecdet/tecdet.html (1 November 2005).

Chang, Briankle. *Deconstructing Communication: Representation, Subject, and Economies of Exchange*. Minneapolis, MN: University of Minnesota Press, 1996.

Chartier, Roger. *Forms and Meanings: Texts, Performances, and Audiences from Codex to Computer*. University Park, PA: University of Pennsylvania Press, 1995.

Chesebro, James W., and Donald G. Bonsall. *Computer-Mediated Communication: Human Relationships in a Computerized World*. Tuscaloosa, AL: The University of Alabama Press, 1989.

Chesher, Chris. "Colonizing Virtual Reality: Construction of the Discourse of Virtual Reality 1984–1992." *Cultronix* 1.1, 1994. http://cultronix.eserver.org/chesher/ (1 November 2005).

Chung, Peter, and Andy Jones, directors. *The Animatrix*. Burbank, CA: Warner Home Video, 2003.

Clark, David L. "Heidegger's Craving: Being-on-Schelling." *Diacritics* 27.3 (1997): 8–33.

Clynes, Manfred E., and Nathan S. Kline. "Cyborgs and Space." In *The Cyborg Handbook*, ed. Chris Hables Gray, 29–34. New York: Routledge, 1995.

Cohen, Eric. "United We Surf: The Clinton Administration and the Business Community Are Eager to Solve a Problem—the 'Digital Divide'—That Does Not Exist." *The Weekly Standard*, 28 February 2000, 26.

Cohen, Richard. Introduction to *Humanism of the Other,* by Emmanuel Levinas. Chicago: University of Illinois Press, 2003.

Compaine, Benjamin. *The Digital Divide: Facing a Crisis or Creating a Myth?* Cambridge, MA: MIT Press, 2001.

Cooley, Charles Horton. *Social Organization.* New York: Schocken Books, 1962.

Cope, Bill, and Mary Kalantzis, eds. *Multiliteracies: Literacy Learning and the Design of Social Futures.* London: Routledge, 2000.

Crabtree, James. "The Digital Divide Is Rubbish—A Kind of Exclusion That Shouldn't Worry Us." *New Statesman,* 14 May 2001, 26.

Cruz-Neira, Carolina, Daniel J. Sandin, Thomas A. DeFanti, Robert V. Kenyon, and John C. Hart. "The CAVE: Audio Visual Experience Automatic Virtual Environment." *Communications of the ACM* 35.6 (June 1992): 64–72.

Culler, Jonathan. *On Deconstruction: Theory and Criticism after Structuralism.* Ithaca, NY: Cornell University Press, 1982.

Davis, Erik. *TechGnosis: Myth, Magic, and Mysticism in the Age of Information.* New York: Three Rivers Press, 1998.

De Landa, Manuel. *War in the Age of Intelligent Machines.* New York: Zone Books, 1991.

Deleuze, Gilles. *Difference and Repetition.* Translated by Paul Patton. New York: Columbia University Press, 1994.

———. *The Fold: Leibniz and the Baroque.* Translated by Tom Conley. Minneapolis, MN: University of Minnesota Press, 1993.

Deleuze, Gilles, and Félix Guattari. *A Thousand Plateaus: Capitalism and Schizophrenia.* Translated by Brian Massumi. Minneapolis, MN: University of Minnesota Press, 1987.

Dennett, Daniel C. *Brainstorms: Philosophical Essays on Mind and Psychology.* Cambridge, MA: MIT Press, 1998.

Derrida, Jacques. "And Say the Animal Responded." Translated by David Willis. In *Zoontologies: The Question of the Animal,* ed. Cary Wolfe, 121–146. Minneapolis, MN: University of Minnesota Press, 2003.

———. "The Animal That Therefore I Am (More to Follow)." *Critical Inquiry* 28 (Winter 2002): 369–418.

———. *Disseminations.* Translated by Barbara Johnson. Chicago: University of Chicago Press, 1981.

———. *Glas.* Translated by John P. Leavey, Jr and Richard Rand. Lincoln, NB: University of Nebraska Press, 1986.

———. *Limited Inc.* Translated by Samuel Weber. Evanston, IL: Northwestern University Press, 1993.

———. *Margins of Philosophy.* Translated by Alan Bass. Chicago: University of Chicago Press, 1982.

———. *Of Grammatology.* Translated by Gayatri Chakravorty Spivak. Baltimore,MD: The Johns Hopkins University Press, 1976.

————. *Paper Machine.* Translated by Rachel Bowlby. Stanford, CA: Stanford University Press, 2005.

————. *Positions.* Translated and annotated by Alan Bass. Chicago: University of Chicago Press, 1981.

————. "The Rhetoric of Drugs." Translated by Michael Israel. In *Points: Interviews, 1974–1994,* ed. Elisabeth Weber, 228–254. Stanford, CA: Stanford University Press, 1995.

————. "Violence and Metaphysics: An Essay on the Thought of Emmanuel Levinas." In *Writing and Difference.* Translated by Alan Bass. Chicago: University of Chicago Press, 1978.

————. *Writing and Difference.* Translated by Alan Bass. Chicago: University of Chicago Press, 1978.

Dery, Mark. "Flame Wars." In *Flame Wars: The Discourse of Cyberculture,* ed. Mark Dery, 1–10. Durham, NC: Duke University Press, 1994.

————. *Escape Velocity: Cyberculture at the End of the Century.* New York: Grove Press, 1996.

Descartes, René. *Discourse on Method.* In *Descartes: Selected Philosophical Writings.* Translated and edited by John Cottingham, Robert Stoothoff, and Dugald Murdoch. Cambridge: Cambridge University Press, 1988.

Dick, Philip K. *Do Androids Dream of Electric Sheep?* New York: Ballantine Books, 1982.

Dill, Karen E., and Jody C. Dill. "Video Game Violence: A Review of the Empirical Literature." *Aggression and Violent Behavior* 3.4 (Winter 1998): 407–428.

Diocaretz, Myriam, and Stefan Herbrechter, eds. *The Matrix in Theory.* Amsterdam: Editions Rodopi B.V., 2006.

Dreyfus, Hubert L. *On the Internet.* New York: Routledge, 2001.

Dreyfus, Hubert L., and Stephen D. Dreyfus. "Existential Phenomenology and the Brave New World of The Matrix." In *Philosophers Explore the Matrix,* ed. Christopher Grau, 71–97. Oxford: Oxford University Press, 2005.

Dyson, Esther. *Release 2.0: A Design for Living in the Digital Age.* New York: Broadway Books, 1997.

Dyson, Ester, George Gilder, George Keyworth, and Alvin Toffler. "Cyberspace and the American Dream: a Magna Carta for the Knowledge Age." *Information Society* 12.3 (1996): 295–308.

Ebo, Bosah. *Cyberghetto or Cyberutopia: Race, Class, and Gender on the Internet.* Westport, CT: Praeger Press, 1998.

Eick, David, and Ronald D. Moore, producers. *Battlestar Galactica.* Season 1. Universal City, CA: Universal Studios, 2005.

Eisenstein, Elizabeth L. "The End of the Book? Some Perspectives on Media Change." *American Scholar* 64.4 (1995): 541–555.

————. *The Printing Press as an Agent of Change: Communications and Cultural*

Transformations in Early-Modern Europe. 2 vols. Cambridge: Cambridge University Press, 1982.

Eisenstein, Zillah. *Global Obscenities: Patriarchy, Capitalism, and the Lure of Cyberfantasy.* New York: New York University Press, 1998.

Elbow, Peter. "The Uses of Binary Thinking." *JAC* 13.1 (1993): 51–78. Also available at http://www.jacweb.org/Archived_volumes/Text_articles/V13_I1_Elbow.html.

Ellis, John M. *Against Deconstruction.* Princeton: Princeton University Press, 1990.

Ellul, Jacques. *The Technological Society.* New York: Vintage, 1964.

Erion, Gerald J., and Barry Smith. "Skepticism, Morality, and The Matrix." In *The Matrix and Philosophy,* ed. William Irwin, 16–27. Chicago: Open Court, 2002.

Faller, Stephen. *Beyond the Matrix: Revolutions and Revelations.* Atlanta, GA: Chalice Press, 2004.

Falzon, Christopher. *Philosophy Goes to the Movies.* New York: Routledge, 2002.

Feenberg, Andrew. *Critical Theory of Technology.* New York: Oxford University Press, 1991.

Feshbach, Seymour. "The Catharsis Hypothesis and Some Consequences of Interaction with Aggressive and Neutral Play Objects." *Journal of Personality* 24 (June 1956): 449–462.

Fidler, Roger F. *Mediamorphosis: Understanding New Media.* Thousand Oaks, CA: Pine Forge Press, 1997.

Finnegan, Ruth. "Communication and Technology." Unit 8 of the Open University Correspondence Course, *Making Sense of Society,* Block 3, *Communication.* Buckingham: Open University Press, 1975.

Fisk, John. Introduction to *Communication Studies.* New York: Routledge, 1994.

Floridi, Luciano. "Information Ethics: On the Philosophical Foundation of Computer Ethics." *Ethics and Information Technology* 1.1 (March 1999): 37–56.

———. "Information Ethics, its Nature and Scope." In *Moral Philosophy and Information Technology,* ed. Jeroen van den Hoven and John Weckert. Cambridge: Cambridge University Press, 2006. Pre-print available from http://www.philosophyofinformation.net/pdf/ieinas.pdf.

Flusser, Vilém. *Die Schrift: Hat Schreiben Zukunft?* Göttingen: Immatrix Publications, 1989.

Fontana, Paul. "Finding God in *The Matrix.*" In *Taking the Red Pill: Science, Philosophy and Religion in The Matrix,* ed. Glenn Yeffeth, 159–184. Dallas, TX: Benbella Books, 2003.

Foucault, Michel. *The Archaeology of Knowledge.* Translated by A. M. Sheridan Smith. New York: Pantheon Books, 1972.

———. *The Order of Things: An Archaeology of the Human Sciences.* Translated by Alan Sheridan. New York: Vintage Books, 1973.

Freeman, Barbara Claire. "Moments of Beating: Addiction and Inscription in Virginia Woolf's 'A Sketch of the Past.'" *Diacritics* 27.3 (1997): 65–76.

Frentz, Thomas S., and Janice Hocker Rushing. "Mother Isn't Quite Herself Today: Myth and Spectacle in The Matrix." *Critical Studies in Media Communication* 19.1 (2002): 64–86.

Gans, David, and R. U. Sirius. "Civilizing the Electronic Frontier: An Interview with Mitch Kapor & John Barlow of the Electronic Frontier Foundation." *Mondo 2000*, 3 (Winter 1991): 45–49.

Gasché, Rodolphe. *Tain of the Mirror:Derrida and the Philosophy of Reflection.* Cambridge, MA: Harvard University Press, 1987.

Gee, James Paul. *Social Linguistics and Literacies.* London: Taylor & Francis, 1996.

Gerbner, George. "Toward a General Model of Communication." *Audio Visual Communication Review* 4.3 (1956): 171–199.

Gibson, William. "Academy Leader." In *Cyberspace: First Steps*, ed. Michael Benedikt, 27–30. Cambridge, MA: MIT Press, 1993.

———. Foreword to *The Matrix: The Shooting Script*, by Andy and Larry Wachowski. New York: Newmarket Press, 2001.

———. *Neuromancer.* New York: Ace Books, 1984.

Global Internet Liberty Campaign. *Bridging the Digital Divide: Internet Access in Central and Eastern Europe.* Washington, DC: Center for Democracy and Technology, 2000.

Godlovitch, Stanley, Roslind Godlovitch, and John Harris. *Animals, Men, and Morals: An Enquiry into the Maltreatment of Non-Humans.* New York: Taplinger, 1972.

Goody, Jack. *Literacy in Traditional Societies.* Cambridge: Cambridge University Press, 1968.

Gore, Al. "Remarks at the Digital Divide Event." 28 April 1998. http://clinton4.nara. gov/textonly/ WH/EOP/OVP/speeches/edtech.html (1 November 2005).

Goslee, Susan. *Losing Ground Bit by Bit: Low-Income Communities in the Information Age.* Washington, DC: Benton Foundation, 1998.

Gracia, Jorge J. E., and Jonathan J. Sanford. "The Metaphysics of The Matrix." In *The Matrix and Philosophy*, ed. William Irwin, 55–65. Chicago: Open Court, 2002.

Graff, Harvey J. *The Labyrinths of Literacy: Reflections on Literacy Past and Present.* London: Bodley Head, 1987.

Graham, Gordon. *The Internet://A Philosophical Inquiry.* New York: Routledge, 1999.

Gramsci, Antonio. *Selections from the Prison Notebooks of Antonio Gramsci.* Translated and edited by Quintin Hoare and Geoffrey Nowell-Smith. London: Lawrence and Wishart, 1971.

Grau, Christopher, ed. *Philosophers Explore the Matrix.* Oxford: Oxford University Press, 2005.

———. "Bad Dreams, Evil Demons, and the Experience Machine: Philosophy and *The Matrix*." In *Philosophers Explore the Matrix*, ed. Christopher Grau, 10–23. Oxford: Oxford University Press, 2005.

Gray, Chris Hables. *Cyborg Citizen*. New York: Routledge, 2002.

———. "Prosthesis/Bricollage/Morph." *ArtLab23,* Spring 2002. http://www.artlab23. net/issue1/Prothesis.html (1 November 2005).

Gray, Chris Hables, and Steven Mentor. "The Cyborg Body Politic and the New World Order." In *Prosthetic Territories: Politics and Hypertechnologies,* ed. Gabriel Brahm Jr. and Mark Driscoll, 219–247. Boulder, CO: Westview Press, 1995.

Gray, Chris Hables, Steven Mentor, and Heidi J. Figueroa-Sarriera. "Cyborgology: Constructing the Knowledge of Cybernetic Organisms." In *The Cyborg Handbook,* ed. Chris Hables Gray, 1–16. New York: Routledge, 1995.

Graybill, Daniel, Janice R. Kirsch, and Edward D. Esselman. "Effects of Playing Violent Versus Non-violent Video Games on the Aggressive Ideation of Aggressive and Non-aggressive Children." *Child Study Journal* 15.3 (1985): 199–205.

"The Great Digital Divide: Broadcasters are at Odds with Congress Over Whether HDTV or Multicasting Will Prevail." *Mediaweek* 7.39, 20 October 1997, 4.

Greene, Brian. *The Fabric of the Cosmos: Space, Time, and the Texture of Reality.* New York: Vintage Books, 2005.

Greenfield, David N. *Virtual Addiction: Help for Netheads, Cyberfreaks, and Those Who Love Them.* Oakland, CA: New Harbinger, 1999.

Griffiths, Mark D. "Internet Addiction: Fact or Fiction?" *The Psychologist* 12.5 (1998): 246–50.

Griswold, Charles L. "Happiness and Cypher's Choice: Is Ignorance Bliss?" In *The Matrix and Philosophy,* ed. William Irwin, 126–137. Chicago: Open Court, 2002.

Gunkel, David J. *Hacking Cyberspace.* Boulder, CO: Westview Press, 2001.

———. "What's the Matter with Books?" *Configurations* 11.3 (Fall 2004): 277–304.

———. "Second Thoughts: Toward A Critique of the Digital Divide." *New Media & Society* 5.4 (December 2003): 499–522.

Gunkel, David J., and Debra Hawhee. "Virtual Alterity and the Reformating of Ethics." *Journal of Mass Media Ethics* 18.3/4 (2003): 173–193.

Gunter, Barrie. "Psychological Effects of Video Games." In *Handbook of Computer Game Studies,* ed. Joost Raessens and Jeffrey Goldstein, 145–160. Cambridge, MA: MIT Press, 2005.

Haber, Karen, ed. *Exploring the Matrix: Visions of the Cyber Present.* New York: St. Martin's Griffin, 2003.

Habermas, Jürgen. *The Inclusion of the Other: Studies in Political Theory.* Translated by Ciaran Cronin et al. Cambridge, MA: MIT Press, 1998.

Hafner, Katie, and Matthew Lyon. *Where Wizards Stay Up Late: The Origins of the Internet.* New York: Simon & Schuster, 1996.

Hall, J. Storrs. "Ethics for Machines." *KurzweilAI.net,* 5 July 2001. http://www. kurzweilai.net/articles/art0218.html (1 November 2005).

Hanson, Robin. "Was Cypher Right? (Part 1): Why We Stay in Our Matrix." In

Taking the Red Pill: Science, Philosophy and Religion in The Matrix, ed. Glenn Yeffeth, 23–32. Dallas, TX: Benbella Books, 2003.

Haraway, Donna J. *Simians, Cyborgs, and Women: The Reinvention of Nature.* New York: Routledge, 1991.

Harmon, Amy. "Daily Life's Digital Divide." *Los Angeles Times,* 3 July 1996, A1.

Hartmann, Frank. *Cyber.Philosophy: Medientheoretische Auslotungen.* Vienna: Passagen Verlag, 1999.

Havelock, Eric A. *Preface to Plato.* Cambridge, MA: Belknap Press, 1963.

Hayles, N. Katherine. *How We Became Posthuman: Virtual Bodies in Cybernetics, Literature, and Informatics.* Chicago: University of Chicago Press, 1999.

———. *Writing Machines.* Cambridge, MA: MIT Press, 2002.

Hawhee, Debra. "Burke on Drugs." *Rhetoric Society Quarterly* 34.1 (2004): 5–28.

Hegel, Georg Wilhelm Friedrich. *Enzyklopädie der philosophischen Wissenschaften im Grundrisse.* Hamburg: Verlag von Felix Meiner, 1969.

———. *Hegel's Logic.* Translated by William Wallace. Oxford: Oxford University Press, 1987.

———. *Phenomenology of Spirit.* Translated by A. V. Miller. Oxford: Oxford University Press, 1977.

———. *The Science of Logic.* Translated by A. V. Miller. Atlantic Highlands, NJ: Humanities Press International, 1989.

Heidegger, Martin. *Being and Time.* Translated by John Macquarrie and Edward Robinson. New York: Harper & Row, 1962.

———. *Die Grundbegriffe der Metaphysik: Welt—Endlichkeit—Einsamkeit.* Gesamtausgabe 29/30. Frankfurt am Main: V. Klostermann, 1983.

———. *Nietzsche: The Will to Power as Art.* Translated by David Farrell Krell. New York: Harper & Row, 1979.

———. *The Question Concerning Technology.* Translated by William Lovitt. New York: Harper Torchbooks, 1977.

Heim, Michael. *Electric Language: A Philosophical Study of Word Processing.* New Haven, CT: Yale University Press, 1999.

———. "The Erotic Ontology of Cyberspace" In *Cyberspace: First Steps,* ed. Michael Benedikt, 59–80. Cambridge, MA: MIT Press, 1993.

———. *The Metaphysics of Virtual Reality.* New York: Oxford University Press, 1993.

———. *Virtual Realism.* New York: Oxford University Press, 1998.

Herring, Susan C., ed. *Computer-Mediated Communication: Linguistic, Social and Cross-Cultural Perspectives.* Philadelphia, PA: John Benjamins Publishing Company, 1996.

Hillis, Ken. *Digital Sensations: Space, Identity, and Embodiment in Virtual Reality.* Minneapolis, MN: University of Minnesota Press, 1999.

Hiltz, Starr Roxanne, and Murray Turoff. *The Networked Nation: Human Com-*

munication via Computer. Reading, MA: Addison-Wesley Publishing Company, 1978.

Hiltz, Starr Roxanne, and Elaine Kerr. *Computer-Mediated Communication Systems: Status and Evaluation.* New York: Academic Press, 1982.

Himma, Kenneth Einar. "There's Something About Mary: The Moral Value of Things qua Information Objects." *Ethics and Information Technology* 6.3 (September 2004): 145–159.

Hoffman, Donna L., Thomas P. Novak, and Ann E. Schlosser. "The Evolution of the Digital Divide: How Gaps in Internet Access May Impact Electronic Commerce." *Journal of Computer-Mediated Communication* 5.3, March 2000. http://jcmc.indiana.edu/vol5/issue3/hoffman.html (1 November 2005).

Holeton, Richard, ed. *Composing Cyberspace: Identity, Community, and Knowledge in the Electronic Age.* New York: McGraw Hill, 1998.

Horowitz, Michael. Editor's Note to *Chaos and Cyberculture,* by Timothy Leary. Berkeley, CA: Ronin Publishing, 1994.

Horsley, Jake. *Matrix Warrior: Being the One.* New York: St. Martin's Griffin, 2003.

Horsfield, Peter. "Continuities and Discontinuities in Ethical Reflections on Digital Virtual Reality." *Journal of Mass Media Ethics* 18.3–4 (2003): 155–172.

Horvath, John. "Delving into the Digital Divide." *Telepolis,* 17 July 2000. http://www.heise.de/tp/r4/artikel/8/8393/1.html (1 November 2005).

Hugo, Victor. *Notre-Dame de Paris.* Translated by John Sturrock. New York: Penguin Putnam, 1978.

Informa Publishing Group. "Absat Bridges Digital Divide with Astra Package: Pay-TV France." *New Media Markets,* 18 September 1997, 3.

Innis, Harold. *The Bias of Communication.* Toronto: University of Toronto Press, 1951.

Internet-a-holics Anonymous. August 1999. http://internetaddiction.com (1 November 2005).

Internet/Computer Addiction Services. June 1999. http://www.icaservices.com (1 November 2005).

Irving, Larry. "Origin of the Term Digital Divide." Digitaldivide@list.benton.org, 3 January 2001. Archived at http://www.rtpnet.org/lists/rtpnet-tact/msg00080.html (1 November 2005).

Irwin, William, ed. *The Matrix and Philosophy.* Chicago: Open Court, 2002.

———. "Computers, Caves, and Oracles: Neo and Socrates." In *The Matrix and Philosophy,* ed. William Irwin, 5–15. Chicago: Open Court, 2002.

———. Dustjacket to *The Matrix and Philosophy.* Chicago: Open Court, 2002.

———. *More Matrix and Philosophy: Revolutions and Reloaded Decoded.* Chicago: Open Court, 2005.

Jakobson, Roman. "Closing Statement: Linguistics and Poetics." In *Style and Language,* ed. Thomas A. Sebeok, 350–377. Cambridge, MA: MIT Press, 1960.

Johnson, Barbara. "Translator's Introduction" to *Disseminations,* by Jacques Derrida. Chicago: University of Chicago Press, 1981.

Jones, Barry. *Sleepers, Wake! Technology and the Future of Work.* New York: Oxford University Press, 1990.

Jones, Steven G., ed. *CyberSociety 2.0: Computer-Mediated Communication and Community.* London: Sage, 1994.

Jones, William G. "Crossing the Digital Divide: Moving From Film to Filmless Radiology." *Journal of Digital Imaging* 12.2 (1999): 47–54.

Kamioka, Nobuo. "Cyberpunk Revisited: William Gibson's Neuromancer and the 'Multimedia Revolution.'" *The Japanese Journal of American Studies* 9 (1998): 53–68.

Kant, Immanuel. *Critique of Practical Reason.* Translated by Lewis White Beck. New York: Macmillan, 1985.

———. *Grounding for the Metaphysics of Morals.* Translated by James W. Ellington, Indianapolis, IN: Hackett Publishing Company, 1983.

Kapell, Matthew, and William G. Doty, eds. *Jacking into the Matrix Franchise: Cultural Reception and Interpretation.* New York: Continuum, 2004.

Katz, James, and P. Aspden, "Motivations for and Barriers to Internet Usage: Results of a National Public Opinion Survey." *Internet Research: Electronic Networking Applications and Policy* 7.3 (1997): 170–188.

Kelly, James Patrick. "Meditations on the Singular Matrix." In *Exploring the Matrix: Visions of the Cyber Present,* ed. Karen Haber, 222–235. New York: St. Martin's Griffin, 2003.

Kelly, Kevin, Adam Heilbrun, and Barbara Stacks. "Virtual Reality: An Interview with Jaron Lanier." *Whole Earth Review* 64 (Fall 1989): 108–119. Available at http:// www.well.com/user/jaron/vrint.html.

Kernan, Alvin. *The Death of Literature.* New Haven, CT: Yale University Press, 1990.

Kestenbaum, G. I., and L. Weinstein. "Personality, Psychopathology, and Developmental Issues in Male Adolescent Video Game Use." *Journal of the American Academy of Child Psychiatry* 24.3 (May 1985): 325–337.

Kierkegaard, Søren. *Concluding Unscientific Postscript.* Translated by David F. Swenson and Walter Lowrie. Princeton, NJ: Princeton University Press, 1968.

———. *Either/Or, Part II.* Translated by Howard V. and Edna H. Hong. Princeton, NJ: Princeton University Press, 1987.

Kiesler, Sara, ed. *Culture of the Internet.* Mahwah, NJ: Lawrence Erlbaum Associates, 1997.

Kittler, Friedrich A. *Gramophone, Film, Typewriter.* Translated by Geoffery Winthrop-Young and Michael Wutz. Stanford, CA: Stanford University Press, 1999.

Krell, David Farrell. *Daimon Life: Heidegger and Life Philosophy.* Bloomington, IN: Indiana University Press, 1992.

Kroker, Arthur, and Michael A. Weinstein. *Data Trash*. New York: St. Martin's Press, 1994.

Kurzweil, Raymond. "The Future of Libraries." In *CyberReader*, ed. Victor J. Vitanza, 291–304. Boston, MA: Allyn and Bacon, 1999.

Landow, George P. *Hypertext: The Convergence of Contemporary Critical Theory and Technology*. Baltimore, MD: The Johns Hopkins University Press, 1992.

Lanham, Richard A. *The Electronic Word: Democracy, Technology, and the Arts*. Chicago: University of Chicago Press, 1993.

Lanier, Jaron. "Homepage of Jaron Lanier." 2005. http://www.jaronlanier.com/index.html (1 November 2005).

Lawrence, Matt. *Like a Splinter in Your Mind: The Philosophy behind the Matrix Trilogy*. Oxford: Blackwell Publishing, 2004.

Leibniz, Gottfried Wilhelm. "Preface to a *Universal Characteristic*." In *G. W. Leibniz: Philosophical Essays*, trans. and ed. Roger Ariew and Daniel Garber, 5–10. Indianapolis, IN: Hackett Publishing Company, 1989.

Lem, Stanisław. *Solaris*. Kraków: Wydawnictwo Literackie, 2002

———. *Summa Technologica*. Kraków: Wydawnictwo Literackie, 1964.

Lenhart, Amanda. "The Ever-Shifting Internet Population: A New Look at Internet Access and the Digital Divide." *Pew Internet American Life Project*. Washington, DC: Pew Research Center, 16 April 2003. http://www.pewinternet.org/pdfs/PIP_Shifting_Net_Pop_Report.pdf.

———. "Who's Not Online?" *Pew Internet American Life Project*. Washington, DC: Pew Research Center, 21 September 2000. http://www.pewinternet.org/pdfs/Pew_Those_Not_Online_Report.pdf.

Lentz, T. M. "The Third Place from the Truth: Plato's Paradoxical Attack on Writing." *Communication Quarterly* 31.4 (Fall 1983): 290–301.

Leonard, Bret, director. *Lawnmower Man*. Hollywood, CA: New Line Cinema, 1992.

Levinas, Emmanuel. *Collected Philosophical Papers*. Translated by Alphonso Lingis. Dordrecht: Martin Nijhoff Publishers, 1987.

———. *Otherwise Than Being Or Beyond Essence*. Translated by Alphonso Lingis. The Hague: Martinus Nijhoff Publishers, 1981.

———. *Totality and Infinity*. Translated by Alphonso Lingis. Pittsburgh, PA: Duquesne University Press, 1969.

Lévi-Strauss, Claude. *The Savage Mind*. Translated by George Weidenfeld. Chicago: University of Chicago Press, 1966.

Lévy, Pierre. *Cyberculture*. Translated by Robert Bononno. Minneapolis, MN: University of Minnesota Press, 2001.

Licklider, J. C. R. "Man-Computer Symbiosis." *IRE Transactions on Human Factors in Electronics* HFE-1 (March 1960): 4–11.

Licklider, J. C. R., and Robert W. Taylor. "The Computer as a Communication Device." *Science and Technology* (April 1968): 21–31.

Liddel, H. G., and R. Scott. *An Intermediate Greek-English Lexicon.* Oxford: Oxford at the Claredon Press, 1991.

Lloyd, Peter B. "Glitches in The Matrix … And How to Fix Them." In *Taking the Red Pill: Science, Philosophy and Religion in The Matrix,* ed. Glenn Yeffeth, 103–124. Dallas, TX: Benbella Books, 2003.

Lorde, Audre. *Sister Outsider: Essays and Speeches.* Berkeley, CA: The Crossing Press, 1984.

Lubar, Steven. *InfoCulture.* Boston, MA: Houghton Mifflin Company, 1993.

Lunenfeld, Peter, ed. *The Digital Dialectic: New Essays on New Media.* Cambridge, MA: MIT Press, 2000.

———. "Screen Grabs: The Digital Dialectic and New Media Theory." In *The Digital Dialectic: New Essays on New Media,* ed. Peter Lunenfeld, xiv–xxi. Cambridge, MA: MIT Press, 2000.

Lurie, Peter. "The Rush to Judgment: Binary Thinking in a Digital Age." *ctheory. net,* 30 March 2004. http://www.ctheory.net/text_file.asp?pick=416 (1 November 2005).

Lyotard, Jean-François. *The Inhuman: Reflections on Time.* Translated by Geoffrey Bennington and Rachel Bowlby. Stanford, CA: Stanford University Press, 1991.

———. *The Postmodern Condition: A Report on Knowledge.* Translated by Geoff Bennington and Brian Massumi. Minneapolis, MN: University of Minnesota Press, 1984.

MacKenzie, Donald, and Judy Wajcman, eds. *The Social Shaping of Technology: How the Refrigerator Got Its Hum.* Buckingham: Open University Press, 1985.

Mallet, Marie-Louise, ed. *L'Animal autobiographique, Autour de Jacques Derrida.* Paris: Editions Galilée, 1999.

Markley, Robert. "Introduction: History, Theory and Virtual Reality." In *Virtual Realities and Their Discontents,* ed. Robert Markley, 1–10. Baltimore, MD: The Johns Hopkins University Press, 1996.

Mattelart, Armand. *Mapping World Communication: War, Progress, Culture.* Translated by Susan Emanuel and James A. Cohen. Minneapolis, MN: University of Minnesota Press, 1994.

———. *The Invention of Communication.* Translated by Susan Emanuel. Minneapolis, MN: University of Minnesota Press, 1996.

McGinn, Colin. "The Matrix of Dreams." In *Philosophers Explore the Matrix,* ed. Christopher Grau, 62–70. Oxford: Oxford University Press, 2005.

McLuhan, Marshall. *The Gutenberg Galaxy: The Making of Typographic Man.* Toronto: University of Toronto Press, 1962.

———. *Understanding Media: The Extensions of Man.* Cambridge, MA: MIT Press, 1995.

McLuhan, Marshall, and Eric McLuhan. *Laws of Media: The New Science.* Toronto: University of Toronto Press, 1988.

McRae, Hamish. "Unleashing the Digital Divide: The Changes in Television Will Change Global Society as we Lose Something that Unifies a Nation." *The Independent,* 17 November 1998, 5.

Meadow, Charles T. *Ink into Bits: A Web of Converging Media.* Lanham, MD: The Scarecrow Press, 1998.

Michel, Bon. "Internet, ou la communauté rétablie." *Le Monde,* 10 February 2001, 1.

Mitchell, William. *City of Bits: Place, Space and the Infobahn.* Cambridge, MA: MIT Press, 1996.

Moore, Dinty W. *The Emperor's Virtual Clothes: The Naked Truth about Internet Culture.* New York: Algonquin Books, 1995.

Moore, George E. *Principia Ethica.* Cambridge: Cambridge University Press, 2000.

Morse, Margaret. *Virtualities: Television, Media Art, and Cyberculture.* Bloomington, IN: Indiana University Press, 1998.

Mueller, Gustav E. "The Hegel Legend of 'Thesis-Antithesis-Synthesis.'" *Journal of the History of Ideas* 19.3 (1958): 411–414.

National Public Radio. "New Poll by National Public Radio (NPR), The Kaiser Family Foundation and Harvard's Kennedy School of Government." *Talk of the Nation,* 29 February 2000, 3:00 pm ET.

Nealon, Jeffrey T. *Alterity Politics: Ethics and Performative Subjectivity.* Durham, NC: Duke University Press, 1998.

———. *Double Reading: Postmodernism after Deconstruction.* Ithaca, NY: Cornell University Press, 1993.

Negroponte, Nicholas. *Being Digital.* New York: Vintage, 1995.

Neumann, Fritz-Wilhelm. "Information Society and the Text: The Predicament of Literary Culture in the Age of Electronic Communication." Erfurt Electronic Studies in English, strategy statement no. 6., 1999. http://webdoc.sub.gwdg.de/edoc/ia/eese/strategy/neumann/6_st.html (1 November 2005).

Newton, Isaac. *Philosophiae Naturalis Principia Mathematica,* ed. Alexandre Koyré and I. Bernard Cohen. Cambridge, MA: Harvard University Press, 1972.

Nietzsche, Friedrich. *Beyond Good and Evil.* Translated by Walter Kaufmann. New York: Vintage Books, 1989.

———. *The Gay Science.* Translated by Walter Kaufmann. New York: Vintage Books, 1974.

———. *Nachgelassene Fragmente 1869–1874.* In *Friedrich Nietzsche Sämtliche Werke Kritische Studienausgabe.* Edited by Giorgio Colli and Mazzino Montinari. Vol. 7. Berlin: Walter de Gruyter, 1980.

———. *The Twilight of the Idols.* In *The Portable Nietzsche.* Translated and edited by Walter Kaufmann. New York: Penguin Books, 1983.

Noble, David W. *The Religion of Technology: The Divinity of Man and the Spirit of Invention.* New York: Penguin Books, 1999.

Norden, Eric. "Marshall McLuhan: A Candid Conversation with the High Priest of Popcult and Metaphysician of the Media." *Playboy,* March 1969, 26–27, 45, 55–56, 61, 63.

Norris, Christopher. *Deconstruction: Theory and Practice.* New York: Methuen, 1982.

Novak, Thomas P., and Donna L. Hoffman. "Bridging the Racial Divide on the Internet." *Science* 280 (17 April 1998): 390–391.

Nozick, Robert. *Anarchy, State, and Utopia.* New York: Basic Books, 1974.

Nunberg, Geoffrey. "Introduction." *The Future of the Book,* ed. Geoffrey Nunberg, 9–20. Berkeley, CA: University of California Press, 1996.

———. "Prefixed Out." Commentary on *Fresh Air.* WHYY radio (17 May, 2002). Transcript available at http://www-csli.stanford.edu/~nunberg/cyber.html.

O'Donnell, James J. *Avatars of the Word: From Papyrus to Cyberspace.* Cambridge, MA: Harvard University Press, 1998.

Oettinger, Anthony G. "Compunications in the National Decision-Making Process." In *Computers, Communications, and the Public Interest,* ed. Martin Greenberger, 73–114. Baltimore, MD: The Johns Hopkins University Press, 1971.

Ogden, Frank. *The Last Book You'll Ever Read: And Other Lessons from the Future.* Toronto: Macfarlane Walter & Ross, 1993.

Ong, Walter J. *Orality and Literacy: The Technologizing of the Word.* New York: Routledge, 1995.

Paik, Haejung, and George Comstock. "The Effects of Television Violence on Antisocial Behavior: A Meta-Analysis." *Communication Research* 21.4 (August 1994): 516–546.

Paley, William. *Natural Theology: Or, Evidences of the Existence and Attributes of the Deity, Collected from the Appearances of Nature.* 10th ed. London: R. Faulder, 1805.

Partridge, John. "Plato's Cave and The Matrix." In *Philosophers Explore the Matrix,* ed. Christopher Grau, 239–257. Oxford: Oxford University Press, 2005.

Paton, H. J. *The Categorical Imperative:A Study in Kant's Moral Philosophy.* Philadelphia, PA: University of Pennsylvania Press, 1971.

Patton, Paul. "Translator's Preface" to *Difference and Repetition,* by Gilles Deleuze. New York: Columbia University Press, 1994.

Peirce, Charles Sanders. *The Collected Papers of Charles Sanders Peirce,* vol. 2. Edited by Charles Hartshorne and Paul Weiss. Cambridge, MA: Harvard University Press, 1932.

Perio, Art. "The Digital Divide and Institutional Racism." *Political Affairs* 80.2 (2001): 4–10.

Plato. *Phaedo.* Translated by Harold North Fowler. Cambridge, MA: Harvard University Press, 1990.

———. *Phaedrus.* Translated by Harold North Fowler. Cambridge, MA: Harvard University Press, 1982.

Plato. *Republic.* Translated by Paul Shorey. Cambridge, MA: Harvard University Press, 1987.

Poole, Gary Andrew. "A New Gulf in American Education, The Digital Divide." *The New York Times,* 29 January 1996, D3, col. 3.

Pool, Ithiel de Sola. Foreword to *The Coming Information Age: An Overview of Technology, Economics, and Politics,* by Wilson P. Dizard. 2nd ed. New York: Longman, 1985.

Porter, David, ed. *Internet Culture.* New York: Routledge, 1997.

Poster, Mark. *What's the Matter with the Internet.* Minneapolis, MN: University of Minnesota Press, 2001.

Postman, Neil. *Building a Bridge to the 18th Century.* New York: Vintage Books, 1999.

———. *Technopoly: The Surrender of Culture to Technology.* New York: Vintage Books, 1993.

Provenzo, Eugene F. *Beyond the Gutenberg Galaxy: Microcomputers and the Emergence of Post-Typographical Culture.* New York: Teachers College Press, 1986.

Proyas, Alex, director. *I, Robot.* Beverly Hills, CA: Twentieth Century Fox Home Video, 2005.

Public Broadcasting System. *Digital Divide.* 28 January 2000. http://www.pbs.org/digitaldivide/ (1 November 2005).

Ratliff, Evan. "The Crusade Against Evolution." *Wired* 12.10, October 2004, 156–161. Also available at http://www.wired.com/wired/archive/12.10/evolution.html.

Regan, Tom. Foreword to *Animal Others: On Ethics, Ontology, and Animal Life,* edited by Peter Steeves. Albany, NY: State University of New York Press, 1999.

Rheingold, Howard. *The Virtual Community: Homesteading on the Electronic Frontier.* New York: Addison-Wesley, 1993.

———. *Virtual Reality.* New York: Summit Books, 1991.

Riddell, Rob. "Doom Goes to War." *Wired* 5.4, April, 1997, 114–118, 164–166. Also available at http://wired-vig.wired.com/wired/archive/5.04/ff_doom_pr.html.

Roberts, John L. "TV: Digital Divide." *Newsweek* 129.16, 1997, 50–51.

Robins, Kevin, and Frank Webster. *Times of the Technoculture: From the Information Society to the Virtual Life.* New York: Routledge, 1999.

Rogers, Everett M., and Sheizaf Rafaeli. "Computers and Communication." In *Information and Behavior,* ed. Brent D. Ruben, 95–112. New Brunswick, NJ: Transaction Books, 1985.

Ronell, Avital. *Crack Wars: Literature, Addiction, Mania.* Lincoln, NB: University of Nebraska Press, 1992.

———. *Telephone Book: Technology, Schizophrenia, Electric Speech.* Lincoln, NB: University of Nebraska Press, 1989.

Rufo, Kenneth. "The Mirror in The Matrix of Media Ecology." *Critical Studies in Media Communication* 20.2 (2003): 117–140.

Rushkoff, Douglas. *Cyberia: Life in the Trenches of Hyperspace.* 2nd ed. Manchester: Clinamen Press, 2002.

Saco, Diana. *Cybering Democracy: Public Space and the Internet.* Minneapolis, MN: University of Minnesota Press, 2002.

Sallis, John. *Delimitations: Phenomenology and the End of Metaphysics.* Bloomington, IN: Indiana University Press, 1986.

Sardar, Ziauddin, and Jerome R. Ravetz, eds. *Cyberfutures: Culture and Politics on the Information Superhighway.* New York: New York University Press, 1996.

Sassi, Sinikka. "Cultural Differentiation or Social Segregation? Four Approaches to the Digital Divide." *New Media and Society* 7.5 (October 2005): 684–700.

Saussure, Ferdinand de. *Course in General Linguistics.* Translated by Wade Baskin. London: Peter Owen, 1959.

Savage-Rumbaugh, Sue, Stuart G. Shanker, and Talbot J. Taylor. *Apes, Language, and the Human Mind.* Oxford: Oxford University Press, 1998.

Schick, Theodore. "Fate, Freedom, and Foreknowledge." In *The Matrix and Philosophy,* ed. William Irwin, 87–98. Chicago: Open Court, 2002.

Schrader, C. "Brücken über den Digital Graben." *Süddeutsche Zeitung,* 5 December 2000, V2/13.

Schuchardt, Read Mercer. "What Is the Matrix?" In *Taking the Red Pill: Science, Philosophy and Religion in The Matrix,* ed. Glenn Yeffeth, 5–22. Dallas, TX: Benbella Books, 2003.

Schuman, Bruce. *Utopian Computer Networking: America's New Central Project,* 19 November 1988. http://origin.org/ucs/text/utopia2.cfm. (1 November 2005).

Scott, Derek. "The Effect of Video Games on Feelings of Aggression." *The Journal of Psychology* 129.2 (March 1995): 121–132.

Scott, Ridley, director. *Blade Runner.* Burbank, CA: Warner Home Video, 1982.

Seay, Chris, and Greg Garrett. *The Gospel Reloaded: Exploring Spirituality and Faith in the Matrix.* Colorado Springs, CO: Piñon Press, 2003.

Sedgwick, Eve Kosofsky. "Epidemics of Will." In *Zone 6: Incorporations,* ed. Jonathan Crary and Sanford Kwinter, 582–595. New York: Urzone, 1992.

Seville, Helen, and Debora Field. "What Can AI Do for Ethics?" Symposium on Artificial Intelligence, Ethics and (Quasi-)Human Rights, Convention of the Society for the Study of Artificial Intelligence and the Simulation of Behaviour (AISB-00). University of Birmingham, UK, 19–20 April 2000. http://www.cs.bham.ac.uk/ ~jab/AISB-00/Rights/Abstracts/seville.html (28 February 2006).

Shachtman, Noah. "EverQuest: The Latest Addiction." *Wired News,* 29 July 1999. http://www.wired.com/news/culture/0,1284,20984,00.html (1 November 2005).

Shannon, Claude E., and Warren Weaver. *The Mathematical Theory of Communication.* Urbana, IL: University of Illinois Press, 1963.

Shapiro, Andrew L. *The Control Revolution: How the Internet Is Putting Individuals in Charge and Changing the World We Know.* New York: PublicAffairs, 1999.

Sherry, John L. "The Effect of Violent Video Games on Aggression: A Meta-Analysis." *Human Communication Research* 27.3 (July 2001): 409–431.

Sidgwick, Henry. *The Methods of Ethics.* Indianapolis, IN: Hackett Publishing Company, 1981.

Silvern, Steven B., and Peter A. Williamson. "The Effects of Video Game Play on Young Children's Aggression, Fantasy, and Prosocial Behavior." *Journal of Applied Developmental Psychology* 8.4 (October–December 1987): 453–462.

Singer, Peter. *Hegel: A Very Short Introduction.* Oxford: Oxford University Press, 2001.

Slouka, Mark. *War of the Worlds: Cyberspace and the High-Tech Assault on Reality.* New York: Basic Books, 1995.

Smith, Merritt Roe, and Leo Marx, eds. *Does Technology Drive History? The Dilemma of Technological Determinism.* Cambridge, MA: MIT Press, 1994.

Soderbergh, Steven, director. *Solaris.* Beverly Hills, CA: Twentieth Century Fox Home Video, 2004.

Somerson, Paul. "Commentary: The Digital Divide is Bunk." *ZDNet,* 17 April 2000. http://www.zdnet.com/zdnn/stories/comment/0,5859,2499151,00.html (2 August 2002).

Sparrow, Robert. "The Turing Triage Test." *Ethics and Information Technology* 6.4 (December 2004): 203–213.

Spinelli, Martin. "Radio Lessons for the Internet." *Postmodern Culture* 6.2, 1996. http://wings.buffalo.edu/epc/authors/spinelli/radio-lessons.html (1 November 2005).

Spivak, Gayatri Chakravorty. "Responsibility." *Boundary 2* 21.3 (1994): 19–64.

Stanovsky, Derek. "Virtual Reality." In *The Blackwell Guide to the Philosophy of Computing and Information,* ed. Luciano Floridi, 167–177. Oxford: Blackwell Publishing, 2004.

Steiner, Peter. "Dog cartoon." *The New Yorker,* 5 July 1993, 61.

Stenger, Nicole. "Mind Is a Leaking Rainbow." In *Cyberspace: First Steps,* ed. Michael Benedikt, 49–58. Cambridge, MA: MIT Press, 1991.

Steward, Shawn. "Diminishing the Digital Divide." *Cellular Business* 14.2 (February 1997): 32–38.

Stewart, Jon, ed. *The Hegel Myths and Legends.* Evanston, IL: Northwestern University Press, 1996.

Stich, Stephen P. *Deconstructing the Mind.* Oxford: Oxford University Press, 1998.

Stone, Allucquère Rosanna. *The War of Desire and Technology at the Close of the Mechanical Age.* Cambridge, MA: MIT Press, 1995.

Street, Brian V. *Literacy in Theory and Practice.* Cambridge: Cambridge University Press, 1984.

Susan Morris Specifications Limited. "Building Deconstruction," 21 April 2001. http://www.gvrd.bc.ca/recycling-and-garbage/pdfs/DeconstructionSpecification.pdf\ (1 November 2005).

Swirski, Peter, ed. *A Stanisław Lem Reader*. Evanston, IL: Northwestern University Press, 1997.

Tarkovsky, Andrei, director. Solaris. New York: Criterion Collection, 2002.

Taylor, Chris. "Digital Divide: So Close Yet so Far." *Time,* 4 December 2000, 120–128.

Taylor, Mark. *About Religion: Economies of Faith in Virtual Culture.* Chicago: University of Chicago Press, 1999.

———. *Erring: A Postmodern A/Theology.* Chicago: University of Chicago Press, 1984.

———. *Hiding.* Chicago: University of Chicago Press, 1997.

Taylor, Mark, and Esa Saarinen. *Imagologies: Media Philosophy.* New York: Routledge, 1994.

Taylor, Paul A., and Jan Ll. Harris. *Digital Matters: The Theory and the Culture of the Matrix.* New York: Routledge, 2005.

Thierer, Adam D. "Nonsense to Say That 'Have-Nots' Need Computers." *The Houston Chronicle,* 3 March 2000, A-41.

Thoreau, Henry David. *Walden and Other Writings.* New York: Bantam Books, 1981.

Toffler, Alvin. *The Third Wave.* New York: Bantam Books, 1980.

Trinh, Minh-ha T. *Woman Native Other.* Bloomington, IN: Indiana University Press, 1989.

Turing, Alan. "Computing Machinery and Intelligence." In *Computer Media and Communication: A Reader,* ed. Paul A. Meyer, 37–58. Oxford: Oxford University Press, 1999.

Turkle, Sherry. *Life on the Screen: Identity in the Age of the Internet.* New York: Simon & Schuster, 1995.

U.S. Department of Commerce. National Telecommunications and Information Administration (NTIA). *Falling Through the Net: A Survey of the 'Have Nots' in Rural and Urban America.* Washington, DC: U.S. Department of Commerce, 1995.

———. National Telecommunications and Information Administration (NTIA). *Falling Through the Net II: New Data on the Digital Divide.* Washington, DC: U.S. Department of Commerce, 1998.

———. National Telecommunications and Information Administration (NTIA). *Falling Through the Net: Defining the Digital Divide.* Washington, DC: U.S. Department of Commerce, 1999.

———. National Telecommunications and Information Administration (NTIA). *Falling Through the Net: Toward Digital Inclusion.* Washington, DC: U.S. Department of Commerce, 2000.

———. National Telecommunications and Information Administration (NTIA). *A Nation Online: How Americans are Expanding Their Use of the Internet.* Washington, DC: U.S. Department of Commerce, 2002.

U.S. Department of Commerce. National Telecommunications and Information Administration (NTIA). *The Emerging Digital Economy.* Washington, DC: US Department of Commerce, 1998.

U.S. House. Committee on Small Business. *The Digital Divide: Bridging the Techno-logy Gap: Hearing before the Subcommittee on Empowerment of the Committee on Small Business.* 106th Cong., 1st sess., 27 July 1999. H. Report 106–25.

———. Committee on Small Business. *The Digital Divide: Field Hearing before the Subcommittee on Empowerment of the Committee on Small Business.* 106th Cong., 1st sess., 25 April 2000. H. Report 106–54.

Vallee, Jacques, and Thaddeus Wilson. *Computer-Based Support of Scientific and Technical Work.* IFTF Rept. No. NASA CR 137879, 1976.

van Dijk, Jan A. G. M. *The Deepening Divide: Inequality in the Information Society.* Thousand Oaks, CA: Sage, 2005.

———. *The Networked Society: Social Aspects of New Media.* Thousand Oaks, CA: Sage Publications, 2000.

Vasiliou, Iakovos. "Reality, What Matters, and *The Matrix.*" In *Philosophers Explore the Matrix,* ed. Christopher Grau, 98–114. Oxford: Oxford University Press, 2005.

Wachowski, Andy, and Larry Wachowski, directors. *The Matrix.* Burbank, CA: Warner Home Video, 1999.

———. *The Matrix Reloaded.* Burbank, CA: Warner Home Video, 2003.

———. *The Matrix Revolutions.* Burbank, CA: Warner Home Video, 2003.

Walsh, Ekaterina O. "The Truth About the Digital Divide." *Forrester Technographics Brief.* Cambridge, MA: Forrester Research, Inc., 2000.

Warschauer, Mark. *Technology and Social Inclusion: Rethinking the Digital Divide.* Cambridge, MA: MIT Press, 2003.

———. "What Is the Digital Divide?" 26 April 2001. http://www.gse.uci.edu/faculty/markw/ dd.pdf (1 November 2005).

Warwick, Kevin. "Cyborg Morals, Cyborg Values, Cyborg Ethics." *Ethics and Infor-mation Technology* 5.3 (2003): 131–137.

———. "The Matrix—Our Future?" In *Philosophers Explore the Matrix,* ed. Chris-topher Grau, 198–207. Oxford: Oxford University Press, 2005.

Watters, Stephen O. *Real Solutions for Overcoming Internet Addictions.* Ann Arbor, MI: Vine Books, 2001.

Weberman, David. "*The Matrix* Simulation and the Postmodern Age." In *The Matrix and Philosophy,* ed. William Irwin, 225–239. Chicago: Open Court, 2002.

Weinman, Lynda. *Deconstructing Web Graphics.* Berkeley, CA: New Riders, 1996.

Weinstone, Ann. "Welcome to the Pharmacy: Addiction, Transcendence, and Vir-tual Reality." *Diacritics* 27.3 (1997): 77–89.

Weir, Peter, director. *Truman Show.* Hollywood, CA: Paramount Pictures, 1998.

Weizenbaum, Joseph. *Computer Power and Human Reason: From Judgment to Cal-culation.* San Francisco, CA: W. H. Freeman, 1976.

Wertheim, Margaret. *The Pearly Gates of Cyberspace: A History of Space from Dante to the Internet.* New York: W. W. Norton & Company, 1999.

Wesley, B. H., and M. S. MacLean. "A Conceptual Model for Communication Research." *Journalism Quarterly* 34 (1957): 31–38.

Whitby, Blay R. "The Virtual Sky Is Not the Limit—The Ethical Implications of Virtual Reality." *Intelligent Tutoring Media* 4.1 (1993): 23–28. Also available at http://www.cogs.susx.ac.uk/users/blayw/VRethics.html.

Whitby, Blay R., and Kane Oliver. "How to Avoid a Robot Takeover: Political and Ethical Choices in the Design and Introduction of Intelligent Artifacts." Symposium on Artificial Intelligence, Ethics and (Quasi-)Human Rights, Convention of the Society for the Study of Artificial Intelligence and the Simulation of Behaviour (AISB-00). University of Birmingham, UK, 19–20 April 2000. http://www.informatics.sussex.ac.uk/users/blayw/BlayAISB00.html (28 February 2006).

Wiener, Norbert. *The Human Use of Human Beings: Cybernetics and Society.* Boston: Da Capo Press, 1988.

Wilhelm, Anthony. "From Crystal Palaces to Silicon Valleys: Market Imperfections and the Enduring Digital Divide." In *Access Denied in the Information Age,* ed. Stephen Lax, 199–217. New York: Palgrave, 2001.

Williams, Frederick. *The Communications Revolution.* London: Sage, 1982.

Witherington, Ben. "Neo-Orthodoxy: Tales of the Reluctant Messiah, Or 'Your Own Personal Jesus.'" In *More Matrix and Philosophy: Revolutions and Reloaded Decoded,* ed. William Irwin, 165–174. Chicago: Open Court, 2005.

Wittig, Rob. *Invisible Rendezvous: Connection and Collaboration in the New Landscape of Electronic Writing.* Hanover, NH: Wesleyan University Press, 1994.

Wolfe, Cary. Introduction to *Zoontologies: The Question of the Animal.* Minneapolis, MN: University of Minnesota Press, 2003.

Wolinsky, Howard. "The Digital Divide." *Chicago Sun-Times,* 17 March 1996, 6.

Woolley, Benjamin. *Virtual Worlds: A Journey in Hype and Hyperreality.* New York: Penguin Books, 1993.

Wresch, William. *Disconnected: Haves and Have Nots in the Information Age.* New Brunswick, NJ: Rutgers University Press, 1996.

Yates, Frances A. *The Art of Memory.* Chicago: University of Chicago Press, 1974.

Yeffeth, Glenn, ed. *Taking the Red Pill: Science, Philosophy and Religion in The Matrix.* Dallas, TX: Benbella Books, 2003.

Young, Kimberly S. *Caught in the Net: How to Recognize the Signs of Internet Addiction—And a Winning Strategy for Recovery.* New York: John Wiley & Sons, 1998.

Zacapa, Eddie. *Matrix Reflections: Choosing Between Reality and Illusion.* Bloomington, IN: Authorhouse, 2005.

Zaleski, Jeffrey P. *The Soul of Cyberspace.* San Francisco, CA: Harper, 1997.

Zettl, Herbert. "Back to Plato's Cave: Virtual Reality." In *Communication and Cy-*

berspace: Social Interactions in an Electronic Environment, ed. Lance Strate, Ron Jacobson, and Stephanie B. Gibson, 83–94. Cresskill, NJ: Hampton Press, 1996.

Žižek, Slavoj. *The Plague of the Fantasies.* New York: Verso, 1997.

———. "Reloaded Revolutions." In *More Matrix and Philosophy: Revolutions and Reloaded Decoded,* ed. William Irwin, 198–208. Chicago: Open Court, 2005.

Zynda, Lyle. "Was Cypher Right? (Part 2): The Nature of Reality and Why It Matters." In *Taking the Red Pill: Science, Philosophy and Religion in The Matrix,* ed. Glenn Yeffeth, 33–44. Dallas, TX: Benbella Books, 2003.

Index